The Collected Edition of
The All-Seeing Eye

For The Year: 1924
Vol. 1. Numbers: 1-6
Modern Problems in the Light of Ancient Wisdom

MANLY P. HALL

Atlas Occulta

ISBN: 9781955087025

© 2022, Atlas Occulta

Al rights reserved. No part of this publication maybe reproduced, translate, store in a retrieval system, or transmitted in any form or by any means, electronic, mechanical, photocopying, recording or otherwise, without prior written permission from the publisher.

PROLOGUE

Manly Palmer Hall (18 March 1901– 29 August 1990) was a Canadian author, lecturer, astrologer and mystic. Over his 70 year career, he gave thousands of lectures, including two at Carnegie Hall, and published over 150 volumes, although is most known for his 1928 work, The Secret Teachings of All Ages. In 1934, he founded The Philosophical Research Society in Los Angeles, which he dedicated to Truth Seekers of All Time, with a research library, lecture hall and publishing house.

Hall's career as a mystic sage began in 1919, when he came to California to be reunited with his mother.He came under the influence of self-styled followers of Rosicrucianism in Oceanside, California. He lived at the Rosicrucian Fellowship founded by Max Heindel but grew suspicious of the order's claims to ancient wisdom and soon moved to Los Angeles. There he fell in with metaphysical seekers and discussion groups. One day young Hall was attracted by a sign advertising phrenology, the discipline that reads human psychology through the shape and contours of the skull. The proprietor of the shop, Sydney J. Brownson, quickly became Halls' mentor and explained magnetism, reincarnation, the aura, the wisdom of the ancients, the mysteries of India and the East and the secret teachings of the church to Hall, who proved to be an excellent disciple.

A noted scholar in the fields of mysticism, alternative religions and the occult. He is best known for his 1928 book, *The Secret Teachings of All Ages: An Encyclopedic Outline of Masonic, Hermetic, Qabbalistic and Rosicrucian Symbolical Philosophy.*

Hall took a closer look into sources that many historians refused to consider – from Masonic and Rosicrucian tracts to alchemical and astrological works – and recent scholarship has justified some of his historic conclusions. Hall clarified ancient ideas that could otherwise seem beyond reach, writing not as a distant judge but as a lover of the rites and mysteries embodied in the old ways.

In 1934, Hall founded the Philosophical Research Society (PRS) in Los Angeles, California, a nonprofit organization dedicated to the study of religion, mythology, metaphysics, and the occult. The PRS still maintains a research library of over 50,000 volumes, and also sells and publishes metaphysical and spiritual books, mostly those authored by Hall. After his death, some of Manly Hall's rare alchemy books were sold to keep the PRS in operation. Acquisition of the Manly Palmer Hall Collection in 1995 provided the Getty Research Institute with one of the world's leading collections of alchemy, esoterica, and hermetica.

In 1942, Hall spoke to an attendance audience at Carnegie Hall, on *The Secret Destiny of America,* which later became a book of the same title. In that book, through a series of stories, he alleged a secret order of philosophers had created the idea of America as a country for religious freedom and self-governance. In one of the stories that Hall cites as evidence of America's exceptionalism, he claims that an angel was present at the signing of the Declaration of Independence, and inspiring them with God's words. President Ronald Reagan is reported to have adopted ideas and phrasing from *The Secret Destiny of America* (1944) in his speeches and essays for his allegorical use of the City upon a Hill.

Hall returned in 1945 for another well-attended lecture at Carnegie Hall, titled: *Plato's Prophecy of Worldwide Democracy.*

He died on August 29, 1990 in Los Angeles, California, USA .

Manly's monthly magazine, *The All Seeing Eye* was a monthly magazine devoted to his writings in search for those fundamental thruths existing in the educational systems, religions, and philosophies of all ages. Each issue contains articles on several topics such as: The Great Pyramid; Magic and Sorcery of the Far East; Translation from the Third Book of Mathesis; The Secret Key to Mystic and Masonic Christianity.

This scarce antiquarian book is a facsimile reprint of the original work. This title is an authentic reproduction of the original printed text in shades of gray and may contain minor errors. **IMPORTANT** <u>Despite the fact that we have attempted to accurately maintain the integrity of the original work, the present reproduction may have minor errors beyond our control like: missing and blurred pages, poor pictures and markings.</u> Because this book is culturally important, we have made available as part of our commitment to protect, preserve and promote knowledge in the world. This title is an authentic reproduction published by Manly Palmer Hall as editor of *The All Seeing Eye.* This work is an exact reproduction of this title reprinted as facsimile edition: Vol.1.Numbers: 1-6. 1924.

Saucerian Publisher was founded with the mission of promoting books in the Paranormal, Hermetica & the Occult Science. Our vision is to preserve the legacy of literary history by reprint editions of books which have already been exhausted or are difficult to obtain. Our goal is to help readers, educators and researchers by bringing back original publications that are difficult to find at reasonable price, while preserving the legacy of universal wisdom..

The All-Seeing Eye

Modern Problems in the Light of Ancient Wisdom

A Monthly Magazine
Written, Edited and
Compiled by
MANLY P. HALL

"Nonsense as a Factor In Soul Growth"
"Atlantis, The Lost Continent"

MAY, 1923

THIS MAGAZINE IS NOT SOLD

THE ALL-SEEING EYE

MODERN PROBLEMS IN THE LIGHT OF ANCIENT WISDOM

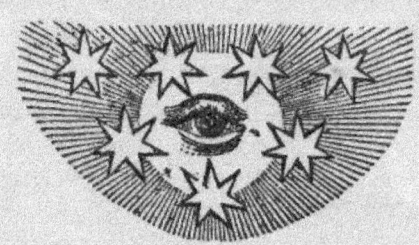

This magazine is published monthly for the purpose of spreading the ancient Wisdom Teachings in a practical way that students may apply to their own lives. It is written, published, and edited by Manly P. Hall and privately published for circulation among his students and those interested in his work.

Those desiring to secure copies of this magazine or who wish to subscribe to it may do so by writing directly to the editor.

This magazine is published and distributed privately to those who make possible with their financial support its publication. The magazine cannot be bought and has no fixed value. Like all of the ancient teachings which it seeks to promulgate it has no comparative value but the students must support it for its own instrinsic merit.

To whom it may concern: It is quite useless to inquire concerning advertising rates or to send manuscripts for publication as this magazine cannot possibly consider either as this is a non-commercial enterprise. All letters and questions, subscriptions, etc., should be mailed to P. O. Box 695, Los Angeles, California, in care of Manly P. Hall, Editor.

The contents of this magazine are copyrighted but permission to copy may be secured through correspondence with the author.

This magazine does not represent nor promulgate any special sect or teaching but is non-sectarian in all of its viewpoints. Suggestions for its improvement will be gladly considered if presented in the proper manner.

TABLE OF CONTENTS

EDITORIAL. Page
 Nonsense as a Factor in Soul Growth 3
 Poem. The Immortality of the Soul 2

ORIENTAL OCCULTISM.
 The Light of Asia 32
 Chinese Cosmogony 7
 The Blue Krishna 8

OCCULT FICTION.
 The Third Eye. An Occult Detective Story 9
 Brothers of the Shining Robe 14
 Chapter One—The Temple of Caves.

MYSTIC MASONRY.
 The Robe of Blue and Gold 17
 The Symbolism of the Triangle on the Mason's Ring 19

SPECIAL ARTICLES.
 A Letter From the Brothers of the Rose Cross. Illustrated 21
 Atlantis, the Lost Continent 23
 Books and Their Place in Occultism
 Music 6

Immortality of the Soul

By an Inmate of Folsom Prison

Sweet mem'ries flash across my mind
   Like dreams of long ago—
Of friendly faces true and kind
   That once I used to know;
But when or where I saw them last
   I cannot always tell—
I know that somewhere in the past
   I knew and loved them well!

     For in my dreams I wander far
       Beyond this mortal sphere,
     Perhaps on some far distant star
       Their spirits hovered near!
     And in my sleep my soul returns
       To scenes it knew of yore,
     And step by step my spirit learns
       Of lives I've lived before.

          My soul has lived since time began,
            And must live on alway—
          Nor can the puny hand of man
            Its onward progress stay!
          Though now I walk the paths of earth,
            My Father's feet have trod—
          Through death my soul shall find rebirth
            In closer touch with God.

               He made the glowing universe,
                 The sun, the stars, the sky—
               He gave the power to hold converse
                 Betwixt my soul and I,
               And only now and then in dreams,
                 I scan futurity,
               And see my soul as true it seems
                 In all its purity!

                    And when the years at last shall roll
                      The shades of earth away,
                    I too shall reach the nearing goal
                      For which I watch and pray.
                    I too shall see that glorious dawn
                      The prophets long foretold,
                    That bids my soul to wander on
                    Through God's bright gate of gold!

Nonsense as a Factor in Soul Growth

THERE ARE TIMES in the unfolding of human consciousness when the student feels and honestly believes that the entire weight of the Eternal Plan, the salvation of God, man, and the universe and the perpetuation of civilization, rests upon his shoulders. He feels that when he passes out Truth will die with him and that his life must be so filled with duties that he has little, if any, time to demonstrate the qualities of the human race. Religion becomes such a weighty problem that he entirely forgets the necessity of humor and the value of mental and spiritual recreation, or, rather, we may say that lack of use has caused his sense of humor to atrophy.

The inevitable result of losing the ability to laugh and to relax the tension of massive thought and incessant labor is unbalance and ultimate spiritual crystalization, commonly known in the world of affairs as freakishness and crankism. The ability of the philosopher to forget his philosophies and the mystic to lay aside his religion and smile with the world over some hopelessly trivial bit of nonsense is the sign of true superphysical greatness and s p i r i t u a l balance.

All students of symbolism know that for ages a long face has been considered symbolical of religion and that the more sad you appear and the more dejected your countenance, the holier you are and the closer you are to a God who has long foresworn laughter. This idea is based upon an entirely erroneous concept of life. The appreciation of humor is a divine faculty, the quick wit that it develops may be used for much deeper works, while the inevitable radiation of cheer which accompanies the happy person is just as important to the growth of humanity as the philosophical concepts which we expound and the problems of compound ratio.

There are those known in the world as "wet blankets," "gloom dispensers" and "Aunty-dolefuls" who in the name of God take all the cheer from life and with their blankets of pessimism totally eclipse the sun which might otherwise send to our hearts at least a solitary ray. If there be an exceptionally high spot in Heaven, a brownstone front in the Great Beyond, we shall undoubtedly find it reserved for those mystics and philosophers, sages and seers, who have not only made man think and pray but have taught him how to laugh.

The world is filled with trials and worries, with long faces and hopeless souls which must be met along tht weary road that leads to Light, but the Powers that be have seen fit to bring laughter into the world to cheer the weary hearts of striving men and women and to make this gift doubly sure have supplied a special set of facial muscles for its expression, and it is the duty of every student not only to promote aestheticism but also to bring into faces furrowed with care and hearts frozen in endless snows the happy smile which is indeed the greatest boon of the gods.

All the greatest philosophers have been noted not only for their quickness of mind but for their sharpness of wit and in truth there is nothing which shows the depth of thought and knowledge of life more than an original joke which has something really funny in it. There is an art in jesting which can only be appreciated after a suffering mortal has listened to what the world calls humor. This art should be listed with the seven immortal arts and sciences.

Let us remember the words of an ancient philosopher who said, when referring to the court jester of a king, "It takes the brightest man in all the land to make the greatest fool." The kingdoms of suffering humanity must have that court fool but few of our so-called religious lights will allow their faces to relax for fear that their dignity may be affected and their congregation dwindle away.

When we laugh from the depths of our soul, relaxing for a moment the nerves and muscles that have so long been at a tension in fighting the battle of life, it is like a gymnasium exercise for the body and a tonic for the soul. The lungs fill with air, the liver receives its "daily dozen," and the face beams with a greater joy because for one moment the purely human has been given expression in a way which can injure none. Even those people who are unconsciously ridiculous will never realize nor be accredited with the honor that is due them from the fact that they have made others laugh, for while their personality is hurt and is many cases their noses are seriously cracked still that laughter will reach to the ends of creation before its last echoes die away at the very footstool of divinity.

It is said that the Christian theology is the only one that has not at least one laughing god in its train and we cannot but feel that there has been a serious omission. The laughter of the gods sounds through all nature which is filled with cheer, it is the sorrows and discouragements of life which turn all things to a leaden gray. Those who radiate this soot colored expression of life are never popular, never happy, seldom useful, and always a bore. The laughter of children is music in the ears of the Almighty and all living things are children who cry one moment and laugh the next, and of those moments which comes closest to the divine,—the joy or the tear? All human beings are like little ones crying over broken dolls and the toys which have fallen to pieces in their hands, but their sorrows are short-lived and soon the bursts of merry laughter shroud the sorrow in forgetfulness. But there are some who cannot forget and it is the duty of all to cheer them on their way, for every heart is filled with sadness and when we, too, are sad it but brings back memories which do not help but always surround us with thoughts of bitterness or remorse.

It is said that animals do not smile but it seems that they do, for every horse and dog and even the old cat purring on the hearth rug have a contented smiling appearance concealed somewhere about their faces. Even the fowls of the farmyard with all their stateliness and dignity have a certain twinkle in their eyes and a certain upward curve at the corner of their bills which is often missing from the human physiognomy, and their dignity is all the greater because of its absurdity while man's absurdities are always greater because of his dignity.

There is a psychology in humor, a moral effect upon all with whom we come in contact. It makes us friends, we are invited to call again in a voice which means it, it brings us closer to the hearts of others, it tries us more tightly to the truly human, it tears down the barriers of creed and caste and gives us a footing in the hearts of others.

There is no greater power which man can evolve than that of seeing all Nature smiling, every plant and flower wreathed in merriness, smiling because his own soul is laughing, filled and overflowing with that exuberance of spirit which marks the true expression of spiritual growth. To see the laughter in nature, the joy in living, the good concealed beneath the ever painful, is a thing not always easy to do. One must have within himself this Fountain of Mirth, which would have lengthened the life of Ponce de Leon had he not shortened his career by the seriousness of his search, which sees in everything not only the deep and mystical but the divinely and sublimely ridiculous.

When our hearts are about to overflow with sorrow, if we could but see with the eyes of the gods we would smile at least. When we are about to be offended by the words and actions of others, if we could but think a moment we would probably make matters much worse for it would be a Herculean task to restrain the laughter which would bring with it the wrath of our opponent.

You may say what you will, it is better far to see the ridiculous in life than the ever sordid, it is better far to laugh at the mistakes of man than to curse the decrees of God, and those who go around brewing cups of hemlock and radiating avalanches of gloom should indeed be listed with the false prophets and the blasphemers of God. The man who cannot find something pleasant to say no matter where he may be, how unpleasant the experience, how uncongenial those around him, or how contrary to his taste the incident in question, should never claim even the first degrees of spirituality. The mystic knows that in the last analysis all opposites blend, tragedy and comedy are one, and their apparently diverse ways are united at the doorway which leads to heights immortal.

So laugh and list among the benefactors of humanity those who often with hearts filled with sadness have realized the sweetness of a smile and the gloriousness of mirth and who have been the fools to make their brothers laugh, their only reward being the realization that for a moment at least a few hearts have forgotten their sorrows and a few lonely wanderers have seen the sunny side of life.

There is nothing more contagious than joy and nothing more infectious than gloom. These two inseparable companions of mankind walk side by side,—gloom noted for its length, joy for its breadth, and their eternal battle for mastery one over the other must be played out in every human heart.

Acid temperaments make acid bodies and the world is filled with intellectual alkalies which seem to stunt all the glories of nature. The reward of gloom is dyspepsia, ankylotic joints, rheumatism, and sour stomach. Those who cannot smile ferment all the world and spoil a glorious crop by their own tiny apple and too often they do this in the name of God. There are thousands whose motto for life is, "If ye smile upon the Sabbath, ye shall weep ere Monday dawn," and other equally sentimental concepts of God's demand of man.

Let us rather use as our motto "A smile a day keeps the doctor away," and the more smiles, the more "undesirables" are excluded from the aura of our association. There are glooms of all kinds revolving in their orbits around us, but until the wet blanket enters our own hearts we are master of them, and if our own lives are sunny the spirits of negation have little chance of entrance there.

One thing about the Devil that we always admire is the fact that he has a most resounding laugh and in spite of all his villianies there is a certain refreshment which comes over us even as we are chilled by his hilarity. He does the most miserable things in the most jovial and likeable way and can even damn us with a smile upon his face, while many of our friends cannot even say "Good morning" without looking like a heavy storm.

Occultists and occult students must realize that when they forget how to be jovial, they lock the door of Heaven and throw away the key.

Music

THERE IS NO POWER that holds so great a sway over the hearts and souls of living things as the charm of music. From the earliest dawn of time when the primitive civilizations of the world were in the making to our modern and apparently more ethical day, the life of man has been softened, his expressions molded to nobler ends, and his emotions raised to more lofty heights by the power of harmony and rhythm. In the early days of the world the children of the earth learned to imitate the eternal music of Nature, the singing of the birds, the moaning of the winds, the swishing of the waves on rock bound shores, the night cries of bird and beast,—all of these blend into a mystic cadence which we may call in truth the endless symphonies of Nature. The powers of creation are eternally musical, their mystic cadences swell from star to star with note divine. All nature, seen and unseen, formed and unformed, listens in rapt awe to the endless symphonies of the Great Unknown.

Then there is another music,—the song of Life, the beating of human hearts, the peals of merry laughter, the broken sobs of sorrow. All these blend into a mystic orchestra, oftimes unheard, which swells in note invisible through eternity to the very footstool of the Divine. Man's nature pours forth from his being with the expression of living music. The old organist allows his fingers to slip over the keys in an apparently unconscious, mechanical way but the very emotions of his soul pour out in divine harmonies from the instrument that registers and seems to live the innermost thoughts of the musician, the innermost symphonies of his soul.

The deep, wailing notes of the violin seem to speak of the master's touch and the very heart of the musician expresses itself in the harmonies that he plays. The heart that is broken in sorrow sends forth sweet melodies that touch the heartstrings, while the ponderous clashes of massive themes speak of the weighty minds that bring them forth.

All life is musical for it is a language universally understood. Its strange discords speak of human hate, its harmony of mutual understanding. Upon the seven stringed lyre of its own being, the human soul plays its harmony celestial; each thought and action is but a note of living music. When we live askew and our natures are unbalanced, the instrument is out of tune because the hands of the master do not rest upon the keys. The Stradivarius is dead until the soft fingers of the violinist draw from its latent soul the mystic yearnings of his own heart. So the bodies of man are like instruments in the hands of master musicians. The spirit within each living thing plays upon its bodies, seeking to build them into more glorious instruments for its own expression that its notes may swell the harmonies of cosmos.

When man's life is a sham, when his heart is cold, all the sounds from his living keyboard are inharmonious and discordant, the keys are out of tune, the strings are broken, and the hands that would play them are shackled by the things of earth. But those who have labored long and suffered much are mellowed like old violins, the ages of sorrow and suffering have brought out the greatest that is in them, and they are masterpieces in a master's hand. Each year the tones grow more mellow and the hand that draws the bow brings more perfect harmonies from its hallowed instrument, until at last in the hands of the Great Musician they pour forth in cords and symphonies sublime, each wondrous melody the reflection of the genius of the soul.

Music is a wonderful thing. It melts the hardened heart, softens the stern lines of the face, brings peace to those who long have suffered, and like the child drifting into sleep, lulled by the soft notes of a lullaby, the soul of man finds rest in the music of his own soul and the divine harmony of Nature's plan.

Chinese Cosmogony

RHEEN OR SHANG-TE is the great Prince or model man; He is the Great Father of Gods and men; He is Heaven or the Kosmos animated by a mind or soul and hence He is a sphere or circle; that being the most perfect figure. All parts of the Kosmos, therefore, viz., Heaven, Earth, Man, Sun, Moon, Stars, Mountains, Rivers, Birds, Beasts, Insects, Reptiles, Trees, Vegetables, etc., are all His parts and members and these are all pervaded and animated by the "One Mind" or Soul of Heaven or Shang-te.

In the state religion Shang-te is worshiped in all His parts, beginning with His triplication Heaven, Earth, and Man.

This philosophy is evidently founded upon the Confucionist idea of man transferred to the universe; as man is composed of mind and body so Heaven or the Kosmos is supposed to be composed of mind and matter, and the mind in each is one and the same, therefore Shang-te designated God or the Divinity within. Hence Confucious states that this Heaven or Shang-te is a gigantic Man, also this Shang-te is a sphere containing the whole universe within Himself and is the highest Numen.

From the "Classic of Chance,"

By the Rev. Cannon McClatchie, M.A.
This sidelight into the mythology and cosmogony of China shows how closely it is correlated with the teachings of the Hebrew Qabbalah and the alchemical and theosophic concepts of life. This Shang-te, the All Prevading manifesting in its multiplicity of forms, is called by many names in many lands but is the same wherever found. This cosmic Being who made man in His own image and whom we honor as the Creator of our universe has been known and studied for hundreds of thousands of years by the ancient peoples of the eastern countries.

Students who analyze religion soon realize that there is but one to analyze and that the most heathenish concept in the world is to believe in heathens.

The ancients of the western world have symbolized the Grand Man as a great figure twisted backward until His head and feet touch, forming a great sphere. There is little doubt that the ultimate form of all things is sphereoid and that the planets which we see in the sky, the sun, etc., are all of them organisms not unlike our own with intelligence, circulation, and consciousness but instead of, like our bodies, being peopled with cells and corpuscles these bodies are peopled with flora and fauna of evolving life.

A true understanding of the mystic philosophies depends upon the willingness of the student to credit all things with intelligence, and to realize that as mind and body expand they eternally express themselves in new environments which are the expressions of need, and that at various times during our growth the forms of our vehicles change.

Man is a universe is himself just as complicated upon a miniature scale as the heavens which unfold around us. Within him are the planets, the great powers of light and darkness and millions of evolving lives,—some have estimated six septillion in the human body. Thus man as he raises his hand to Shang-te, the Father of Light, and the globe-shaped Spirit of Creation, within whose Being we live and move and have our being, must also realize that he himself is Shang-te and that the universe wonderful beyond conception which expresses itself as his bodies is in truth built in the image of the Father, and that he himself is not only a God in the making but is already a great spiritual power to the millions of lives seeking expression through his extension of consciousness.

The Blue Krishna

IN PICTURING the Christ Child of India, Shri-Krishna, the Blue Lotus, we find that He is always painted as having a blue skin. Now let us consider briefly the reason for this rather unusual symbolism. Why the Lord of Love playing upon His flute with Radha in the woods is always colored with this bluish light has caused considerable speculation among students of occult philosophy.

The reason for this is said to be that blue is the symbol of the Father, the highest of the three primary colors. All great spiritual workers are said to be under the protection of the Father, or, as the East would say, enfolded in the cape of Brahma. This blue spiritual wall which divides the Great Ones from men is symbolized by the Oriental by coloring the body of Krishna, the incarnation of Vishnu, the second Principle of the Indian Trinity, a pale blue color.

Briefly, it is said to mean that between that soul and the world there was forever a wall, and that while Krishna came to the world He was not of the world but belonged in the home of the Gods. This beautiful symbolism applies to the problems of life. There are many who are in the world, and while apparently they are one with us still they know and we often feel that there is a wall between us. This is the wall of spirit, the wall of greater light and truth which spiritually divides the living from the dead. Those who come to us from behind the veil still wander with us but the blue veil of spirit conceals them, the blue light of spirit shines out from their being, and while they labor with us they are concealed forever behind the blue veil of immortality.

Each will one day step behind this veil and the blue folds of the Father's cape will stand between us and the world as protection and relief. Then we too shall labor in the world concealed forever and divided from mortal man by the blue veil of Krishna, the Blue Lotus of India.

Would Man Gain Anything By Living Forever In One Body?

AS SOON as the average student realizes that there are certain powers which transcend material things or apparently do so and discovers that there are those who remain for indefinite periods in one body, the student immediately desires to do the same thing because, after all, living and dying appear as very inconvenient phases in the evolution of man. Perpetual life seems to be a novelty which has attracted a number of people who should have much better sense and the fountain of eternal youth is sought for as earnestly now as in the days of Ponce de Leon. But let the student always remember that these great things are effects and that the only cause which can bring them about is mastery and adeptship. Until he lives right, thinks right and becomes master of those lower desires and passions and emotions which wreck his life he can never hope to lengthen it by spiritual powers.

There are many lessons for man to learn besides those of this plane of nature and in other worlds he learns and studies while the stage is being set here for the next great step in his unfoldment and if he was forced to remain here age in and age out with no one that he knew and the incessant monotony which to him now seems a novelty he would soon pray for death as now he prays for life. But when he has learned to be of use through the ages, when he has completely given up all desire to live for himself alone, when he has become so useful in the Great Plan that he is needed every moment for the good of all, then he will be able to live forever and to do useful works in many worlds to come.

The Third Eye

BANG! The shot sounded through hotel like a clap of thunder in the dead silence of the winter night. A moment later there came a dull thud as of something falling and the loose fixtures in the hotel room shook. Then came the soft patter of footsteps in the hallway, a woman's holf broken sob, then all was still again.

The sound of the shot aroused every one in the building, doors opened, and frightened faces appeared in the frames of light.

"What has happened?"

"Is someone killed?"

"Was it a shot?"

"I don't know, do you?"

From mouth to mouth the questions flew alosg the hallway like wildfire, but on one could be found who seemed in a position to answer them.

It was then that with a tremendous gust of personality Mr. Jeremiah Johnson, the house detective, appeared upon the scene with a glorious blue-green dressing gown draped over pink-striped pajamas. In one hand he carried a revolver while with the other he endeavored to make his scanty attire cover as much ground as possible, not forgetting to brush the nickle-plated star which he fastened conspicuously on the blue-green background of his bizarre attire.

"Where did the shot come from?" he demanded in a booming voice as he scuffed his way in bedroom slippers to the center of the hall and gazed around.

"That is precisely the information with which we desire you to supply us," answered a distinguished looking gentleman, dressed in an iron-grey Vandyke and blue nightshirt, as he gave the house detective a careful inspection through gold pince-nez and then vanished in the direction of his wardrobe.

The detective looked along the hall at the opened doors and startled faces; registering professional poise and then his eyes fastened themselves upon two portals side by side at the extreme end of the corridor. They were the only two upon the entire floor that had remained closed during the excitement. Many pairs of eyes followed the rather Bohemian figure of Jeremiah as he laid his course for these doors. In a second he was pounding on one of them; he waited a second and knocked again but no answer sounded from within. He tried the door but found it locked so turned his attention to the other. He rapped upon this also but silence alone rewarded his effort. Trying this one and finding it unfastened, Jeremiah opened the door and stepped inside. The portal screen closed behind his back.

About a minute slipped by although it seemed much longer to the watchers in the hall. Then the door reopened and the detective stepped out but it was with a look of horror on his pale and drawn face that Jeremiah Johnson half staggered into the hallway leaning upon the wall for support.

"What was it?" all asked in one breath.

"Yes," reiterated the gentleman with the Vandyke who had reappeared upon the scene, a necktie and smoking jacket added to his wardrobe, "we would be—ah—much obliged if you would elucidate this perplexing problem."

"Murder," muttered the detective, as turning he locked the door with his passkey, "go back to your rooms everyone and remain there until the inspectors arrive." And without further word Jeremiah Johnson disappeared a trail of pink and green in the direction of the elevator.

"I wonder who the dead person is?" asked a kindly appearing old lady halfway down the hall.

"I don't know," came a shrill voice from across, "but I think it's just too romantic for words!"

"Brrrrrrrr," muttered the distinguished

gentleman with the Vandyke as his knees shook together, "really if they must murder in this hotel, I would certainly consider it a favor if they would turn on the steam heat first. This is a most undesirable moment for a crime."

As no one could cast any light upon the mystery, one by one the doors closed until the only sound breaking the stillness was a whisper now and then which trickled through some keyhole.

An hour later four very puzzled men stood in the center of the room where the tragedy had occurred. Before them on the floor, illuminated by a reading lamp, lay the dead man fully dressed with a bullethole in his back. There were no signs of weapons or apparent motive for the crime, nothing had been touched in the room and as usual the officers could not find the clue upon which to base their further investigations. One of the detectives turned to the hotel inspector, "Have you been able to secure any information concerning the murdered man?"

"Very little," replied Johnson, "the name he signed on the hotel register was Professor Amos Martin. I hear he is a scientist and a globe trotter. I have also gathered from my examination here that he is an author and connected in research work with several well-known universities. He is just back from several years in the Orient. On the table you will find the beginning of the latest book that he was writing. It was to be called "The Third Eye" and is apparently of a very scientific nature. He seems to be basing it on some Eastern sacred writings or something of that sort. So far as I have been able to discover he was not married, has no relatives, and is a long way from his original home. He appears to be well fixed financially and has been in the hotel three days short of a month."

At the word "Orient" the detectives pricked up their ears and looked at each other in a significant way.

"You say he was just back from the Far East? That is a very important point. Do you know whether there are any Orientals in this neighborhood at the present time, especially stopping at the hotel?"

"Oh, yes! Why didn't I think of it before? There is a Chinaman here who came soon after the Professor's arrival who is supposed to be assisting him in the completion of his great book. He may have been with him last night."

"Where is his room?" asked one of the detectives.

"Wait a minute and I'll find out," replied Jeremiah as he slipped quickly from the room.

While awaiting the return of the house detective, the other three walked over to the desk upon which lay a great mass of typewritten manuscripts. One of them picked up a sheet and read:

"The Third Eye is a small ductless gland in the brain, known to modern science as the pineal gland. In India, China, Thibet I have come across great scientists who have so developed this gland, which is much more powerful than the physical eye, that they can see through solid walls and into the very secrets of the human mind."

"Humph," muttered the detective, scratching his head. He then took a long breath and continued:

"Few people realize the powers which work through this eye when it is awakened. If they did, greater attempts would be made to revivify this partly atrophied organ of cognition. This is only possible, according to those who have awakened this power, through the turning upward of the forces playing through the segments of the spinal canal. These forces dilate the gland which then becomes a superorgan of sense orientation. In the eastern countries much time has been spent in the awakening and training of this very important gland and the purpose of my book is to show the western world the value of this little known organ."

The detective looked at his companions, then down at the dead man on the floor, a rather peculiar expression playing on his face, then shrugging his shoulders he held the paper under the light and continued:

"There are certain superphysical powers known to the ancients which the western world little understands, but these secrets are still in possession of certain priests and eastern scientists whom I have met during my travels. It is of these mysterious ones that I would write. They are found most frequently in Northern India, Burma, and China, and among the Llamas of Thibet. They have powers of sight far beyond those of the average individual. Their lives as aesthetics and hermits and their self-sacrifices and rigid purification have given them powers over their own being and also over others, which are perfectly uncanny to those unacquainted with the hidden side of human nature and the powers of the universe."

"Oh, tommyrot!" laughed the officer as he threw the paper back among its fellows, "some people are getting dippy over this sort of stuff nowadays. And he looked like a nice, sane, sensible sort of man," and the detectives gazed down on the face of the murdered Professor. "But this is the way they all get when they delve into these things. They either go insane or get killed or something."

At the same instant the house detective returned apparently quite excited, "Why," he exclaimed, "it's all clear now. That Chinaman had the room right next to this one. I hear that he spent nearly all of his time with the Professor and was here with him up to a late hour last night. There's no use talking, boys, when we get him there'll be another feather in the cap of this department." Jeremiah brought his fist down on the big table, his excitement registering through the blow and sending the papers of the late Professor's book skidding around in mad frenzy on the floor.

"My, but I'd like to get my hands on that Chink now!" As Jeremiah Johnson expressed the thoughts flooding his innermost soul, there came a soft knock at the door which the house detective swung open and then stepped back giving a gasp of amazement.

In the doorway stood a tall Chinese dressed in a long Mandarin gown of sober color but rich in texture. On his massive head was a tiny black cap while a glorious peacock feather hung down his back. In his hand he carried a beautiful fan inlaid with mother-of-pearl which was closed and which he used as a pointer. It was his face, however, which caused the amazement and that uncanny feeling which seemed to pour out from him wherever he went. He had the dome and brow of a philosopher and his eyes, while almond, were wide apart and of such great size and brilliancy that they could be but poorly hidden by the dark shell-rim glasses that he wore. Under his drooping mustache his mouth was fixed in a true oriental smile, a pleasant but absolutely blank expression which hinted many things but never committed itself.

He spoke in a soft, purring voice, English worthy of a college-bred man, "My honorable friend expresses a desire to see me, so I take great pleasure in coming. It is an honor to have important persons such as house detectives and you worthy gentlemen of the police desire my presence."

Some way the thought came into the detectives' minds that this Oriental was deliberately ridiculing them, but his tone was so exemplary and his manner so polite that there was no chance of taking offense, even though Jeremiah fancied he saw the upper lip of the Chinaman quiver slightly at times although this might have been only his imagination.

"Are you S———?" asked the hotel inspector in as sharp and brisk a tone as he could with a sense of a certain personal discomfort and an inexplainable feeling of smallness which had crept over him since the entrance of this gifted Chinese.

The Oriental bowed low, "Ah, the honorable gentleman has taken the pains to learn my unworthy name. So much attention overwhelms me and I can only reply by saying that I shall pray to my ancestors for your eternal salvation and the extension of your labors."

"Save your prayers for yourself," muttered the detective, "I believe you're going to need them worse than I do in the near future."

"Ah, most honorable gentleman, refuse not the prayers of thy lowly servant," and the Chinese bowed again, "for in my country prayers returned are often needed by those who give them back." At the same instant his eyes fell on the murdered man man for the first time.

"Ah," he exclaimed, and the almond eyes became mere slits, "Murdered?" he turned to the detective, "Oh, so many times I have warned him to be more careful and told him what the immortal Confucius, the giver of all wisdom, said, but it was of no avail it seems."

"Of what did you warn him?" The Chinese tapped his jade thumb ring with his fan and bowing low took the liberty of picking a small white thread from the inspector's coat sleeve before making a reply, "Oh, only this, that he had certain weaknesses of which I was aware and I have told him often that some day these little indiscretions would most likely cost him his life, and," the Chinese twisted his foot and gazed at the toe of it as it protruded from his Mandarin cape, "and," he repeated, smiling blandly, "it appears to have done so."

"Um-m," muttered one of the detectives, "so our deceased client was subject to indiscretions?" he turned to the Chinese and bowed sarcastically. "Will you please be a little more explicit?"

The Chinese merely shrugged his arched shoulders and with long, slender fingers picked up a sheet of paper from the table. It was the title page of the Professor's book.

"I should advise my honored friends of the detective force to secure a copy of this most esteemed work should the Gods decree that it ever be finished, for I am seriously afraid that this useful organ is not properly developed in the brain of our most worthy friend, the hotel inspector."

The detectives looked at each other not quite sure how to act with this Oriental who it now seemed was also slightly unbalanced. But as they themselves had nothing to work on in the form of information they mentally decided that they could not be any worse off so concluded to allow the Chinese to go on.

"Do you know who murdered him?" demanded all in one voice of the Cihnese.

"No, no, no," answered the Oriental as he opened his glorious fan to blow away some of the smoke from Jeremiah's none too select cigar, "but I think I can find out for you if you wish me to do so."

The detectives looked at each other and then one of them spoke, "Go on, but remember whatever you say here will be used against you."

"Oh, I don't think so," replied the Oriental, "for this is a matter between honorable friends and as gentlemen I am going to ask you to forget what I have said when I go. In fact, to make this easier I shall even assist you in the forgetting." The Oriental walked to the center of the room and removing his black cap with its glorious peacock feather, he hunched his shoulders and bent his back until the dome of his massive head was pointing directly at the dead man.

The officers then saw that the top part of his head was shaven clean for a piece about the size of a silver dollar and that on this spot a small green snake was traced in dark pigment. With his eyes closed and the crown of his head pointing first in this way and then in that, the Chinese noiselessly slipped about the room and finally spoke in his soft, musical voice.

"It was precisely as I feared. A lady called upon the Professor, my esteemed friend, last evening. How many times have I warned my worthy brother of letters, even going to the extremity of presenting him with a beautiful book of proverbs by

Lao Tze and underlining in red those pertaining to his indiscretions. It was not the first visit of the fair lady but she had married and came to tell the Professor that their friendship was at an end. My honorable friend was so unwise he could not understand the warnings that I gave him although I have prayed to my ancestors to preserve him. He and the lady had a little misunderstanding, shall we say, there was a slight struggle which would not have occurred had he been a Chinese gentleman. My worthy friend losing his temper knocked the lady down with undue expression of western energy, unpardonable in the East, and turned his back. Now it seems that they lady's husband being out a great deal of the time had loaned her one of his revolvers to be used in case of burglars or other emergency. She had brought this with her and when my unfortunate friend turned his back she shot him and dropping the revolver with a scream ran from the room."

"That's a very pretty story," muttered one of the detectives, "but you forget one thing, Chinky, where's the gun?"

"It is still in the room," answered the Chinese, and the Oriental turned his head first in a general circle which he steadily decreased in size until it stopped on Jeremiah Johnson, the house detective.

"The revolver is in the upper pocket of this gentleman's coat where he has hidden it. He concealed it because upon entering the room for the first time he recognized it as the one he had given his wife."

The hotel inspector collapsed.

"How did you know?" he gasped.

The Chinese bowed himself towards the door, the smile still playing around his mouth.

"I should advise our friends, the honorable detectives, to carefully read that little book of tommyrot which my belated friend will not now be able to complete upon the interesting subject of "The Third Eye."

He slowly closed the door, saying as he passed out, "I do not think any of you will use the information I have given you against me but should that be your intention I can only pray to my fathers for assistance."

The four detectives stood alone, blank expressions on their faces.

"What happened?" asked Jeremiah Johnson as he looked down at the revolver in his hand.

"I don't know," replied the other three.

"Say, was that Chink in here or not?"

"I don't know.'

"Then where did the gun come from? Whose is it?"

The oldest of the four detectives scratched his head and turned to the other three, "What have we been doing this last half hour? It seems like I've been asleep. I can't remerber anything."

"It is the same with me," answered one after the other in turn.

They looked down upon the dead man and there upon the ground beside him lay the title page of his book. In the meantime the Chinese, his hands crossed in his sleeves, shuffled slowly down the corridor, his face set in the placid satisfaction of the Oriental.

"I really do hope that these honored gentlemen will not use anything that I have said against me. In fact, I very much believe they will not be able to do so, for my good brothers in the western world have short memories—on problems of this nature. Poor Professor, if he had only developed that Third Eye a little himself he might have been spared by the gods to complete that honorable work!"

The Brothers of the Shining Robe

Chapter I
The Temple of Caves

WHY I CAME into the world with this deep seated wanderlust I have never been able to explain. Relatives and friends said that it was the blood of ten generations of soldiers and fighters for the British crown, but I have always believed that these things are not inherited but rather are the results of peculiar phases of individuality, the true explanation of which has only come to me in later years. Suffice it to say by way of introduction that I have been a wanderer upon the face of the earth,—from the South Sea Islands to the great salmon fisheries of Alaska and Columbia, from plague stricken Burma to the Deserts of Mexico, from Tartary to Algeria, from the blue lagoons of Venice to the domes and mosques of Constantinople, I have wandered in an endless search.

I came into this world with a larger fortune than is good for most, the younger son of an Earl. None of the responsibilities of my family worried me for it seemed improbable, with two elder brothers, that the cares and problems of an estate would ever descend upon my shoulders. So year after year I wandered over three-quarters of the known globe. At last one sultry evening I found myself standing on a point of rock jutting out from the sides of a great cliff, before me unrolling in majestic grandeur rose the snow-topped glaciers of the Himalayas. Straight in front the sheer crest of Mt. Everest shot heavenward and the rays of the fast setting sun bathed it in purple and rose shadows so that its glacial peak gleamed like the diamonds in the crowns of Emperors.

The strange land of the East had always held a fascination for me, and now I stood looking out at this great expanse of natural majesty hundreds of miles from the nearest white man merely as the result of fancy. During my wanderings in Northern and Central India, which had occupied some five years I had come closer to a true understanding of the Oriental mind than many white men. I had eaten with them, slept with them, prayed with them, tended, with practical kniwledge which is the inherent right of the western world, their sick, read their books, loved them and hated with them, and as the result I believe I can honestly say that to some degree at least I know the East.

While talking one day with one of their learned and holy men he told me a little, with the trust of many months of friendship, of the centerground of their faith, pointing to where the blue haze of the sky was broken by the line of mountains, in a voice filled with awe and reverence he told me of the sacred Temple of the Caves. He said that there lived in this ancient monastery a very wise man beloved of God and the mouthpiece of Brahma. Then he became silent and would say no more, but my inquisitiveness was aroused and I asked many learned Brahmans to give me more details of this sacred temple, but all shook their heads and despite their high regard either knew nothing or refused to reveal that which they did know. It was that short legend, those few involuntary words of the old mendicant, that changed the destiny of my life, for with the impetuosity which remained with me even after the days of my youth, I decided to wander these hills and mountains until I myself found the Temple of the Caves and spoke with this great wise man whom legend told me lived there.

My readers would suppose that a simple thing like this was of small importance, but to a mind like mine which knew nothing of the responsibilities of one phase of life the mere carrying out of a desire was all important.

As evening fell on the day in question, I stood on the crag of rocks overlooking the valley in whose dark and gloomy depths a fine mountain stream fed by the glaciers flowed on in silence to spread later and be lost in the marshlands below. Five months I had climbed through the mountains, among the caves of the holy men, through cities long deserted, through jungles and among broken rocks, and like many other searchers who had gone before found no trace of the thing I sought. At my feet on the boulder lay a heap of human bones. Some other wanderer had ended his pilgrimage where I had but started mine. Slowly the beautiful view vanished in the haze of night and a pale blue light from the waning moon took the place of the sun, and slowly turning I descended again to the plateau some fifty feet below.

As I did so my eyes wandered upward past a great cleft of rock where I had been standing. Walls of granite and stone rose nearly a thousand feet in rough, broken grandeur. But as I stood gazing out and up a strange feeling possessed me. I do not know whether you have ever felt when alone that someone was standing behind you looking at you, but this feeling suddenly swept over me and in the eerie stillness I felt I was not alone, and yet as far as I could see in the pale moonlight no living thing was visible.

Suddenly over the rough ground at my feet a dark shadow passed as though a great bird had soared over the cliffs and rocks but the shadow was not that of a bird. It was that of a tall human being passing silently somewhere between me and the moon. Looking quickly to the top of the cliff, I was in time to see a stately whiterobed figure with long gray beard and white turban pass the field of vision between me and the light and vanish between two great rocky boulders.

Around this figure hovered a number of flashing, dancing lights of shining white and after he had gone for several seconds the opening gleamed and glowed as though by some hidden fire. Then even that vanished

I cannot explain the reason but the thought crossed my mind in a flash that this figure was in some way connected with the place I sought, and regardless of tearing my hands and clothing I climbed as rapidly as possible upward and in some ten minutes stood where the shining one had been. I found that I was in a natural hallway of rock which reminded me of the roofless temples of Karnac. On each side massive pillars of natural stone rose from thirty to fifty feet above me to be lost in the shadows of night, and the tiny, winding path led straight into the side of a lofty hill invisible from below.

I hesitated for I realied that it is not always safe to enter the temples of the East, but my hand closing over the hilt of my revolver reassured me, and with the bravado which shows lack of better sense I took a hitch at my belt and started up the mountain.

I must have gone nearly a mile in gloom which grew ever deeper before I realized that the walls had closed above me and that that I was no longer in a great canyon or cleft but was in a cave. There was no sign of human being and save for the narrow path it seemed that no living thing had ever entered there. My matches had given out but I had taken the precaution to pick up a broken stick which I had lighted and with this firebrand I kept on my way. The ruddy light of my torch made each outcropping rock appear to be a living thing.

Suddenly I stopped,—another light was added to that of my torch. Outlined against the smooth stone wall was a lighted doorway reflected from some angle invisible from my present position and in the doorway was the silhouette of a tall, thin figure whose hands seemed clasped upon his breast. Drawing my revolver I started to advance and suddenly a cold chill ran up and down my spine,—I could not move. My eyes, my hands and feet could move but I could go neither forward nor backward. As far as I could see there was nothing to prevent me but when I tried to take a forward step it seemed that I struck a wall which no power of mine could pass through. Then slowly a strange numbing sensation passed over me, my revolver dropped from a hand that could no longer hold it, and my firebrand struck the ground with it. I could do nothing but gaze at the red shadow outlined on the wall, a shadow which told by its flickering motion that it was caused by a blazing fire.

Slowly the figure moved and around an elbow of the rock there appeared a solitary being, the strangest that my eyes have ever looked upon. The man was nearly six and a half feet tall, robed from head to foot in a glistening, shining, pearl grey garment which in the moonlight outside I had mistaken for white. Around his head was a turban, one end of which fell upon his shoulder. His age none could tell but he appeared to be beyond the prime of life for his full black beard was flecked with grey as was his hair that fell contrary to custom on his shoulders from under the edge of his turban.

As I looked at him it seemed that my eyes too were paralyzed for in spite of all the efforts that I made I could not take them from his face. His eyes, though large and piercing, still held in them a look of gentleness and kindness. The feeling of fear changed to a strange attraction and warmth and comfort surrounded me the moment he turned his face to mine. All around his body which seemed powerful but spare, strange flickering shadows seemed to twist and turn. I felt in spite of myself and my disregard for heathen ideals that if I had not been paralyzed I would have been on my knees before him for there was something in that cave which no words of mine can express.

He slowly came forward and taking me by the hand motioned me to advance. As he did so it seemed that the metal fetters and bonds dropped from me, my consciousness and power of locomotion returned, and with perfect ease I followed him where before I could not go, and passing through an arch of natural stone I entered into one of the strangest rooms I believe that human being was ever in.

(To be continued)

"THE SACRED MAGIC OF THE QABBALLAH"
The Science of the Divine Names.
By
Manly P. Hall

In this work the study of numbers and the Hebrew alphabet is taken up in a way never before undertaken. No system of numerology or cabalism is promulgated but a few underlying principles are given here useful to all students of mystic, occult and cabbalistic philosophy. The work is divided into three parts as listed below:

Part One .... The Key to the Sacred Wisdom.

A Study of the flaming letters of the Hebrew alphabet, the creation of the Sacred Name, the mystey of the vowel points and the unwritten books of Moses.

Part Two .... The Origin and Mystery of Numbers.

Under this heading are grouped the natural laws as they are expressed in numbers from 1 to 10, and the application of these laws to the problems of daily living.

Part Three .... The Power of Invocation and
The Science of the Sacred Names.

In this part of the work transcendental magic is completely unveiled and the ancient rituals of calling up spirits is exposed and the true meaning of transcendentalism and the finding of the lost Word is presented to the student, including the invocation of Christ. A most unique and unusual document containing over fifty pages, neatly bound in an art cardboard cover. This work should be in the library of all occult students, not to be believed but to be considered.

As is the case with our other publications you must fix your own price for the work, not to cover your share of the responsibility but that the entire work may go on and you and others may be in a position to receive the work which we are putting out.

Masonry: "The Robe Of Blue and Gold"

THREE SILENT BEINGS hidden in the depths of the Unknown weave eternally the thread of human fate, three sisters known to the world as the Norns or Fates incessantly twist between their fingers a tiny cord which is one day to be woven into a living garment, the coronation robe of a king. Under many names this garment is known among the mystics and occult students of the world. To some it is the simple yellow robe of Buddhahood, by the ancient Jews it was symbolized as the robe of the High Priest and the garment of glory unto the Lord, while to the Masonic Brother it is the Robe of Blue and Gold, the Star of Bethlehem, the wedding garment of the spirit.

Three Fates weave this living garment and man himself is the creator of his fates. The triple thread of thought, action, and desire binds him when he enters into the sacred place or seeks admittance to the Lodge, but later this same cord is woven into the wedding garment whose purified folds shroud the sacred spark of his being.

We all like to be well dressed and robes of velvet and ermine seem to us symbols of rank and glory, but many an ermine cape has covered an empty heart while many a crown has rested on a tyrant's brow and many a velvet cloak has gowned an empty void. These symbols are earthly things and in the worlds of matter are too often misplaced. But the true coronation robe, the true garments of the Mason, are not of earth for his robe of glory tells of spiritual growth. The garments of the High Priest of the Tabernacle were but symbols of the bodies of men, which purified and transmuted glorify the life within, and the little sliver bells tinkled with never ending music from the fringe of his vestments, their silver note telling of a harmonious life while the breastplate reflected the gleams of Heavenly Truth from its many-sided gems.

There is one garment without a seam which was worn often by the Masonic Brothers of old, in the day of the Essenes when the monastry of the lowly Nazarenes rose in gloomy grandeur from the steep sides of Mount Tabor to be reflected in the silent waters of the Dead Sea. This one-piece garment woven without a seam is the spiral thread of human life, which, when purified by right motive and right living, becomes a tiny line of golden light which weaves eternally the purified garment of regenerated bodies. Like the white of the lambskin apron it stands for the simple, the pure, and the harmless, the requirements of the Master Mason, who must give up forever the pomp and vanity of this world and seek to weave with his own soul that simple one-piece robe which marks the Master.

We can still see the lowly Nazarene in His spotless robe of white, a garment no king could buy but worthy of a god. This robe is woven by the daily actions of our lives, each expression weaving a thread, black or white, according to our actions and the motives which prompted them.

As the Master Mason labors in accordance with his vows, he slowly weaves this spotless robe out of the transmuted expressions of his energies. It is this white robe which prepares and sanctifies him for the robe of glory which can only be worn over the spotless, seamless garment of his purified life.

Now comes the moment when the candidate, purified and regenerated, begins to radiate the life powers of the divine. From him pour forth streams of light and a great aura of many colored fires surrounds him with its radiance. This wonderful garment of which all earthly robes are but symbols is built of the highest qualities of human nature, the noblest of ideals, the greatest of aspirations, the purification of bodies, the unselfish service to others. All these things build into the Mason spiritual powers which radiate as a wonderful body of living fire. This is the Robe of Glory, this is the garment of Blue and Gold, which shining out as a five-pointed star of light heralds the birth of the Christ within. Man is then, indeed, a Sun of God pouring out through the tubes of his own being the life rays which are the Light of men.

This spiritual ray, striking hearts that long were cold raises them from the dead; it is the living light which illuminates those still buried in the darkness of materiality; it is the power whch raises by the Grip of the Lion's Paw; it is the Great Light which seeks forever the spark within all living things and finding it awakens again dead ideals with the power of the Master's word. Then the Master Mason becomes, indeed, the Sun in Leo and reaching downward into the darkness of crystallization and materiality raises his murdered Builder from the dead by the grip of the Master Mason.

As the sun awakens the seedlings in the ground, so this Son of Man, glowing with the Light divine, pours out from his own purified being the mystic spears of redeeming light which awaken the seeds of hope and truth and nobler lives in others where discouragement and suffering have too often brought down the temple and buried beneath its debris the true reason for being and the true motive for growth.

It is this robe which enfolds all things, warming them and preserving them with its light and life as the glorious robe of the sun, the symbol of all life, bathes and warms all things with its glow. Man is a god in the making and on the potter's wheel he is being molded as in the mystic myths of Egypt. As his light shines out to lift and preserve all things, he accepts the triple crown of godhood and joins the throng of Master Masons who in their garments of glory, the Robes of Blue and Gold, are seeking to illuminate the darkness of night with the triple light of the Masonic Lodge.

Ceaselessly the Norns spin the thread of human fate. Age in and age out upon the loom of destiny are woven the living garments of God. Some are rich in glorious colors and wondrous fabrics, others are broken and frayed before they leave the loom. But all are woven by the Three Sisters, thought, action, and desire, which in the hands of the ignorant build around them walls of mud and bricks of slime, while in the hands of the pure of heart this living thread is woven into raiments celestial and garments divine.

Do what we will, we cannot stop the nimble fingers that twist the threads but we can take the thread and use it as we will. The wool may be red with the blood of others, it may be dark with the uncertainties of life, but if we will we may restore its whiteness and weave from it the seamless garment of a perfect life.

Blessed are they that know and know that they know, for they are wise; blessed are they who know not and know that they know not, for they can be instructed; cursed are those who know not and know not that they know not for they are foolish; cursed are they who know and know not that they know, for they are asleep, and who shall awaken them?

The Triangle on the Mason's Ring

ALL CREATED THINGS express themselves through a trinity as the Yod, the Eternal Flame, manifests through the triangle of differentiation. The triangle is used in practically all the Mystery Schools, representing the three outpourings of the Unmanifest. The triple scepter and the threefold crown also symbolize the same general principles. Radiating out from man, the equilateral triangle symbolizes:

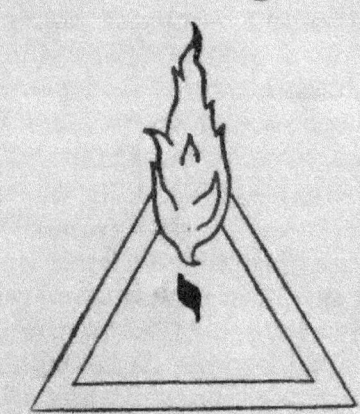

First side—
Mastery of the celestial world—Heaven.

Second side—
Mastery of the material world—Earth.

Third side
Mastery of the denomiacial world—Hell.

Taking the three general divisions of Heaven, Earth, and Hell, as they are played out in nature, we find them symbolical in the religions and philosophies of the world of the following principles:

Heaven, the superior	Earth, balanced	Hell, the inferior
Above	Center	Below
God	Man	Demon
Spirit	Mind	Matter
Sulphur	Mercury	Salt
Brain	Heart	Procreative System
Fire	Earth	Water
Altruism	Balance	Egotism
To be raised	Equilibrium	To be Lowered
Light	Firemist	Darkness
East	South	West
Vitalization	Vitalized matter	Crystalization
Oxygenization	Blending	Carbonization
Regeneration	Generation	Degeneration
Light	Shade	Darkness
Thought	Heart Sentiments	The Strength of Hand

The Great Triangle of human existence consists of the powers that bring in, the powers which preserve, and the forces which take out. These three form the Trinity of religious thought and have been personified as three phases of the Godhead, namely:

The Father	The Son	The Holy Ghost
The Creator	The Preserver	The Destroyer
Brahma	Vishnu	Shiva
Odin	Balder	Thor
Blue	Yellow	Red

These three are expressions of God whose color is indigo and who manifests in this world through His Three Witnesses which we know as the Triangle.

To a Mason the triangle is symbolical of balance. It teaches him that as a student of the mystic and the occult it is his duty to balance and harmonize all of these series of extremes, each one of which is dependent upon the others. All opposites are dependent one upon the other for existence and the initiate is one who has blended and unified all diversity. These three sides of the triangle represent the three kings of the Masonic temple glorifying their God but they also become murderers and prison walls when they are preverted through human ignorance and the animal tendencies.
animals tendencies.

(To be continued.)

The Magical Mountain of the Moon

SCHOLÆ MAGICÆ TYPVS.

From the Rare Work, "Lumen de Lumine" by Eugenius
Philalethes, London, 1651

A Letter From the Brothers of the Rose Cross

Concerning the Invisible Magical Mountain and the Treasure Therein Contained

EVERY MAN naturally desires a superiority, to have treasures of gold and silver, and to seem great in the eyes of the world. God, indeed, created all things for the use of man that he might rule over them and acknowledge therein the singular goodness and omnipotence of God, give Him thanks for His benefits, honor him and praise Him. But there is no man looks after these things, otherwise than by spending his days idly, they would enjoy them without any previous labor and danger, neither do they look for them out of that place where God hath treasured them up who expects also that man should seek for them there and to those that seek will He give them. But there is not any that labors for a profession in that place, therefore these riches are not found, for the way to this place and the place itself hath been unknown for a long time and it is hidden from the greatest part of the world. But notwithstanding it be difficult to find out this way and place, yet the place should be sought after. But it is not the will of God to conceal anything from those that are His, and therefore in this last age, before the final judgment comes, all these things shall be manifested to those that are worthy: As He Himself (though obscurely, lest it should be manifest to the unworthy) hath spoken in a certain place; there is nothing covered that shall not be revealed and hidden that shall not be known. We, therefore, being moved by the spirit of God do declare the will of God to the world which we have also already performed, (a) and published in several languages. But most men either revile or condemn that our manifesto or else waving the spirit of God they expect the proposals thereof from us, supposing we will straightway teach them how to make gold by art or furnish them with ample treasure, whereby they may live pompously in the face of the world, swagger, and make wars, turn vultures, gluttons, and drunkards, live unchastely and defile their whole life with several other things, all which things are contrary to the blessed will of God. These men should have learned from those ten Virgins (whereof five that were foolish demanded oil for their lamps from those five that were wise) how that the case is much otherwise. It is expedient that every man should labor for this treasure by the assistance of God, and his own particular search and industry. But the perverse intentions of these fellows we understand out of their own writings, by the singular grace and revelation of God; we do stop our ears and wrap ourselves as it were in clouds to avoid the bellowings and howlings of those men, who in vain cry out for gold. And hence, indeed, it comes to pass that they brand us with infinite calumnies and slanders which notwithstandings we do not resent but God in His good time will judge them for it. But after that we had well known (though unknown to you) and perceived also by your writings how diligent you are to pursue the Holy Scripture and seek the true knowledge of God; we have also above many thousands thought you worthy of some answer, and we signify this much to you by the will of God and the admonition of the Holy Ghost.

There is a mountain situated in the midst of the earth or center of the world which is both small and great. It is soft also above measure hard and stony, it is far off and near at hand but by the Providence of God invisible. In it are hidden most ample treasures which the world is not able to value. This mountain by envy of the Devil who always opposes the glory of God and the happiness of man is compassed about with very cruel beasts and other ravenous birds whoch make the way thither both difficult and dangerous: and therefore hitherto because the time is not yet come the way thither could not be sought after nor found out but now at last the way is to be found by those that are worthy but notwithstanding by every man's self labor and endeavors.

To this mountain you shall go in a certain night (when it comes) most long and most dark and see that you prepare yourself by prayer. Insist upon the way that leads to the mountain but ask not of any man where the way lies, only follow your guide who will offer himself to you and will meet you in the way, but you shall not know him. This guide will bring you to the mountain at midnight when all things are silent and dark. It is necessary that you arm yourself with a resolute, heroic courage lest you fear those things that will happen and so fall back. You need no sword nor any bodily weapon, only call upon God sincerely and heartily. When you have discovered the mountain the first miracle that will appear is this: a most vehement and very great wind that will shake the mountain and shatter the rocks to pieces; you shall be encountered also by lions and dragons and other terrible beasts but fear not any of these things. Be resolute and take heed that you return not, for your guide who brought you hither will not suffer any evil to befall you. As for the treasure, it is not yet discovered but it is very near. After this wind will come an earthquake that will overthrow those things which the wind has left and make all flat but be sure that you fall not off. The earthquake being past there shall follow a fire that will consume the earthly rubbish and discover the treasure but as yet you cannot see it. After all these things and near the daybreak there shall be a great calm and you shall see the day star arise and the dawning will appear and you shall perceive a great treasure. The chiefest thing in it and the most perfect is a certain exalted tincture with which the world (if it served God and were worthy of such gifts) might be tinged and turned into most pure gold.

This tincture being used as your guide shall teach you will make you young when you are old and you shall perceive no disease in any part of your body. By means of this tincture also you shall find pearls of that excellency which cannot be imaged. But do not you arrogate anything to yourselves because of your present power but be contented with that which your guide shall communicate to you. Praise God perpetually for this His gift and have a special care that you use it not for worldly pride but employ it in such works which are contrary to the world. Use it rightly and enjoy it so as if you had it not, live a temperate life and beware of all sin, otherwise your guide will forsake you and you shall be deprived of this happiness. For know this of a truth whosoever abuses this tincture and lives not exemplary, purely and devoutly before man shall lose this benefit and scarce any hope will there be left ever to recover it afterwards.

This letter was written by the Brothers of the Rose Cross to Eugenius Philalethes and appears in his work now rare and out of date Lumen de Lumine, published in London, 1651, and in next month's issue we will consider the occult and Rosicrucian interpretation of this symbolical letter.

Atlantis, The Lost Continent

Very few people know of this wonderful land now one with the land of forgotten things for today there is very little to remind us of this ancient continent that was once so fair and greater even than ours in glory and beauty, a land filled with happy homes, with peasants, statesmen and philosophers, and all those things which we now think of in connection with the highest and greatest phases of life.

This great continent now lost, the great land of Atlantis, is now somewhere miles beneath the ocean and over it pass our great ocean liners and sailing ships. Strange sea creatures now play through the pillars of its ancient temples, weeds and mosses are twined around its ancient gateways, its libraries containing the sacred tomes of ages have vanished from the light of day and are now known only to the finny denizens of the deep, a land of desolation miles under the surface of the sea-blue waters, its wondrous arches thick with coral and its statues deep beneath the shifting sands of the ocean bottom.

In truth it is a continent that is gone, a land forgotten save by a few poets whose ancient songs tell of its vanished glory. Can we say that it is lost? No, nothing in nature can be lost, but great changes have come in the eternal program of divinity. As a land it is no more but as a memory it will remain forever in the soul of the mystic while the wondrous lesson that it teaches is well worth the glory that is gone.

Nature is like the changing surface of the sea and the waves that come and go. Today a thing is, tomorrow it is no more, but somewhere in the endless vistas of the infinite the thing that once has been shall always be. In a new environment, in settings changed, its life goes on manifesting the powers of the Creator. The broken flower is gone, not dead; it has vanished but is not lost. Somewhere mid stick or star it will bloom again. In other lands it will carry on its work of charming the eyes of the world and building ever more stately mansions and more complex organisms to give greater expression to its tiny life; its message is eternal and its life is without an end.

In order to understand the sublime message and the wondrous mystery of Atlantis it is necessary to realize the indestructibility of all things, and while its continent now lies beneath the ocean its work still goes on, its memory remains, its finger prints are on the marble slabs of eternity. Its work is never done but when it needs new fields for its endeavors, nobler channels for its expression, it goes on to other worlds, to other lands, to other beings, and its empty, broken shell moulds from the sight of men.

Let us picture for a moment this lost continent inhabited by a strange race, a few broken remnants of which still wander the earth, tottering slowly towards the veil of oblivion. Here and there still walks a Red Man, the remnants of a dying people. The ancient Egyptian of the Pharoahs is gone and now there lives in his place another people; the glory of Egypt is crumbled to the dust and the Temples of the Rising Sun are buried beneath its desert sands. The ancient Red Man is fast vainshing from our midst, he is no more, his last great stronghold in the Western Americas has been broken and as a dying wanderer he passes silently into the eternal West. Many are they who have hastened the day of his destruction, many are there today who have upon their hearts and hands the blood of this ancient people. But the law works eternally and those who have helped to bring about the destruction of even the least of these ancient peoples shall live to see their own land in ruins, and the time will come when the white race shall lie down in an endless tomb to be listed with the forgotten, to be laid side by side with the mighty kings of Atlantis. But that does not concern us at the moment.

Let us picture the Red Man in the days of his glory. A few remnants of broken temples on the Peninsula of Yucatan, a few deserted altars amid the snow peaks of the Andes, here and there a lonely pyramid rising from a desert waste, a sphinx of stone that never speaks, a handful of dried bones, a few old philosophies and heaps of broken stone, are all that is left to tell us of an ancient civilization upon whom the wrath of the gods was loosened and whose annihilation is practically complete. They had brewed their cups of poison which they themselves drained to the dregs. Their iniquity overflowed and they vanished as all must do.

Let us pass again back through the ages to the dawn of human thought, let us read again their record in the living powers of nature. As we gaze into the eternal mystery we see great mountains rise from the blue waters of the Atlantic; great plains clothed in verdure glorious appear from the darkness of the tomb; wondrous cities with twisting spiral minarets rise upward to the sky; colleges and universities paved in marble dot the fairest of all lands; great coliseums and amphitheatres, which modern man has never sought to build, rise out of the mists and bring back memories of days gone by. A beautiful land stretches before our eyes, a continent that blossoms as a rose, which extended all over that great area where now the mighty Atlantic rolls.

Far up in Iceland and Scandinavia, from Nova Scotia and Labrador, through banks of ice and snow great mountains rise, peopled with strange, wild beings. Further South the beautiful lands of the temperate zone rise out of the deep, from the British Isles to the coast of the United States, a great host of phantoms rise from the forgotten past, a mighty race of copper colored beings. Down through Egypt and South Africa they pass in steady streams; even through South America they wandred mid fertile fields which they tilled and over wondrous mountains that they climbed. A mighty race of happy, laughing people, strong of arm, great of heart, glorious in ideals. They were the Red Men that are now fast disappearing in the setting sun.

There amidst them great nations were established, princely governments were built, great universities spread knowledge to the corners of creation, kings and emperors in robes of silk and gold, in jewels and diamonds the heritage of gods, ruled over mighty peoples as numberless as blades of grass.

Here there came into being the Priest Kings of ancient times; the divine servants of the gods with the snakes upon their brows ruled Atlantis in the days of its glory, for it was not a land as we know it but a world of demigods, a land of masters. Life as we know it now was very different in the world in which they lived. Their civilization was wild, massive, and grand. The ignorance of many but the divine wisdom of a few marked the civilization of that ancient Empire.

Duriing those days great giants labored on the earth. Man was no puny being as he is today but stood rather like the one-eyed Cyclop gods of Homer and the strange beings of the Odyssey and Iliad. There the Frost Giants of Scandinavia walked the earth in the millions of years that are past. And the glorious, grand, and wonderful truth is, that these giants are not dead, the Hercules of myth still lives, the bodies have changed but so surely as these ancient peoples wandered the earth in the dawn of this day of creation so surely we are those peoples.

You and I have wandered amid the temples of Atlantis. The City of the Golden Gates has open its portals that we might enter. We are the ones whose footsteps sounded on its streets of marble in the days of the greatest race that yet has been. Row after row of pillars, mile upon mile of fiuted columns, millions of domed roofs, marked the civilization of Atlantis. Then the pyramids were in their glory and the casing stones had not yet known the vandalism of neglect. On ancient tablets now lost, in languages forgotten were engraved the history of mighty things, of the world in its making, of the glory of gods and sages that walked with men.

You and I were there in the ages listed with the dead, we wandered through the pillars of the ancient temples, in the robes of glory we stood before the altar fires, we gazed down from the mountain tops in pride and glory upon the works of our hands. Stone by stone we built the City of the Golden Gates, we were the Atlanteans who raised temples on the mountain peaks to the glory of our gods. Through the ages we labored, as slaves we have known the master's whip, as kings we have held the sceptre, and today we are living the things we once were as we raise our eyes and gaze into the future as of old from the mountain peaks of Atlantis.

In order that we may appreciate the civilization of the ancients, it is necessary for us to accept the great fundamental principle of the continuity of life. Those unwilling to accept this principle can never learn the mysteries of Atlantis, they can never know why that continent came and vanished again. In order to find the true reason, we must gaze back to the things we were and realize again how the altar fires in the temples burned low and dying buried beneath them the nations of the dead.

Let us try to picture one of the great Atlanteans,—his massive frame, his glorious brow, his eyes filled with the lustre of primitive life, unhampered by the ties which bury races, unbroken by the millstone of today's affairs, which in this land of ours are grinding human hearts to feed ambition. They had many things that we have lost, we have many things they never knew.

The reason for it all is that man must grow along many lines. If it were only necessary for him to have a glorious body and strength divine then the world would have ended with Atlantis or its end might have come in the days of classic Greece and the work would have been well finished, but there were other things to do.

Today we are the fifth great race of beings that have inhabited our world, the Atlanteans were the fourth, they lived their day and now have passed on to endless sleep, but the spirit continues its march eternal. Man has not yet reached the grandeur of Atlantis in the new civilization with which he works, but one day in the mystic future he will pass beyond anything that ever was before, and, having reached the heights of all, the white race will draw its shroud around it and vanish to make way for other peoples and other works, but the same spirits will remain.

Let us learn the lesson of Atlantis and build again in the mirror of the mind the things that brought about its grand destruction in the seventh day of its creation. We are the breakers of new ground but 'ere we go on we must review the old, we must live again that great power of concrete thought which was the crowning genius of Atlantis, we must remember its phillosophies and sciences. Then shall we be crowned with a new power to which end all races are striving,—the power of creative genius, the power of abstract thought, the power to unite, and that spiritual eye which sees the oneness of life and the brotherhood of man.

The keynote of Atlantis was the survival of the fittest, its great ones were great because the weak were weaker, but in our day a new power is being added. We have not yet reached the glory of the Aztec king before the coming of the white race, but we will reach it and pass beyond it with the great power of compassion crowning us more gloriously than ever, but, in passing, let us learn the lessons on the way.

Our world today stands as Atlantis stood, our buildings rise upward, their many towers pointing to the skies, our libraries are filled with ancient wisdom, our scientists and philosophers are exploring the mysteries of nature, again we fly through the air and under the sea, again we walk the path that Atlantis walked, but we must go on, we must survive to the glory of a greater work. The great birthright of every people is to labor with new things. This new world has dreams which Atlantis never dared to conceive and possibilities undreamt of by the men of old. But to do great things we must have the courage of conviction and the power to pave the way. You see we have other works to do in other ways. For a day we have forgotten the things we were, a veil conceals the past that we may learn the new thing in a different way. We are unfolding new powers, building new faculties, mastering new arts, creating new ideals.

The old soul, its years measured by the labors it has done, is now confronted with a great problem. It is our duty to take the best that Atlantis had to give, to learn the mysteries that Lemuria, now lost beneath the waters of Australasia, gave us in times more ancient even than Atlantis, and use them as steps to build upon their top a new temple based upon the foundations of the old. To go higher, to reach ever heavenward, is the age-long cry of the mysteries. It is the same cry that sounded through the temples of Atlantis. It is the fulfillment of this inner urge that makes necessary new experiences, that bring new worlds out of the waters and causes others, their labors finished, to vanish from the sight of men.

In Atlantis many of the things we call sublime would have formed but kindergarten classes amid those ancient philosophers. White-domed temples of education filled Atlantis. Every city not matter how small was crowned by its universities and colleges and in the City of the Golden Gates were the divine sources of learning which initiated those who came out of the world into the way of the gods. We have taught many things they did not know but they taught things which today we cannot remember but still have hidden in our souls to be used again when the moment arises. Or mayhaps we were thoughtless then as we are now and today we little realize life because we never lived or studied it then. Therefore we wander through the mazes of religion, our spiritual teachers contradict each other eternally, and when we read the mysteries of Revelation we believe the writer must have written for himself alone. We wander betwixt sacred philosophies and moral ethics which are sealed truths that mean nothing to our souls. We were the drones amid the hives of learning as oftimes we are today, so now we know what we learned then and tomorrow we shall be known by what we learn today.

We can tell the world how to live but we cannot make them live it. Those who were told but did not practice, today know not the lessons that they might have learned.

There was in the City of the Golden Gates a temple dedicated to the worship of Light, the divine principle of human knowledge. This Light was served by the priestcraft, it was served also by the legislator, it was honored and adored by all the powers of that ancient land. From between the pillars of this temple came forth the Priest Kings. Here humbly before the altar they prayed that the divine light from the seven stars might come down to them, but the years went by and materiality took the place of spirituality. Then came the handwriting on the wall, the stars in their courses upon the heavens penned strange, celestial words upon the blue field of eternity, and the priests raising their crucifixes, cried, "Behold! the Sun-God is murdered, the Light is passing over into darkness!"

Then the great cataclysms came that shook this mighty people to the very foundations of their world. The savages from the North and South fought with the civilized people who tried to enslave and defraud them. They were driven back but the debt of blood was upon the hands of Atlantis and the priests of the ancient temples cried in the marketplaces, "With the spilling of blood Atlantis has sealed its doom!"

Its high spiritual ideals were buried beneath materiality, death and pestilence walked in its ways, degeneracy and lust overran its people, and its nations were drenched in blood.

There are many kinds of blood. There is that which comes from broken hearts, there is the life blood that pours from the soul, there is the blood of our fellowmen, and all this was loosened by the falling peoples of Atlantis. Again the warning of the gods broke upon it, its nations were split and torn, but more and more the black light took the place of the white. Slowly the divine Priest King lost his touch with God, his connection with divine powers which mold the destiny of worlds was broken, the priestcraft lost its sacred word, the name of the Living God; the light went out upon the altars; magic and sorcery took the place of the sacred mysteries and from the gods no longer flowed the life which makes nations live.

A new people was born out of the land of darkness to carry the dying fires and the Shekinah's glory out of the lost land. All glorious things it seems must sometime wither; all the flowers that bloom must one day fade. Blessed are those who know that the fading flower but marks the passing of a life to a more glorious work, for man need not be always in the trough of the sea but may step from the crest of one wave to the crest of the next. So a new race was born to take charge of those who were true, and the Great White Brotherhood slowly formed a new people amid the falling temple pillars of the old, and the sacred Ark with the Cherubim sacred to the Lord passed slowly onward to the West. Around them gathered the faithful ones and the Great Light went out in the land of darkness which again was shattered by mighty cataclysms. Its people were torn by an unknown fire; none knew what that fire was for they had not read the handwriting on the wall; they had not heard the warning which the white-robed priests had spoken to them from the housetops nor the sacred words which were chanted from the temple steps for their ranklings and dissensions had drowned its note.

But the voice had sounded from the temples of Atlantis, saying, "Thou art weighed in the balance and found wanting." The Great White Brotherhood worked on however in a mysterious way and a new continent was unrolled for the chosen peoples, a great pathway was made in the waters and those who still served the noble and true passed onward into the promised land.

All that was left of the Continent of Atlantis was a single island. At last about 9000 B.C., or a little later, this dying remnant of Atlantis sank and in less than twenty-four hours millions of souls were freed from their molds of clay.

Now comes the problem. With all their arts and sciences crystalization crept in, which is the end of all that lives, the crystalization of thought, vitality, and growth. Nothing has to crystalize but all things do that stagnate. Today we face the same problems that brought about the destruction of Atlantis in the ages that are past. Our lands stretch out in peace and plenty and we too feel secure. Nothing, surely, can happen to us! Yet the moment no man knoweth. But one thing we do know, either the work must be done and done well, either the soul must learn its lessons or else new environments are necessary to make completion possible.

When we allow the fires upon our altars to die out, when we allow our higher beings to starve, then we are failing in the great work. Then again will the thunderbolts of Jove be loosened and the eternal scythe reap in its harvest.

Let us consider some of the causes that brought about the destruction of Atlantis. The first was blood. All those who live by the sword shall perish by the sword and with the first drop of blood that man sheds comes the price,—his own must flow. Blood feeds the flames of passion and when the animal in man is fed he becomes as a ravening wolf and the Four Horsemen ride forth again on their journey of destruction. Only peace can bring peace and that must come from man himself. We are all the body of the Father, we are all the Christ in flesh, and when each of us does as he should things will prosper, not with the transcending prosperity that rises up and then disappears like a comet but with the slow, gradual growth that marks the spreading oak. Unless man learns the ways of peace the day is not far off when the blue waves will break over his homes and the Light will go on to other lands.

The second necessity of man is to find the lost art of beauty. Probably you do not know what beauty means, for beauty is a mystic thing. We can look at a man like Lincoln, as homely as the fence rails that he split, and yet there is beauty there. We can look around us and many are there whom we call handsome but beauty is not there. There is much prettiness but little beauty. As we look at the gods of Greece and Rome we find what the world has long called beauty, but when you look at the eyes you will find a blank for the sculptures did not fill them in. Few realize what beauty is or how subtle are its ways. None know it who have it; none realize who really possess it. It is something that shines out and molds man into an expression of itself. Gold trinkets, ribbons, and a powderpuff are not the secrets of beauty. Beauty is of the soul and we need more of it. We must have more of that beauty that molds form into the ideal. The eyes of form see the beauty of form alone but the true mystic realizes that the source of beauty is not the form, it is the soul that shines within. We may look over the world at those who are now judged as the beautiful, the handsome, the distinguished, and yet always there is something missing, and it was the loss of that something that sank the Continent of Atlantis. We must have more beauty and the world must realize more and more that "Beauty is as beauty does." Never mind how perfect the form if the soul and mind be not there it is an empty shell. It is a dead thing without a reason for its being. The beauty of harmony based upon strength, the beauty of peace strong on the foundation of compassion, the beauty of purity supported by knowledge, is missing. It was missing with the later Atlanteans and if we would not follow in their footsteps we must find it again today.

We must mold our lives into that divine glory we seek under the name of Christ, into the grandeur that was found in the temples of the ancients where a beautiful life molded a body worthy of a Greek god. The beauty of compassion, of love, and of spiritual thought is sadly missing in the world today. It is the first to go. We hardly know when it goes; slowly it fades away and with it fades the strength of a people. Long before the inharmony breaks forth as a ravenous flood, this subtle something vanishes in the night. It is the handwriting on the wall, a warning to all who live, for when beauty goes with it goes the strength of a people. We can bring it back, this elusive thing, this Psyche, floating over the marshlands, veiled in a mystic haze, a something unseen but felt. It must come back, if our age is to reach the goal it seeks.

There is something else also that must return,—the universities of Atlantis must be built again. We must raise again the schools of learning, by learning how to live, for the ignorant are dead and there are none so ignorant as those who will not learn, there are none so blind as those who will not see. Yet we forget, but let this thought be in our minds, those who forget shall be forgotten. Our world is filled with forgetfull people who forget by habit, they have forgotten so long that now they cannot remember, but in some way they must be helped to learn. We must understand the meaning of education, educo, to draw forth, not to cram in, to bring out that which we have already built within. From the heart of our beings blaze forth the fires of Atlantis, in our souls is the history of peoples as we have lived it. We must remember it, we must draw forth that knowledge, for the great things we would build can only be raised upon the things we know. If we are to create dream castles in the ethers we must bring back again the power of dreaming. We cannot imagine that which we have never known or think of that which we have never been, therefore education means to draw forth and profit by the things that we have been and the lessons that we have learned.

This world must learn. If it learns as Atlantis did it will die, but if it profits by the lessons of Atlantis it will live, and each of us were the Atlanteans and have studied the lessons that can save our lands. It is no longer a problem of what we want to do, it is what we should do, it is what the duties of nature demand of us. In the name of the gods we must act. Let us remember the blood that sank Atlantis. Blood is heat, strife, and confusion. It is the life force of the universe, it is the Lamb of God slain for the sins of the world, it is the power of a people. We must take the golden chalice and catching in it the life blood that now we waste return it to the altar of our God.

Then too we must have beauty, beauty of thought, glory of ideal. The loves of men must give place to the loves of God, the passions of our age must be transmuted into the compassions of the gods, form must give place to spirit, or again we shall be numbered with the dust.

We must have education, if we do not we shall find out to our sorrow that the strength of a people depends upon the knowledge that it applies; not upon hopes, wishes, or the willy-nilly blowing of concepts but upon the solid rock of truth must our nations stand.

Man is a slave of his fears, a servant of ignorance, and a grovelling wretch at the feet of the Unknown. He must rise and taking his light explore the recesses of each mystic cave. Each individual, if he does not know how to live, to eat, to think, must find out; the gods will never tell him unless he hears the voices of the gods in the wisdow of his fellowmen. The way of knowledge, brotherhood, and service, the way of purity and truth, alone can liberate us from the wheels of birth and death. We may talk of our shortcuts, backdoors, second stories, patent medicine spirituality, canned religion, just-as-goods, etc., to say nothing of the advanced spiritual teachings which transcend common sense, but unless we live the life to which we aspire we shall be numbered with Atlantis.

It is more important to know these things by far than rounds and periods, for upon them rests life itself. We are governed by the laws of cause and effect and today we are building the causes which sank the Atlantean world and we can expect nothing better for ourselves. We must realize that the earth beneath our feet is indeed the Son of Necessity born that man may live. It will mold itself into the needs of man but his needs are seldom his wants. Humanity needs a good housecleaning but they do not want it, and it must either come about through our loving service and labors with our fellowman or the thunderbolts of Jove.

Let the spiritual fires of our universities rise from the planes of matter, let the grandeur of ancient Greece be ours, let us so live that we shall be a credit to creation and to the plan that brought us into being. As Luther Burbank converted the cactus with its prickly thorns into a nutritious food product by removing the sting, so let us transmute the powers of the people that they may rebuild and recreate. It is more important far to help someone who is not able to help himself than to have been cloistered for hours with the sages. We warn all occultists and true students that their place is in the world working and not in the temple praying, that their duty is to make the world their temple, to don the white armor of purity and ideals, and armed with the greatest of all weapons, which leaves no sting, the sword of truth, knowledge, and light, to go out and labor for the right.

We cannot escape the sorrows of the world but we can go out and change its tears to laughter and be in a happier world that we ourselves have made.

So as we stand on the cliffs of lost Atlantis and see the restless sea breaking upon the shore and hear the dark waves which are like the surgings of a lost people, let us realize that they are our own broken lives and that our own voices speak to us from the depths of the waters salty with the bitterness of the tears of millions who allowed black magic to replace the true mysteries, even as we do today. Black magic means the perversion of things. When we use energy to destroy, when we tear down the dream castles of those we love, when we fill our lives with sordidness, we are black magicians. When we take the powers of God and use them to deceive our fellowmen, when we use the powers God gave us to free our souls, to cast down, then we are black magicians who have not learned our lesson from the sinking of Atlantis.

Let us open wides the gates, let the gates of brass swing open and man come forth. Let the tombstones be rolled away and the divine in man be released from the shackles that now bind him, let the divine in us be liberated, and Christ call unto the lower man, "Lazarus, come forth!" Let our ideals be gleaming lights upon the hilltops. We must tear up the thistles and briars before it is too late and plant flowers in their place and dedicate our lives to helping, serving, lifting, purifying, and glorifying, mentally, physically, and spiritually, all with whom we come in contact. We shall then be listed with the white robed Brothers, who, carrying the sacred relics, pass with them into the promised land.

A new race is to be born. Who will be its parents? There are few of earth who are ready to give to the new land a proper birthright. Let us remember once more the three things which bring with them the loss of all, the price of blood, the loss of beauty, and the perversion of education which sank an Empire greater far than our own, and that the same power will sink this continent unless in each individual peace and brotherhood takes the place of blood and hate, beauty of spirit replaces sordidness of life, and that great eternal light, knowledge, supplants human ignorance.

Books and Their Place in Occultism

OF ALL THE THINGS in the universe which mold themselves into the expression of individual likes and dislikes, there are none with such elastic consciousness as books for regardless of our feelings or the conditions which have colored the day we always find something congenial in the pages of a good book. There are no truer friends than volumes whose treasured contents have become etched into our souls. The average individual's idea of a friend is someone who will agree with them and a book is the most obliging of all. If you feel lazy the book will be most uninteresting, if you feel mean, meanness gleams from every page, if sarcasm holds you in its grasp every word of the author seems a satire, while if you feel hungry for a certain line of information the book is eager to give it to you.

Those who have found joy in reading and bringing into play upon their lives the wisdom of past ages as it is immortalized in ancient tomes have reached a great point in the growth of their being. But, above all, if we realize that the book gives to us that which we have given it, we then understand that mirrored in its pages are the thoughts and ideals of our own lives.

In reading ancient books we see pass before our mind's eye the thoughts of others brought down to us through the ages from races and cultures now extinct, yet to all of them we must give understanding through the light within our own soul and with the keys of our own being unlock their sealed pages.

There is no more wonderful place in all the world than the bookstores such as we find in the old countries, with rows and rows of musty volumes, where stepladders lead up to shades unknown, and ancient tomes some of which have slept upon their shelves since the days of Cromwell line the walls as far as the eye can see. The hands that wrote them are long since laid to rest and many an aged philosopher has put them aside to wander in some distant land, yet the thoughts, ideals, and aspirations of thousands live again for posterity through the words in their books. They are dead and yet they live eternally in their thoughts and these thoughts live on through the ages in the leaves of their books.

We feel a certain reverence and awe as we enter one of these hallowed spots, the curiosity shops of the human mind. We can feel that the shades and shadows of author and poet hover still around the children of their genius. A subdued hush falls upon our being as we stand before a mighty book, for it seems that we are in the presence of a great and superior thing. Before us stands a throbbing brain stored with information and its old bindings seem to enfold the massive brows of philosophers.

As we go to various parts of these ancient shops we find many wondrous things, beautiful books illuminated with glorious faces and flowered letters by monks in their meditation, when lives were spent in the writing of a single work. Some are in ancient parchments, others in old block bindings, while a few here and there have been desecrated by the hands of man and their torn and tattered pages speak of the vandalism of human nature.

These old books bring back to us the days that are past and tie the breathing, living today to the yesterdays numbered with the dead. All these wondrous relics of thought recall sacred memories as they stand like silent headstones on the drooping shelves, for in truth bookstores are graveyards of the human mind. As cemeteries are filled with the children of men so these old book stores conceal in their numberless niches, shrouded in darkness, the children of human thought. But the thoughts live on eternally and within the rude coffins of their ancient bindings they wait to be liberated by those who love them.

Let us roll away the stones which mark their resting place and with the light of our own thoughts and the vision of our own lives carry on these beauteous truths. Many of them are the dying bequests of those who have given all for man, written at a time when every penstroke was a hardship, when to express a thought or an ideal was to court destruction at the stake or wheel. These books stand as living testimonials of the courage of great souls, for they are the last word to the world of poets and mystics, the dreamers of the ages who have suffered much and given all that their dreams might survive to posterity.

Good books, indeed, are treasures for the very soul of the author speaks through the pages that he wrote. Today, alas, books with great ideals and noble thoughts are few but in those days they were the labors of a lifetime and their every word was illuminated by the blood of the author. Every book has behind it a quaint pathos which is irrestisibly fascinating to those students who have developed organs of veneration. Why should man not feel reverence as he clasps in his hands the life work of another human being who now lies silently in some little churchyard while the thing for which he gave so much rests undusted on the shelves?

If the clairvoyant could but go there he would see lives and wars, hates and fears, loves and sorrows, living again among the lives around him, speaking again from the silent walls while loving hands behind the veil still fondly guard the children of their souls.

There are many reasons why we should love to wander among these old bookstores and digging into the past bring forth these treasured writings, for in some mystic way they seem to whisper of the libraries lost in the darkness of the human soul. Among the mystics there are those who spend their lives in doing nothing but preparing and preserving ancient writings, and far from the sight of our ordinary lives these great souls have dedicated their beings to the transcribing again from the akashic records of nature the mystic truths now lost to mankind.

The average individual does not know how to read a book, if he did he would not read so many. Reading is an art and there are few indeed who know how to glean the treasures from the printed page. Books have to be read as they were written, thought for thought, spirit for spirit, and to know the works of philosophers we must ourselves be philosophers. To understand the meaning of ancient truths our minds must be attuned to the souls who wrote them. One who really reads belongs to the realms of the immortals for every sentence is something to be lived for years, every thought a child entrusted to our care. Few, indeed, ever learn the mystery of the wondrous lives immortal concealed beneath their broken covers. An old book is an oracle which not only gives forth the thoughts of the author but whispers in the voice of the age in which it was written the living story of human progression.

The rows of ancient books that fill the curiosity shops of Europe sink into oblivion beside the cosmic library of human consciousness, the lost libraries of the human soul. Up in the dusty attic of the human brain is a room filled with ancient heirlooms, memories of a forgotten day, and in this room a library is stored away. It is not seen by everyone and even its existence is dreamed of but by few, but there you will find under the cobwebs of time the rare occult tomes of other days, the sacred books of mystery and magic, philosopry and art, which are missing from the bookshelves of the world. In this little room, stored away, are the lost library of Alexandria, the sacred books of the Incas and the Aztecs, and the mystic scriptures of the ancients. All these are the rightful possessions of every living soul. If only man would break through the dust of ages and enter once more that little room! This is the great library of thought, immortal in the human mind, and books are merely thoughts put on paper.

Each day we inscribe in the great Book

of Life the history of our world as seen through the eyes of the soul, each life we turn a page and store away the ancient manuscripts somewhere in the darkened attics of the past. As we walk the path that leads to greater understanding and the light within shines forth more brightly we find ourselves amid these ancient rooms, surrounded by these mystic tomes, and if we would read we have but to take them from their shelves and within their dusty pages is the history of our being. In the brain of man is an inexhaustible fund of knowledge and truth hidden away and accessible only to those who have found the knock that will open the door. Millions of years man has been writing this library, tracing its letters in flames and tears. Some wonderful day we shall find this little room and there surrounded with the ideals of the past we shall know again the things that we have done and the powers that we have been. Then we shall realize that our labors have never been lost for in this great domed library of our own consciousness on records of living ether is stored away our every thought and action, and like the ancient volumes on the bookshelves we have but to take them out and read again the message they contain.

The Light of Asia

THERE IS no more beautiful character in the world than that of Buddha, immortalized by Arnold's wonderful poem, "The Light of Asia." As the Christian worlds, divided by so many barriers from the East, seek to walk the path that leads to Light, they ofttimes overlook this great Light which has shone on over half the known world and the wonderful message which he has given out to the children of men.

God works in many ways, through many vehicles, in many lands, but if there ever was one through whom the Almighty labored it was the Prince Sidartha, the Compassionate Lord of the Lotus. His teachings filled with truths divine in no way combat the principles of Christianity but rather give to the western world keys with the aid of which it may labor more successfully.

To this Great One we owe our greatest understanding of the doctrine of Reincarnation, one of the fundamental principles of spiritual growth. This hypothesis is generally neglected not because of its improbability but because it is so different from the accepted concepts which we have. There is no real reason for our disputing it; nowhere in our sacred Scriptures are there any words against it but in many places it appears that an understanding of this law was taken for granted.

Reincarnation is the only concept of life which is universal in opportunity, personal in responsibility, impersonal as to environment, and all-promising in its possibilities. The accepting of this law, while it does not bring Heaven closer, forever dissipates the concept of Hell eternal, the bugaboo of the Christian religion. It gives noble incentive to greater labors, it promises sure rewards for work well done, it is socialistic in its concept, and the entire doctrine of Reincarnation as it has been presented by Buddha, the great Oriental educator and non-radical socialist, can be stated as follows:

The doctrine of Reincarnation teaches equal opportunities for all and special privileges for none, success being the reward for work well done and failure the result of indolence. Buddha, in giving to man this law, has presented the only concept of life which could be acceptable to a just Creator aand still explain the inequalities of human consciousness.

Therefore we are grateful to the bearer for the Light which he has brought,—who brings it matters not for the Light is of Heaven. And as these concepts of life become universalized we shall recognize the Light of Asia as one of the Lights of the world.

"The Lost Keys of Masonry"

By

MANLY P. HALL

In this work an attempt has been made to dig from the ruins of Speculative Masonry the lost keys to the operative craft. In it the three degrees of the Blue Lodge are taken up separately, their requirements explained and the real meaning of the Masonic allegory given out for the benefit of Masons and Masonic students. The book contains a preface by a well-known Los Angeles Mason.

The following headings are discussed in the work:

        Prologue, the Masonic allegory, "In the Fields of Chaos."
    Chapter One—"The Candidate."
    Chapter Two—"The Entered Apprentice."
    Chapter Three—"The Fellow Craft."
    Chapter Four—"The Master Mason."
    Chapter Five—"The Qualifications of a True Mason."
    Epilogue—"In the Temple of Cosmos."

The entire presented in a sensible, comprehensive manner which can be understood by those not otherwise acquainted with the subject.

The book is handsomely illustrated with a four-color plate of the human body showing the position of the three Masonic Lodges on the cosmic man, also other pictures in black and white. The book is handsomely bound in solid cover with three-color cover design.

The work contains about eighty pages printed in two colors with a very fine quality of art paper.

Like all of our other works this book is only securable through the free-will offering of those desiring to secure it. Each person is placed upon his own honor and only reminded that the perpetuation of the work depends upon the cheerful co-operation of the workers.

These booklets by the same author may be secured by sending to Postoffice Box 695, Los Angeles, California, care of Manly P. Hall.

Price. These publications are not for sale but may be secured through voluntary contribution to help meet the cost of publication.

The Breastplate of the High Priest

A discussion of Old Testament symbolism showing how the spiritual powers of nature reflect themselves through the spiritual centers in the human body which we know as the jewels in the breastplate of Aaron. This booklet is out of print but an attempt will be made to secure a few copies for any desiring them. Illustrated.

Buddha, the Divine Wanderer

A new application of the life of the Prince of India as it is worked out in the individual growth of every student who is in truth seeking for the Yellow Robe.

Krishna and the Battle of Kurushetra

The Song Celestial with its wonderful story of the Battle of Life interpreted for students of practical religion. The mystery of the Blue Krishna and his work with men.

The Father of the Gods

A mystic allegory based upon the mythology of the peoples of Norway and Sweden and the legend of Odin the All-Father of the Northlands.

Questions and Answers, Part One
Questions and Answers, Part Two
Questions and Answers, Part Three

In these three booklets have been gathered about fifty of the thousands of questions answered in the past work gathered together for the benefit of students.

Occult Masonry

This booklet consists of the condensed notes on a class in mystic Masonry given in Los Angeles. It covers a number of important Masonic smybols and the supply is rapidly being exhausted.

Wands and Serpents

The explanation of the serpent of Genesis and serpent-worship as it is found among the mystery religions of the world and in the Christian Bible. Illustrated.

The Analysis of the Book of Revelation

A short study in this little understood book in the Bible, five lessons in one folder as given in class work during the past year.

The Unfoldment of Man

A study of the evolution of the body and mind and the causes which bring about mental and physical growth, a practical work for practical people.

Occult Psychology

Notes of an advanced class on this subject dealing in a comprehensive way with ten of its fundamental principles as given to students of classes in Los Angeles on this very important subject.

Parsifal and the Sacred Spear

An entirely new view of Wagner's wonderful opera with its three wonderful acts as they are applied to the three grand divisions of human life, the Legend of the Holy Grail, which will interest in its interpretation both mystics and music lovers.

Faust, the Eternal Drama

This booklet is a companion to the above and forms the second of a series of opera interpretations of which more will follow. The mystic drama by Goethe is analyzed from the standpoint of its application to the problem of individual advancement and its wonderful warning explained to the reader.

The All-Seeing Eye

Modern Problems in the Light of Ancient Wisdom

A Monthly Magazine
Written, Edited and
Compiled by
MANLY P. HALL

JUNE, 1923

THIS MAGAZINE IS NOT SOLD

THE ALL-SEEING EYE

MODERN PROBLEMS IN THE LIGHT OF ANCIENT WISDOM

VOL. 1   LOS ANGELES, CALIF., JUNE, 1923   No. 2

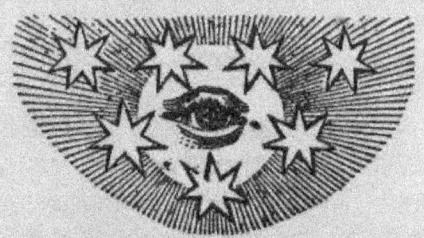

This magazine is published monthly for the purpose of spreading the ancient Wisdom Teachings in a practical way that students may apply to their own lives. It is written, published, and edited by Manly P. Hall and privately published for circulation among his students and those interested in his work.

Those desiring to secure copies of this magazine or who wish to subscribe to it may do so by writing directly to the editor.

This magazine is published and distributed privately to those who make possible with their financial support its publication. The magazine cannot be bought and has no fixed value. Like all of the ancient teachings which it seeks to promulgate it has no comparative value but the students must support it for its own instrinsic merit.

To whom it may concern: It is quite useless to inquire concerning advertising rates or to send manuscripts for publication as this magazine cannot possibly consider either as this is a non-commercial enterprise. All letters and questions, subscriptions, etc., should be mailed to P. O. Box 695, Los Angeles, California, in care of Manly P. Hall, Editor.

The contents of this magazine are copyrighted but permission to copy may be secured through correspondence with the author.

This magazine does not represent nor promulgate any special sect or teaching but is non-sectarian in all of its viewpoints. Suggestions for its improvement will be gladly considered if presented in the proper manner.

TABLE OF CONTENTS

	Page
EDITORIAL—Highbrows and Low Morals	3
POEM—The Masters	2
OCCULT FICTION—Brothers of the Shining Robe, Chapter One, The Temple of Caves (Continued)	15
A LITTLE EPISODE FROM LIFE	14
MYSTIC MASONRY—The Shrine	18
ASTROLOGY—The Key Words of the Sign of Aries	25

SPECIAL ARTICLES

Art	6
Man, the Human Violin	7
Brothers of the Rose Cross, Their Letter Continued	12
Plate from Robert Fludd.	
Adam and Eve and the Flaming Sword	20
The Mystery of Initiation	21
Broken Dolls	27
Ships That Pass in the Night	28
THE PEARLY GATES GAZETTE	32

ARTICLES THAT WILL APPEAR IN THE FOLLOWING ISSUES OF THIS MAGAZINE.

Occult and Practical Eugenics.
The Divine Masquerader.
Green Fire.
Cranks and Crankisms as Factors in Indigestion.

Just Lonely.
The Dope Problem.
What Will the Harvest Be?
Orpheus and the Celestial Harmonies.
And Many Others.

THE MASTER

Alone 'mid the throng that surrounds him,
    A figure silent and meek,
While the battle of life surges round him,
    Still he walks in the ways of the weak.

A soft, sweet look from tender eyes,
    The clasp of a comrade's hand,
A word of hope from a world of sighs,
    A heart that can understand.

By this he is known in the world of men
    As one of that mystic band
Who has turned back to trod again
    Life's ever-changing sand.

Where he walks the world seems brighter,
    Better for his having trod,
While sorrowing souls grow a little lighter
    For having felt their God.

With never a fear, he walks the way
    That leads to the heights above
Where the light of Truth holds perfect sway
    'Mid the selfless hearts of love.

This is the way that the Masters go
    To the light through a battle won,
Far up from the shade in the depths below
    On the path of the Rising Sun.

EDITORIAL

Highbrows and Low Morals

DURING THE COURSE of human events it has come under our personal observation that a certain Mr. Belshazzar Jinx, whose intellectuality and power of analytical reasoning is of international repute, was arrested last night by Officer Murphy who found him intoxicated rushing up and down the main street of a small town with a revolver in each hand shooting wildly. Such a thing came as a wonderful surprise to us for we had fondly believed Mr. Jinx to be the soul of spirituality and learning. To be more explicit as to his strong qualities, he is one of our leading paleontologists, a university man draped with sheepskins and with so many letters after his name that he requires a six-inch calling card, while his small frame seems bent under the weight of honorary degrees. He had been dean of this, honorary president of that, and somebody or something else of the other, and is considered one of the most promising of our men of renown.

We had placed Mr. Jinx on a pedestal and pointed him out as one of the most blossoming of our scientific possibilities. When we heard that he was in for thirty days without bail our idol was shattered into a million pieces and we felt for a short time at least that the world would come to an end. The very idea that Mr. Belshazzar Jinx with his colossal, philosophical dome and his superlative education being so hopelessly lacking in self-control, and our ideas of social decency tore forever this man of letters from our list of speaking and thinking acquaintances.

As we were slowly recovering from this amazing revelation we received another shock. Mortimer J. Highbrow, Jr., one of our leading religious lights, wonderfully balanced between mystical theology and Chaldean archaeology, whose knowledge was of a nature most complete, and in whose inspiring sermons we had reached heights where our souls had never dared to tread on account of the rarified atmosphere of the high altitudes, had been called into court as the leading light and star of a divorce suit in which he was being sued by a mere member of the ignorant society for alienation of affections. This thunderclap was almost too great to be endured. That Mortimer J. should have done anything like this was beyond the wildest dreams of his worst enemy. Even Mortimer J. himself seemed to be a little amazed at his own audacity, but when we visited court the next morning we found him a most dejected looking individual fighting in a sort of dazed way for liberty against insurmountable evidence.

We went away shaking our heads and sad beyond expression only to meet a good friend, one of those human broadcasting stations, who was running over with a still later bit of news. One of our famous occult teachers, whose knowledge of rounds and periods was something terrific and who had worked out by trigonometry the length of a Night of Brahma, had just vanished from the light of men for ten years as the result of a bootleg still being found in his cellar.

Our heads were spinning around as one after the other the world's highbrows apparently demonstrated their low morals, but the capping of the climax occurred when Miss Algernida DuBarry, one of the sweetest exponents of Divine Love, was sued for divorce by her doting spouse as the result of having fractured his skull with a bootjack during a friendly argument.

We left the sight of men for several hours and within the darkness of our own sanctum sanctorum sought an answer to this inexplainable problem which has undoubtedly confronted a large percentage of mystic students who have seen their idols collapse ignominiously at some unexpected moment. After many hours of deliberation we reached a solution which relieved somewhat the ache of our soul. You know this is not only a problem of the worth of a teacher but from a very personal standpoint it is quite a blow to our dignity to witness the weird and woozy actions of those whom we hold up as scintillating examples of human erudition. One after another we have seen our patron saints un-haloed, run out of town on rails, or tarred and feathered in the public square for some surpassing bit of inexcusable villiany, or else we found them sneaking out of the backdoor of certain unsavory places with their hats down over their eyes and their collars turned up. And slowly a peculiar feeling comes over us which clutches us in a grip of terror, we begin to fear that we may become a genius ourselves some day and be found sneaking into the second story of a church to steal the prayer books or cutting the stones out of the stained glass windows.

Practically every genius that we know occasionally demonstrates individual eccentricities or else someone whom we know informs us of their failings. Several of our leading religious shrines are raided occasionally and many an illuminated one has been brought up before the police court to plead not guilty of doing something which it is proved they did. What is the answer to this soul-perplexing, heart-rending problem? These are the conclusions we have reached:

Science has now proven that genius is a mild form of insanity or at least tends in that direction, and we have never found a person yet who could be too long-headed without being hollow somewhere along the line. When they get too broad they get shallow and mud-flats border the stream, when they get too deep they get narrow and fall into ruts, and when they get too high they cease to watch their feet and soon slip over some philosophical or sentimental banana peel and are hurled headlong flaming from the ethereal skies. If they get too deeply immersed in their problems and only an occasional bubble comes up to the surface, a seismic cataclysm usually follows. When they get too deeply wound up in rare specimens, Latin verbs, or split infinitives, and too busy analyzing the embryonic life of a strombolis gigantis, about that time some other man sues them for something, they wake up with some weird domestic problem, or else they come out of their lethargy long enough to realize they murdered someone in the night or have robbed the leading bank.

There are two reasons for this strange condition, it seems. The first is the unequal development of mental faculties and the fact that the energies which have been drawn to a certain point to feed a brain center, which is being heavily used while certain scientific or philosophical work is being carried out, flood back again to other parts of the body when this work is discontinued. When there is no other legitimate channel for its expression the body does not absorb this energy in a well balanced manner and it breaks out through some part of the being not under control and usually results in some unwise and unbalanced action.

If Balshazzar could have cut wood as well as he talked Latin he would not now be making little ones out of big ones at the county jail; if a well-known lawyer in a small town had played golf as well as he argued he wouldn't have knocked the court clerk over the judge's stand when a certain trial was over. But these one-sided people do not realize the ebb and flow of energies within themselves, which, when they have only one thing they can do, must in time burst out somewhere along the line. Then, Mrs. G. talking to Mrs. F. over the back fence will say, "I just know he's been that way for years and we did'nt know it, the hypocrite, but I always knew he was crooked underneath, he had such a mean look in his eye," et cetera, when in truth the individual discussed is a good, kind-hearted, well-meaning, and hard-working individual, Professor of Bacteriology in a leading university until they found him one morning rolling moth-balls around his room, playing dolls or drunk. Sometimes one of our leading lights in scientific circles is found in a dope den for no other reason at all than that his unbalanced nature as the result of his unnatural life had mastered him through his own disorganized energies.

When a man is mastered by an art or science he is insane and there are few masters of philosophies and religion who are not in truth slaves to their concepts until finally their religion runs them amuck, or, as it was said on the Western plains during the early days, they got "locoed" and we find them doing all kinds of things which they should not do and working up scandals generally.

The need of balance is one of the greatest considerations for the occulist. It is the easiest thing in the world to get so twisted up in theory and argument, science or theology, that the individual becomes mildly insane and hopelessly irresponsible.

The second reason for the degeneration of reputation and complete ruination of celebrities is that compendium of Christian charity which is turned upon them by their loving and sincere disciples. Mr. and Mrs. Buzzzzz are always with us and will probaby remain until the last great dawn of eternity folds them in its sable mantle, and their last words will be, "M'dear, did you hear about buz-buz-?" If anyone can remain thirty days famous without someone making him infamous, if he can boast a reputation for one month in philosophy, religion, or politics, there is but one explanation. It is the direct result of the fact that so much has been found out about him that his doting followers do not know what to say first. Of course, if by chance he happens to be a little short of scandals it only requires a few hours to produce them. The rocking-chair and smoking-room brigade specialize in this work and the record at the present time is two hundred scandals per rock.

A reputation is one of those peculiarly subtle things which like your appendix you do not know you have until you lose it, and strange to say it is taken from you by your nearest and dearest beloved. It is usually a loving friend, a helpful and accommodating relative, or one of these illustrious individuals noted for religious inclinations or leanings whose tongue being hung in the middle and wagging both ways strips you of every vestige or respectability and leaves you shivering before the world, the perfect picture of dejection and misery.

Therefore, between these two evils, your weak points and your strong friends, there is very little chance for a highbrow to keep both ends of his reputation above water. As fast as he gets his philosophy up, either he or someone else pulls his private life down until finally he lands in a padded cell where he remains counting sunbeams and praying the Lord with Abraham Lincoln to deliver him from his friends.

Of course, these may seem exceptional cases but the principle remains, and we cannot be too careful not only of our own lives but in our thoughts and actions with others because each is fighting a great battle, and many a great soul has been completely broken by the harsh words and thoughtless actions of others, when its own battle against the powers of unbalance was as much as it could shoulder.

Art

THERE IS NO POWER that holds a greater sway over the hearts of men than the subtle mystery of color. Who has not stood before the child of a great master and seen on the canvas before him the creation of the master genius? Raphael, Murillo, Titian—their souls have left on mortal canvas traced by the endless motion of their subtle fingers visions from somewhere behind the veil of human consciousness.

Few there are who have the power to know the heart of the master painter whose pictures are not of earth but are the rapt visions of seers illuminated by the great Light brought close through years of dreaming and hours of meditation. As we gaze upon some hallowed painting, a Madonna or some face of Rembrandt, it seems to live, to speak to us from the depths of its gilded frame. We cannot help but feel that art is not of man but of God, that a power unseen works through the master's fingers, a hand unknown mixes the pigments of the pallet. There is no power but God, no creator but the One Divine, who can blend colors into these mystic harmonies which touch the strings of the soul, and it must be true that God made artists to picture Him.

There are few old masters today who like the ones of centuries gone by have beheld with broader vision the grandeur of the universe and whose skilled fingers have placed upon canvas and carved into stone the visions that filled their souls. They were the master artists who bowed in reverence before One who with colors no mortals ever used, with the artist's eye far greater than human sense, the hand more skilled than any earthly fingers, paints eternally in colors indescribable life and all living things. He is the Genius and all that mortal artists can hope is to reproduce His art but never to excel it. Who of earth can paint with the colors of the sunset? What artist of mortal school can discover the wondrous pigments that shade the autumn leaf? Where is the hand of skill consummate? Where is the eye which divines the perfect blending?

There is but one great Artist and He is the Master of the human school, and above all mortal instructors there is one true Genius of living art. Today this Master lives incarnate in the creations of His students. Through brush and pen He lives for His heart is ever filled with a mystic harmony which has been expressed by few of this world as it is revealed in the brush strokes of Guidio Rene, in the massive marbles of Michelangelo, or in the simple Angelus of Millet.

But there is a more glorious art within the soul of man which paints anew all things of nature. There is a master school which paints not on canvas that perishes but on the living background of the human soul. There are fingers that with the deft touch of the true genius paint again with bright color cheeks that have long been paled. There are souls who bring sunshine again to the dark clouds of sorrow, there are master painters who dry the eyes that weep and with the brush of love remove furrows from the souls of men.

Here and there is a great genius who comes to the world to paint that one eternal masterpiece of the gods. In colors rich with light and truth he takes away the shadows from the canvas and with the inspired touch of genius paints all life in living colors. These are the Master's immortal, the truly great artists, who are pupils of that one great Genius whose nameless paintings are the basis of all human aspiration.

Man the Human Violin

ALL existing things divide themselves into two general classes, objective and receptive. For all times the outpouring, vitalizing power or that expression which is the source of light, power, and motion we call spirit, the divine Father, the positive expression of existing things. It is called positive because it expresses mentally, physically, or spiritually animated qualities; it is called the spirit that goes forth and that which goes forth has always been symbolized as positive and is known as the Father-ray. Opposed to this principle is the divine negative element. This negative element represents cessation of animation for it is the basis of matter, and matter is spirit the rate of vibration of which has been slowed down by one of two reasons, either obstruction to the passage of spirit or else the rates of vibration have so far to go before reaching the end of their wave that the slowing of these rates produces matter. In other words, so-called matter is a crystallization of energy which crystallization inhibits its expression. Matter is a globular substance in which the latent life germ is incapable of expressing itself through the walls of negation or not-being. This negative element depends upon the vitalization of external energy for the liberation of its own latent life. Therefore, matter is said to be divinely receptive and is referred to by the ancients as the divine Mother principle. For ages life and the fiery sun globe have represented the fierce, blazing Father while the verdant, liquid sustained earth, the reposing place of the spirits of life has been referred to as the moist and harmless receptive principle of nature which is known to all students as the Mother of spirit. All matter enfolds within itself a germ of life, thus matter is the incubator which protects and like a wall or shell surrounds latent life qualities with protecting substances. Matter, being life asleep, is incapable of individual self-expression while in latency, consequently it depends upon the life within it for its expression, and matter manifests the state of growth reached by its indwelling, central, flame-born consciousness. For this reason spirit has been symbolized as self-expressing force which striking against the walls of negation is thrown back from these as are the notes of music from the sounding-board of a violin.

All the way down through the ages the Wisdom Teachings have taught that the unfolding of the body is necessary to the clearness and beauty of the notes of spirit, which as rates of vibration and spirited substance in motion strike this natural sounding board. In other words, we may symbolize spirit as the divine musician, which, in the intelligent kingdoms of nature, is incessantly playing upon and expressing itself through the medium of harmonies which depend for their sweetness upon the quality of matter and its arrangement as it expresses itself in bodies.

The same rates of vibration vary in physical expression in accordance with the quality, shape, and size of the instrument which is played. The same rates of vibration do not produce the same sound on all instruments, the same spiritual influx which makes one man a saint leaves another a sinner. The same thing which produces divine harmony will produce divine discord if the instrument is not what it should be.

Life expresses itself in the world of affairs in many ways but its beauty is always limited by the quality of the instrument through which it is manifesting. We cannot see vibration, neither can we see spirit which expresses itself through vibration, but spirit manifests in the world of affairs as thought, action, and desire, and we are either charmed or irritated not by the ideals of the musician but upon the registering of these ideals in the world of concrete things, and this is only possible through a material vehicle of expression. Our daily lives are visible, tangible, comprehensive evidences of things unseen and unknown which can be wholly felt or believed only on the abstract planes of consciousness. The most beautiful thoughts are often unrevealed because the thinker has no words to express them; most glorious melodies are lost to the world because the one who feels them is incapable of expressing them musically.

Man's vehicles of expression must always limit the life and while he may dream on forever beautiful dreams, if he does not properly attune his instrument he dreams for himself alone, and oftimes he cannot even formulate clearly within his own mind the dreams which fill his soul.

Vibration is caused by the animation of substances and the setting of air or ether in motion. Every word that comes out of our mouths is toned by the mouth. It is changed and often ruined by the shape of the teeth, the position of the tongue, and the quality of the sound-box at the back of the mouth. As the rates of vibration pass out of the throat into the various chambers of the head and chest they produce the various tones which we admire or dislike. Wherever there is impediment in the natural expression of vibration we have the so-called nasal tone, which is out of tune because it isn't nasal, and the passages being stopped up inhibits the flow of the vitalized energies. The results of developing the cavities in the head and chest are the building of resonant tones which striking the ear-drum in a harmonious way we recognize as melodies and harmonies, and every known tone is the result of air in motion passing through chambers differing from each other in two things. First, size, shape, and location; second, the quality of the material forming their walls.

In the beginning it is said that man was created through the outbreathing of God, who, as He outpours the vibrations from the celestial sound-box of cosmos, becomes the great Father principle of creation for He is sending forth the sparks of life from His own mouth. These strike matter and the various combinations of these two forces produce the differentiation in form, shape, and quality. All the varying expressions of life in form of which we can conceive are the result of motion striking the lack of motion, the result being spiritual, mental, or physical harmonies or sounds, which are tuned according to the sounding board of cosmic root subtance upon which these harmonies strike in their search for expression.

The same sound wave we hear in a cornet passes also through the bass horn but the notes of the latter are heavier and deeper and in many ways different, the only cause being that the general form, magnitude, and orifices of the two instruments are different in size and shape. The same setting in motion of atmosphere takes place and the same noted energy is used in drawing the bows of both a cello and a violin but the result of the action differs on account of the difference in the instruments.

In the spiritual things of life the same principle is true. Man is completely limited by the quality of the instrument upon which he is seeking to play the celestial harmonies. There are no two individuals who ever have been or ever will be exactly the same in their thoughts, desires, and actions, and these in turn mold the instrument of matter into an expression of their own quality which results in the distinct individuality of specie. In spiritual things we find a perfect analogy, for the spiritual waves of living substances in motion are molding eternally their own keyboard into an expression of themselves and this keyboard is in turn defining and limiting the expression of its own creator.

Spirit or God is an intelligent force which being creative itself bequeathes the power of creation upon everything which expresses it. Man is a creator every time he animates substances and he animates certain substances with every expression of active energy, mental, physical, or spiritual. Whenever he speaks or even thinks the result is a chain of vibratory waves which on the various planes of nature mold the vehicles of man into expressions of their own intrinsic vibratory power. These vehicles in turn are the concrete expressions of man's innermost ideals, and the spirit, the I Am, manifesting imperfectly through the not-self or what are called the spiritual centers of the body, is hampered in turn in its own expression by the limitations which its thoughts, actions, and desires place upon the unfoldment of its bodies.

The sounding board makes the instrument. Thought, action, and desire create the sounding board and the sounding board limits the expression of the divine in man. Our bodies are the sounding boards and as vehicles of consciousness the three bodies are under the control of individual intelligences. Each of these intelligences is twofold in its expression, selfish and selfless. When each body strives for individual mastery then we have unbalance in people whose thoughts, actions, or emotions run away with them and who who cannot control their own bodies. When this condition is present it means that the sounding board is being limited by bodily intelligences which are in turn limiting the spirit of man which should be served by these intelligences.

If, on the other hand, the body consciousness centers of thought, emotion, and action are selfless in their expression and governed wisely and selectively by the spiritual consciousness and used always to build more stately mansions for the soul, then the sounding board is limited only by the spiritual consciousness itself and quickly responds to every note which strikes it, and harmony will be the eternal result for if the body is married to the spirit, their union being unimpeded by expression of individual bodies, the result is that each body becomes a pen in the hand of a ready writer which will always be in harmony with itself if not interrupted by inharmonious relations between centers of sense consciousness.

The true musician realizes that quality does not depend upon pedigree alone, neither does harmony depend upon commercial value, but that the value of a violin is in its tone. Our bodies are violins upon which the spirit plays varying harmonies and discords until finally they attune themselves with the music of the spheres. As the violin depends for tone upon the quality of the materials composing it and the harmony depends upon the tone, so the bodies of men depend for their quality upon the things which are incorporated into them mentally, physically and spiritually. Man's most valuable asset at this time is the tail appendage of consciousness which he calls the physical body. If it be poorly constructed the individual who inhabits it will never be a functioning genius for he will always be limited in some way by the organic quality of his vehicles, and the result will be a series of squeaks and rasps which grate not only upon the ears of the musician but upon the whole world which hears consciously or unconsciously his discordant expressions.

The centers of the four bodies within us can be called the strings of the instrument and the spiritual consciousness within our being plays upon these centers, and they in turn through their vibratory qualities produce in the finely evolved individual the same spiritual, bell-like tones that physically sound out from a master's violin. Two things are absolutely necessary to the full-of the genius and the instrument worthy of a master. The result of this combination is divine harmony. But if you take a genius and give him a cheap instrument, though his technique be perfect, he will never be satisfied either with the instrumnt or with himslf. In fact, a truly great musician would refuse to play on a cheap instrument, it would grate against his soul. Then, again, take a master of music and give him a cheap violin and there will be within him a repugnance, he is disgraced, for with the soul of genius there comes something else, and although he be blindfolded and not allowed to touch the strings the master musician will feel the quality of his instrument. Then let us look at it in another way. Suppose you take an instrument worth thousands of dollars and give it to someone who cannot play, does the value of the instrument make him a musician? No. In all nature two things are needed, the instrument and the player. These are the basis of all expression and in nature they are called spirit and matter. The existence of either means struggle until there is a mutual harmony and an agreement of quality between the two. A good body in the hands of a sleeping spirit is like a grand violin in the hands of an amateur; a beautiful soul in a shapeless body filled with inharmony and discord is likened to a master with a cheap instrument. The result is always inharmony.

Many instruments look alike but they are not, for many lack the soul of the maker. There are two ways of making instruments. There are those just made to sell, maybe turned out at the rate of fifty a day, they look just like the greater instruments that it has taken a lifetime to build, but they are not the same. Then there are the instruments made by those who loved their craft, who labored for the joy of building, and who raised these children of their souls with the same tenderness and care that loving parents bestow upon their children, for the great musicians love their instruments and the great makers feel that they have built gods.

In the same way there are two kinds of people living in the world. There are those who work as fast as they can to get things done. They do not care whether they build well, if they get through it's all right. They labor because they must eat. And there are others who get spiritual because they believe it is the only way to escape work and hard knocks. They are just like the people who build instruments to sell. The soul is missing that in some mystic way adds beauty to its tone. Then there are those who do not care how much they labor for they serve for the joy of serving, they build for the joy of building, to them their labors are divine, they almost worship the creations of their hand, to them their creations have a soul—their soul. And though the workmanship may be unskilled, often the instrument is more beautiful than some mechanically made masterpiece.

It is the same with our bodies. There are bodies thrown together, pressed together, crammed together, and there are are bodies that are gathered through ages of experience, the sublime desire of the spirit to unfold the godhood within itself, not just to get through but for the joy of the building. All these considerations play their part in the making of the master's intrument, and every student must realize that the most glorious work is not to unfold the spirit but to unfold bodies through which the spirit may speak for the spirit can never be greater than the temple where it is enshrined. There can be no soul where there are no bodies, no life where there is no shape, no color where there is no substance. Remove the worlds of material things and you will leave just the life itself which cannot even know itself, for in taking away matter you have removed the brain through which mind thinks, you have removed the mind which is also a thing of matter through which spirit speaks, for this is a great truth: If you remove not-being, being can never know itself.

Let us picture for a moment a great and wonderful violin, one of those master instruments which have come down to us through the ages. Many a broken heart has wept alone clasping it to his breast, many a lone life has whispered its innermost dreams through the strings of an ancient instrument, for it is beloved by its user and worshipped by its maker. It is said that Stradivarius, probably one of the greatest known violin makers, expressed himself in the following way: "God made Antonio to make violins." It is sad to think how few love the living temple of their own body as the old musician cherishes his beloved violin. It is said that Antonio Stradivarius made his greatest violins from the bell-post of an old church and that the wood was many years old when it was cut down, for it is known that great violins are made out of wood that is seasoned. Whenever there is water or moisture in the wood the tone is injured and the master's instrument must be made of seasoned wood.

All musicians know that a violin grows sweeter with age. People do not realize this fact but it is true. The tones of these instruments which have lasted hundreds of years are sweeter far than any made today. For the tone changes, every hour it grows mellower and sweeter, and the old violin weighs much less than the new one for it has dried out until it is merely a shell devoid of self-expression, it is nothing but a sounding board which registers each fine vibratory tone.

Now the spiritual consciousness of man is a very peculiar thing. Every expression of the bodies is sharp and harsh until finally with age the spiritual consciousness of man becomes master of the selfless body. It is experience, growth, sorrow, the things with which man battles through the ages which mold the body and the mind into the more seasoned and spiritual instrument. All the outside contacts of life build certain qualities in man and as he wanders through the ages the instrument of his body grows sweeter and sweeter as in spiritual powers as he grows older and older. The soul and the body of man are mellowed through the ages like great violins. The rough edges, the false tones, the selfish phase of the instrument, the great I Am, are nothing more or less than a drop of water in the wood, a bit of resin which is the sour note all through the ages, until at last after experience and growth and bitter sorrows the self part goes forever and the soul is all that is left. The bodies have gone and from them has been born a wondrous, selfless thing—the true companion of the self—and this is the divine instrument of the master genius and upon the strings of its selfless sounding board he plays the harmonies celestial.

The world is filled with people who grate upon us and who seem unsavory. The explanation is this, the instrument is new, and it has not been mellowed. The same deft fingers are trying to play it, the same sweet spirit tries to express itself but it cannot for the depth of tone is not yet there. We should not feel that our brothers are below us for their violins when mellowed may be wonderful instruments and they have not been laboring as they might, maybe, and then again we all have a sour note somewhere. Everyone has a flaw in his being which injures the tone of his instrument, but as the ages go by these flaws seem to disappear and for some unknown reason the violin that was sour when new is sweet and mellow when old. Many an instrument has been discarded by its maker as of no use and many, many years later, hundreds perhaps, it was taken out and found to have a master tone.

There is a wonderful lesson in this for everyone. You and I are like Antonio, the Lord has made us to make violins. Like Antonio, God has given us the work of making bodies, each complex organism is a master's labors through the ages, it is the eternal problem of spiritual consciousness and some day in the mystic future we shall learn to make a perfect instrument. Many people do not think, oftimes they do not want to think, they do not like to feel the responsibility of creation rests upon them. And yet it does. It is our duty and each of us must build a master instrument which is to give perfect expression to the genius within his own soul.

Then comes another great consideration. Take a great violin and crack it and the sound is gone until it is repaired and often then it is more beautiful than before. It is the same way we take an indiivdual, a child for instance, and abuse and break that instrument, or not being strong enough for the battle it is damaged by the blows of life and the sweetness is gone, oftimes it is many ages before the soul can repair the break caused by the thoughtless actions of others.

(To be continued.)

The Magical Mountain of the Moon

A Letter From the Brothers of the R. C.
to
Eugenius Philalethes
(Continued)

IN LAST MONTH'S EDITION of this magazine we published the letter from the Brothers as it is found in the original edition of "Lumen de Lumine," and now it is well to consider what Thomas Vaughan, who uses the penname of Philalethes, has to say concerning this mystical and magical Mountain of the Moon. On page 24 of his book, published in 1651, we find the following statement:

"This is the emblematical, magical type which Thalia delivered to me in the invisible guiana. The first and superior part of it represents the mountains of the moon. The philosophers commonly call them the mountains of India on whose tops grow their secret and famous Lunaria; it is an herb easy to find but that men are blind for it discovers itself and shines after night like pearls. The earth of these mountains is very red beyond all expression, it is full of crystalline rocks which the philosophers call their glass and their stone: birds and fish say they bring it to them. Of these mountains speaks Hali the Arabian, a most excellent, judicious author. Vade fili ad Montes India ad Cavernas suas, accipe ex eis lapides honoratos qui liquefiunt in Aqut, quando commis centur eis. Go, my son, to the mountains of India and to their quarries or caverns and take thence our precious stones which dissolve or melt in water when they are mingled therewith. Much indeed might be spoken concerning these mountains if it were lawful to publish their mysteries, but one thing I shall not forbear to tell you. They are very dangerous places after night for they are haunted with fires and other strange apparitions, occasioned (as I am told by the Magi) by certain spirits which dabble licivitiously with the sperm of the world and imprint their imagination in it producing many times fantastic and monstrous generations. The access and pilgrimage to this place with the difficulties which attend them are faithfully and majestically described by the Brothers of R. C. Their language indeed is very simple and with most men perhaps contemptible, but to speak finely was no part of their design, their learning lies not in phrase but in the sense and that is it which I have proposed to the consideration of the reader."

After having read this slight introduction by the renowned alchemist and mystic, it would be well for the reader to consider again the letter which was published in last month's edition and then let us study the general symbolism of the entire work.

Among all the ancient peoples mountains were held sacred and the points most sacred to every land were its lofty hills. Among the ancient Greeks the temple of their gods was upon the top of Mount Olympus where far above the clouds the gods dwelt and labored with man, coming down occasionally into the valley to sojourn with and direct the energies of their children. Among the Scandinavians we find Asgard, the home of the twelve gods, far upon the top of a magical mountain which was symbolized as the highest point of the world. We are all acquainted with the sacred mountain of the Jewish people, Mount Sinai, where the Lord spoke to Moses, and Mount Moriah over the brow of which Hiram Abiff, the Masonic hero, was buried. Among the Orientals we have Mount Moru, and the world still turns in awe to the shadowy heights of the Himalayas where many people yet believe the gods to dwell. The knights of the Holy Grail had their castle far up among the crags of Mount Salvart in ancient Spain, and among the Andes of the western world we still find the ruins of massive altars at the very top of pyramids and mountains.

The entire story of the magical mountains is based upon the analogy between the world and man. Each individual is a universe, a god, a planet, an infinitesmal bit of something all in one. We find the human body to be the plan of the temple, it is undoubtedly the symbol of Calvary, and where the head of man is in the ancient churches there were steps leading up to an altar. There are three worlds of human consciousness in which man is particularly interested. There is Hel, the land of darkness and dissolution, the land of dead things, lighted only by the fires of perversion; then there is the middle garden of the earth-world which man knows, the world of purely human affairs; then far up on the heights of a lofty mountain is the heaven world of man with the skull as its dome. Now, all the powers which man really uses are centered upon the top of the mountain of his body in the domed temple of his own head. It is within this superior world of which the lower is a counterpart, for all the functions of the human body and its organs are duplicated in the brain, that the treasure of great price is concealed. The path that leads to light is the path taken by the consciousness of man up through the red mountain of his own body into the superior, mystical world concealed upon its top. The twelve convolutions of the brain are the twelve disciples or gods who govern and regulate the destiny of human affairs, and it is the passing of the spiritual consciousness upward through the thirty-three segments of the spinal column that constitutes the path of initiation up through the Magical Mountain of the Moon. It is known to alchemists and all students that the world is divided into two general divisions,—the sun and the moon. The sun has to do with spiritual things while the moon affects material things, and here it is important to note that the magical mountain of the bodies forms the living throne upon the very crest and in the very heart of which is concealed the "quintessia vitra," the philosopher's elixir. The passing upward of the consciousness of the individual through regenerated thought and action is by means of the mastery of things. He grows through mastery, and initiation is the mastery of certain elements by the consciousness or spiritual power within.

It is stated above in the letter that the path which leads to this mountain is beset with many dangers and any student who has attempted to walk the spiritual path realizes that this is true. The terrible beasts, dragons, and reptiles represent our own lower natures which are ever between us and the path that leads to higher things. There is, as it is said, but one weapon with which we can fight them and this is the weapon of truth, light, and non-resistance. The only way of overcoming evil is through the boycott system as the student will discover before he reaches the goal he seeks.

Three tests confronted the candidate according to this allegory, three great natural elements were called into play, a very mighty wind, a terrific earthquake, and a consuming fire. These may very briefly be explained as thought which along spiritual lines breaks up the rocks of crystallization, this thought being symbolized by air which blowing the clouds across the sky was symbolized by the ancients as the ideas of man in the blue dome of the skull. As the result of this thought there is the expression of physical action and the action of physical bodies, which are commonly listed under the heading of earth conditions and are symbolized as the earthquake, which, more spiritually interpreted, represents the changes which take place in the physical organism when the candidate begins his active, spiritual work. The fire is the spiritual power generated by the previous processes which loosened upon the individual by his thoughts and actions immediately burns away whatever is not fit for its own works, the alchemy of transmutation within its own soul.

The rising of the day star symbolizes the extension of the soul which has been referred to as the "star body" by the ancients. Through the rising of the Light, the spiritual center of consciousness within him, after having passed through the three grand initiations of the Father, Son, and Holy Ghost, air, fire, and earth, man is then enabled to see within himself the Magical Mountain of the Moon and the wondrous treasure that is contained upon its top. These treasures are entirely of a spiritual nature and have nothing to do with material things, the gold and precious stones referred to symbolizing the awakened centers which are jewel-like and the streams of transmuted vital energies which the ancients called gold, and it is this gold which is said to pave the streets of the New Jerusalem.

In next month's magazine we shall continue the consideration of this mystic message of the Magical Mountain of the Moon and the mystery of the Magi referred to by Philalethes in his wonderful book.

A Little Episode from Life

IN EVERY LARGE CITY of the world we see those solitary figures which whisper of life's tragedy. On almost every street corner we find someone sick, blind, or poor, asking for the consideration and kindness of others. Among the eastern peoples we hear the eternal cry, "Alms! In the name of Allah!" and in our western world there are many who hold out their hands asking those who have to aid those who have not. In every land there are those for whom the battle of life has been too severe and one after another they sink down beside the way and ask our aid that they may live. The Master expressed a great truth when He said to His disciples, "The poor ye shall have with you always."

Huddled on the street corners we find them and while some no doubt use these methods to evade honest labor, still there are many broken souls who if it were not for the coins of the passersby would find life cold, indeed, and we should remember the bond of brotherhood that ties all living beings together, for it is better by far to give to a dozen who do not need than to miss the truly worthy one.

There is a little drama played out here as in all things of life, a little story that should etch itself into the soul, and I want to tell you of one little drama witnessed on a street corner just a few days ago.

In a darkened doorway away from the passing throng a little old lady sat on a broken stool, her face was tired and worn, pinched with suffering and poverty, and while many may seek in the road of begging sympathy and easy money this little soul bore the stamp of sincerity. She had an accordian on which she was playing and a little tin cup for the coins of thoughtful persons. She was playing old-fashioned tunes and it is to be admitted that she did not play them well nor was the little broken voice in tune with the squeaky notes of the cheap accordian, still there was a certain pathos, a certain sweetness and softness which spoke of sorrow and suffering and disappointment. Who can say what stretched behind in the years that had passed? Who can tell of children now in other parts of the world, maybe dead, possibly only thoughtless? Who can know the shattered hopes, the broken idols, the crushed ideals, hidden away beneath that tattered shawl of camel's hair? And still there must have been hidden beneath that broken body the star of hope which even in the cold desolation of life still shines eternal in the human heart. . . . This little figure whispered of better days, of years more filled with joy than those which stretch before her. It may be in truth that she should be in the home for the old; very possibly her present position was the result of her own mistake, in some way it must have been, but that is not the drama with which we are interested.

As we stood there listening to the plaintive wail of the cheap accordian we watched the throngs go by as the drama played itself out. First comes a stout busi-

(Continued on Page 30)

Brothers Of the Shining Robe

Chapter One

The Temple of Caves, Continued

I CREDIT MYSELF with being in a position to know, for I have been in the Catacombs of Rome, through the dungeons of the Coliseum, in the Palace of the Doges, and through the vaulted chambers of the Pyramids. So far as the eyes could see, the room stretched on in avenues and rows of natural pillars carved into gigantic elephants holding up with raised tusks and trunks the ceiling above. On one side of me was a great god with hundreds of arms and whose hundreds of heads gazed down from the vaulted archway. On the other side sat the Elephant God upon a couch of lions.

In the center of this great room stood a massive stone bowl, the pedestal of which was a great green cobra carved from marble. In the bowl blazed a fire of many colors, the light of which I had seen reflected on the wall without. Around the edge of this great room which grew dimly visible as my eyes became accustomed to the darkness, I saw twelve great doorways leading into recesses which I could not fathom, and at once the thought came into my mind, one which I hardly dared to believe myself, that I was in the Temple of the Caves cut from the heart of a living mountain.

There was no one in sight save my lonely guide and he led me silently across the great room and along the temple pillars to where a great shrine opened in the wall and here three great mysterious Beings looked down from recesses which had no end. You might call them gods or idols in the outer world, but they did not seem such here and to this day I do not know whether they were made of stone or of strange living substances. If they were stone they were of some other kind than that which is known in the world for they glowed and gleamed and seemed never still, not with the reflected light of the fire but with a glow and blaze from within themselves.

The Three together supported a great frame which seemed of solid gold and around the frame great serpents twined and within was a strange, bluish, transparent haze of unknown depth.

My curiosity, which was of true European type and incapable of the stoic attitude of the East, overcame me and in spite of what might be the result of my actions, I stepped forward to examine the relics and reaching out my hand sought to touch the mirror, for that was the only thing which it seemed to resemble in my mind.

Then a smile came over me, a smile, however, filled with terror and awe. I had sought to step forward but I had not moved, I had tried to raise my hand but it did not lift, and I realized that I was in a place unknown to the outer world and that the laws which govern ordinary man were not effective here.

My companion now broke the silence for the first time and although I spoke both Hindustani and Sanskrit he addressed me in flawless English.

"Well, my friend, this is the first time that you have seen me but it is not the first time I have known you. A strange series of apparent coincidences have occurred, not only within the last short span of years but in the ages that are past. All things work as the gods decree and before the coming of the Compassionate Ones, when these great stone walls had not yet had the builder's hand upon them, the work which we do today was ordained. Look back over your life and its restless wandering and can you not see the hand of Destiny which is molding you, has molded you, until today you stand within the shrine of the living god in the Temple of the Caves? Forever, there has been between you and man the blue veil of the gods and the restless wandering of your own soul must have whispered that you were not as other men. Some great reason yet unknown you must realize has been the potent factor of your being. I have been watching you and in this silent room have guided you in the ways of light. I have been near you in loves and fears, preparing a great way that later you shall walk. In this strange mirror, not of glass but of living ethers, I will show you the reason for all things, the labors that have stretched behind, the works to come, how you are fulfilling vows you made when worlds were in the forming, and why now you have been called out of the multitudes of men, for I put the words in the mendicant's heart that led you here. You do not know us or believe in the sacred ways and yet before this body returns to the earth from which it came you shall be listed with the Compassionate Ones."

Chapter Two
The Mirror of Eeternity

I LISTENED with close attention while my strange companion made the remarks which concluded the preceding chapter. I was not a religious man, I did not understand nor particularly care about the spiritual things of life. From the time when I first entered the world I had been told that I was supremely selfish, and all the conditions of my childhood tended to bring out my egotism, self-aggrandizement, and laziness, and I felt that I had been pretty true to my early teachings.

Still at his words I felt a tugging at some invisible cord within my own being and in spite of myself my eyes turned to the strange, blue haze which filled the frame supported by the three gods.

In the old guide I recognized the great saint referred to by holy men and I remained silent as he continued his discourse.

"I know, my son, that you do not understand or rather that you fail to remember the things which I am telling you, therefore be very attentive to my words. The fact that you alone out of all the holy men of India are the first in nearly forty years to find this sacred place proves beyond all words that a great reason lies behind your coming, and in order that you too may understand all that lies around you I shall tell you of this sacred mirror.

"In the days now gone by when the gods lived with men, when the great devas from the higher plane and the Manu himself walked the earth in flesh, he built himself in a single night this wondrous temple and left in it his most precious gifts of which this wondrous glass which reflects the worlds invisible to the eyes of men is not the least. From the ever-changing substances of nature this glass draws forth each hidden secret and is indeed the Mirror of Eternity. For, know you, that there surrounds and interpenetrates the world which we know other worlds that we do not see, and this mirror while of this world is sanctified in other worlds and shows to those who look the records of Brahma's Day preserved within the living beings of earth. Look!"—and he pointed at the fathomless depths.

As he spoke great swirling, twisting clouds appeared in the bottomless abyss of the sacred mirror. I looked and before my eyes there slowly formed out of the whirling clouds a strange world that stretched into the infinity of darkness. It was a world of broken things, great, twisted, gnawed trees of types unknown, their trunks blackened as though by fire, raised their branches like supplicating arms. Great cloudy, smouldering flames burst forth from cracks and crevices in the rocks and in the air great banks of sulphurous smoke tinted by the flames formed into twisting clouds of oily red. In my ears was the moaning and sighing of the winds and the dashing of the waves upon a broken shore.

I tried to recall from somewhere out of the past this strange scene but nowhere, even among the volcano and lava beds of Vesuvius and Etna, had such clouds of smoke ever gathered.

"What is this strange scene?" I asked my guide.

"That, my son, is called the Land of the Lonely Ones," answered the Oriental, "Although the eyes of mortal cannot see it, what you now behold is built of the thoughts and desires of the people of earth. You are now gazing on the home of men as it has been seen by the Compassionate Ones. From this strange land of death and dissolution there pour forth the spirits of the flame, the demons of war, the miseries, strife, and contention which fill the world. It is here that the work you are to do begins, it is here in the world of Causes that the Compassionate Ones labor for their brothers."

I gazed at the picture again and a strange chill came over my being. It was so cold, so cheerless, so dead, and yet from within came the echo of an accusing voice, and although I was loath to admit it I realized that beneath the life I lived my own being wandered in a wilderness as gloomy and desolate as the scene I beheld.

As I watched I saw a tiny, golden star shine out through the darkness. Whereever its beams fell the broken, confused mass of ragged rocks melted away with its glow and the deep, angry red of the smouldering fires turned golden with its warmth. As I looked more closely I saw that this little star was carried in the form of a lantern by a strange, mystic figure which walked or rather floated over the scene of desolation.

"Who is that?" I muttered under my breath.

"Watch," answered my strange companion.

(To be continued)

"THE SACRED MAGIC OF THE QABBALLAH"
The Science of the Divine Names.
By
Manly P. Hall

In this work the study of numbers and the Hebrew alphabet is taken up in a way never before undertaken. No system of numerology or cabalism is promulgated but a few underlying principles are given here useful to all students of mystic, occult and cabalistic philosophy. The work is divided into three parts as listed below:

Part One ....The Key to the Sacred Wisdom.

A Study of the flaming letters of the Hebrew alphabet, the creation of the Sacred Name, the mystey of the vowel points and the unwritten books of Moses.

Part Two..........................The Origin and Mystery of Numbers.

Under this heading are grouped the natural laws as they are expressed in numbers from 1 to 10, and the application of these laws to the problems of daily living.

Part Three......................The Power of Invocation and
                                The Science of the Sacred Names.

In this part of the work transcendental magic is completely unveiled and the ancient rituals of calling up spirits is exposed and the true meaning of transcendentalism and the finding of the lost Word is present to the student, including the invocation of Christ. A most unique and unusual document containing over fifty pages, neatly bound in an art cardboard cover. This work should be in the library of all occult students, not to be believed but to be considered.

As is the case with our other publications you must fix your own price for the work, not to cover your share of the responsibility but that the entire work may go on and you and others may be in a position to receive the work which we are putting out.

This month's issue also contains a rare occult plate taken from the writings of Robert Fludd, the English Rosicrucian and alchemist. The original is dated 1619.

The description of this plate will appear in next month's magazine.

OCCULT MASONRY

The Shrine

AMONG THE MASONIC CRAFTS there are many wonderful degrees but none has a deeper or more beautiful sentiment than the Mohammedan Shrine. Let us drop for the present the social side of Masonry for it is only an accessory which means nothing to the true art and science of the active craft. The Mason is a builder throughout eternity, and in the beautiful degree of the Shrine a wonderful thought is given to him which should assist him to better thinking and better living, otherwise its profound significance in Masonry is lost to the craft.

Let us go back to the ancient peoples where practically all of the modern symbolism had its origin, and here we find many wonderful facts concerning the mystery of the Shrine.

Man is eternally a worker, but to what end? That is a question which only mystics and philosophers can answer. What is the great reward for years of sorrow and labor? What is man's recompense for his works and his life? The answer is that man is a builder of Shrines.

From the beginning of time to the end of eternity man is building a wondrous altar piece for his living temple; he is fashioning a wonderful and glorious decoration to adorn an empty niche. In other words, with thought, action and desire, through his thousands and millions of years of growth he is laboring consciously or unconsciously to a single end. This end is the preparing of a holy place to be the dwelling of the Most High. Therefore, in spirit and in truth man is a Shriner, a builder of shrines.

Now, in many ways man carries on his appointed destiny, and all through the ages he is building eternally many things, and on all planes of nature he is laying up treasures with which to adorn this wondrous altar piece,—the living shrine of his own soul.

In India there are many wonderful shrines of gold and jewels, brass and glorious lacquers, stone and wood, carved by the hands of the faithful into ornaments and decorations to embellish and make more grand the altars of the gods they worship. It is said that only the heathen build shrines but we know that this is not true, for only the finest, the purest, the most noble of human beings can build a shrine, and not even the end of time as we know it shall bring to completion the shrine building of the soul.

Now, the world as we know it at the present time is the great rough block from which man must cut this beautiful shrine. With love, compassion, joy, and a deeper understanding of the mysteries of life, he must take the brutal, the cruel, the rough, and the unfinished, and with the vision of the true seer carve with loving thoughts, joyful hands, and a contrite spirit, this rough and broken mass into the glorious shrine of spirit.

Let man realize that he is building a strange and subtle thing and a new power and zeal inspires his efforts. Its wonderful pillars he carves from the granite blocks of matter. With thought, word, and actions he decorates it and glorifies it until it becomes a thing of beauty and grandeur. Into the settings he has fashioned, he places the stones of knowledge and love, each flower, each little figure, carved by loving hands for the glory of his God. As he works through the ages he realizes that his own body, the world in which he lives, and the world of his friends and those around him are the materials from which this shrine must be built. It is from the dross of his own soul that he must cut the golden key, and his own being must become the glorious setting to contain the most precious of all jewels,—the Pearl of Great Price and the Philosopher's Stone.

Man is ever human and being human he is impatient, thoughtless, and unsettled as to the reason for his own being. Therefore, he makes a great mistake, a sad and terrible mistake, yet who shall blame him for it? It is a mistake which seems almost godlike and which sometimes even the Masters make, and yet how can we judge them? When man builds this sacred shrine he fails to realize there is but one thing worthy to fill that hallowed spot. Some god of earth he seeks to raise to heaven's height, enshrined beside the Infinite, a cherished thought, a loved one of this world, who has called to him or who has heard the whisper of his soul.

But how can a god of clay fill a shrine of gold? The answer lies in the broken heart at the foot of the shrine, when the one we sought to raise to the height of a god proves to be only a creature of earth. How many hours and years of sorrow man must experience when he allows the human to fill the shrine of the Divine! None can answer that problem save those who have seen the shrine shattered and the figure crumble which they worshipped as a God. Therefore, the shriner learns that that sacred place is the dwelling of the Most High and that there can be no other gods before Him.

As man labors through the ages to build the shrine he must never seek to fill it with an idol of wood or stone which he glorifies as the divine, for soon the beloved lies at his feet a broken ruin, only less broken than the heart of the worshipper.

Close to his heart man must keep the ones he adores, deep in his soul should he etch the picture of those who are dear, but never let him place within this hallowed shrine any save the living God. Our world is filled with those who have known the pain of a broken heart because something of earth came too close to the things of God. Broken we lie at the feet of our idols, crushed and disconsolate, and for years we do not labor with the shrine because it seems that whatever we build into it, a glorious love or life, is shattered into a thousand places and nought have we in our hands but broken clay. The soul of the dreamer is broken with the idol at his feet, the heart of love is cold as it sees the creature of its adoration fall a heap of broken dust before it.

But there is the mystery of the shrine. Through the ages man is to build this glorious altar but not to fill it. Man will never know, it seems, the glory of being able to fill that shrine with those adored. His is the work to build it, to finish it with all the beauty and grandeur that his soul may know, but forever the empty niche must face him, never to be filled. Forever he seems to be building a golden ring around an empty void, but from his hands there shall come a strange craftsmanship. The mercy seat shall be built into the shrine, and as the last touch is completed and the architect lays aside his plans, the shrine-builder shall kneel in adoration before his works and know at last the mystery of the Shrine.

In the heart of the altar he has finished, in the niche of that sacred shrine, a great Light shall come and descend upon him. It is the Light he cannot build, it is the presence of the Lord, which nothing of earth can give him. Whatever else he may worship becomes as nothing before that mystic thing and whoever in this world he cherished no longer fills the shrine, for each loved thing has an altar, everything we cherish has its own little worshipping place in the heart. The shrine of the soul is for the spirit alone, and when man has finished his work and built his temple after the order of the Most High, then shall the spirit of the Lord inhabit it and the shrine shall be filled forever.

No longer will the idol crumble for now the ideal fills the shrine, no longer will man's heart be broken as those he trusts fail him in the moment of his extremity, for the presence in the shrine will never leave it but as a pillar of flame by night and a column of smoke by day the shriner is ever protected by the Light of God.

So in Masonry we have the privilege and duty of building this mystic shrine, the living temple of the living God, and the beauty of this wonderful Mohammedan degree is as sweet and as divine as any Christian concept. So, seekers of the Great Light, let us make our pilgrimage to Mecca and there pay our homage to the green banner of the prophet, and then wrapping the veil around our turbans or fez let us return to build more wonderful and more mystic shrines as we labor in the completion of the great one which is to be within us the dwelling place of the living God, for there is no God but Allah and Mohammed is his prophet.

Five times a day the Moslem calls to prayer, five times the son of Islam faces the Kabba and there offers up his prayer to the living God. Let us pray to the same God that the time may not be far off when we shall more truly build His shrine that He may dwell within it.

Adam and Eve and the Flaming Sword

I DO NOT SUPPOSE there is anyone who does not speculate, at least a little, over the story of the cherubim with the flaming sword that guarded the way to the gates of Eden to prevent the return of our primal ancestors to their heavenly home. The same little story is played out every day of our lives if we will but see it.

First, Eden represents paradise or heaven, that particular form of earthly joy which is the direct result of man's living in accordance with the plan of his being. In other words, when man is in a harmonious state of consciousness, when his organism is properly balanced, etc., he then lives in a new world of his own creation or rather to which he has become attuned through his life, and this is in fact the garden of the Lord.

Man has been cast out of the garden of balance and peace by his perversions, and the flaming sword of Eden undoubtedly represents the descending spirit fire which drives the spiritual consciousness of man out of his peace and joy. The cherubim with the flaming sword that stood at the gates of Eden had four heads. These four heads symbolize the four bodies of man, while the flaming sword is the fire of passion. It is the emotion body of man, uncurbed and unregenerated, that stands as a flaming sword between him and the higher worlds. Nearly all the suffering in the world at the present time is the result of emotion in which individuals have lost control of themselves and have allowed the passion body to dominate their lives. So long as this is permitted, the cherubim with the flaming sword will stand between the spiritual consciousness of man and the realization of his ideals. It is only when this body is mastered that peace can return.

When man masters his lower being the down-pointing sword is turned upward through spiritual regeneration and man is then able to enter again the garden of the Lord. But so long as we are a slave to our lower natures and to the animal fires, just so long does the flaming sword stand between us and our true spiritual home, and we are forced to wander the earth dressed in the skins of animals until as purified egos we pass through the fire of the flaming sword and the bodies which like the Sphinx of old guard the entrance to the higher worlds.

The Mystery of Initiation

DURING THE LAST few years a great wave of mysticism has swept over the world. The heart of mankind is hungry for greater knowledge, the soul yearning for fuller understanding, has sought to tear away the veil which forever drapes the figure of Wisdom. Man has sought to learn those mystic truths so long lost to the world, and in his study and search he has found that there are strange and mysterious beings known to the world as Initiates. Among the ancient works and the mystery schools of those peoples now dead, strange ceremonies called initiations were given in some mysterious way and the popular mind has come to believe that there is a mystic rite, an initiative ceremonial, which makes man one with the immortals, and in the name of this wonderful and mystic concept terrible crimes have been committeed against the spiritual and occult teachings. There is probably no word in the English language that has been so abused, so misused, so often used and so little understood, as the word "Initiation." Every dream, every phantom form, every unusual happening, has been called the initiation and all over the world temples have sprung up in the name of the mystery schools to initiate candidates into the Wisdom teachings, some of them without cost but in the majority of cases a heavy fee accompanies the initiation in which for, say, $25.00 the candidate is dubbed "Sir Somebody" or made a leading luminary in some mystic shrine.

The result of this perversion is that the sacredness, the beauty, and the true realization of the meaning of initiation has been lost to the world, for it is very true that there are none who can so damage a religion or an idea as those who claim to be its followers. How long it will take the world to learn that initiations are not ceremonials it is difficult to say, but sometime each individual must realize that swinging robes and incense burners and other trimmings do not constitute initiation, and that no one on the face of the earth could buy it for the fortune of Croesus nor in any way receive it until he himself by his life has become worthy of its mystic blessing.

There are few in this world who know what real initiation is, and there are fewer still who having discovered it really want to so live that this mystic rite may be unfolded within their souls. The true initiate is a very wondrous and mysterious being and any words that we can say concerning such a one are very poor, in deed. Those who have not already walked the path can have but a feeble idea of what an initiate really is, for such a one has unfolded within himself or herself, as the case may be, certain principles of which the average layman knows nothing. The powers of life and death, the powers of destruction and construction, the mystic principles of integration and disintegration, all these are in the hands of the Great Ones of God. The knowledge of life is the mystic power of the Initiate, for only those who have walked the ways of many can ever know what the laurels of initiation mean. Only when his heart is filled with love for humanity and with the great suffering and great peace of those who know, can he so express the powers within himself that he is of use in so great a plan.

The Initiate has the mindless mind of spirit which thinks only the thoughts of life, to the source of which he each day draws nearer; he is filled with the understanding of nature's plan for her children and only this knowledge holds in check a heart that would otherwise break with sorrow. He knows that strange, sweet melancholy, that mystic feeling few have ever realized, such as must have filled the soul of Jesus as He wept over Jerusalem. The true initiate is initiated by God and not by man and he will give his life, his soul, his very being, to lift the suffering in the name of the Father.

It is only those who have a heart great enough to enfold all creation, a consciousness as great and broad as life itself, who are even on the road to initiation, those whose very being is a mirror of the Divine, whose every thought is to save, whose every power is expanded to raise, whose every action is a blessing, who reach out with hands ever stronger to aid suffering humanity. Those and those alone know the true meaning of initiation. Those whose eyes have never seen suffering, those whose hearts have never been broken, those who are tied by earthly ambitions, can never receive that celestial influx of life which comes to those who have prepared their vehicles in the way of the law and the great love.

The Initiate is slowly reaching out into the Great Unknown, lighting each corner of chaos with his own glory, bathing all life in the warmth of his own soul, limited only by his own unfoldment. On through the ages he is dispelling ignorance and darkness by the ever broadening sphere of his own light. It is those who have dedicated their lives and being to feed the flame of the Eternal One that its light may shine more brightly whom we call the Initiates and, oh, how few they are! How few have given up the kingdoms of the earth! How few are ready to give up earthly desires to walk the path that leads to Divinity, holding out the little alms-dish of the Buddha for the words of wisdom and love that are given to those who seek for help that they in turn may serve. To those who seek it in any other way than this, initiation is only a terrible demon. The student may gain growth, the wisdom or so-called power of the Adept may come to him, but still if selfishness is his motive he is cursed to suffer and to go without the things of this world as well as the other, for he is cursed with knowledge, and knowledge brings with it a weight that few shoulders are strong enough to bear.

It is only when that mystic thing comes, the strange, spiritual power of initiation, that to man is given the strength to carry knowledge in the way of light. There are only a few who are ready to take up the cross and follow in the footsteps of those who have consecrated their lives to their fellowmen. There are only a few with strength enough to see the veil of the future lifted and remain sane. There are few who could see the veil of their own destiny raised and still have strength enough to walk the way, and even to those who can stand this great light there comes the still greater test of standing alone in the high places of the world without even the staff of comradeship, for the initiate is ever alone but when truly ordained of the spirit is never lonely.

For with this knowledge that no tongue can speak, no coin of man can buy, there comes something else, a still whisper, the word of eternal life that passes eternally through the soul of the saved. While the Initiate sees the bleeding hearts of his fellowman and the breaking and tearing of living things, he still sees the eternal justice of all things, to him there comes the realization that all is working for good. He sees the divine hand working through the apparent chaos of things and that behind the human discord there is the divine reason.

Can we face this Great Unknown as the Great Ones have faced it? Can we pass through with the glorious vision of Nirvana forever before us? If we can we are on the path upward that leads to the feet of the Great Ones who look down on man with never-changing eyes of love. Very few are there in the world today who are ready to make the great renunciation which the world knows as initiation.

There comes a time in every soul when there is a parting of the ways, and there are few who will take the stony path, give up the kingdoms of earth, and ascend the rocky crags to the feet of the Liberator. Those who take that path are the true essence of the life we live. Eventually, all will take the path as the light dawns upon them.

If we would take that silent way we must renounce the selfishness of materiality and slowly and painfully meet bravely the buffets of the world and go on and on in the endless paths that leads into the Unknown. It is those who have done this, sacrificing all without a murmur, whom we know as the Initiates, and we owe them respect and love for they are in truth our Elder Brothers who have gone a little ways before that they may come back and show us the path to tread.

A time comes when each soul after having passed the first degrees of initiation receives the greatest test of all. It is when he reaches the veil that divides him from the world. Nirvana with all its blessings shines before him while those wandering in the wilderness cry out for help from the darkness below. He stands at the parting of the ways—which path will he choose? The path of initiation is forever the path of sacrifice. No glory, no power, just a selfless willingness to serve the highest. In the robes of the mendicant the Initiate returns to wander the earth and serve others. While they are apparently imperfect and torn and slandered by the world, yet the hosts of heaven look down and bless them. Those who give up all, even the paradise well earned and the rest that is theirs and come back to walk in the muck and mire,—they are the Initiates. It is at that moment the Star of Bethlehem shines out to tell that another Son of God is born among men.

There are many on earth who have made this great renunciation. They have given up peace to walk the streets in rags, to be laughed at and ridiculed, to teach the few who would listen. They have gained great knowledge and great intellect but still they live and speak of simple things. We only see them occasionally and we say that these great ones have been blessed but we do not know the price that they have paid, how they have bathed their souls in tears, how they have been garbed only in their own blood and crucified by their own disciples. This is the price of initiation and it is through these things great souls are born.

We have grown to think that there is only one Son of God but we are all his children, and when one really takes the path that leads to Light, the voice of the Father speaks spiritually within his soul, saying, "This is my Beloved Son in whom I am well pleased." It is only then that the candidate climbs the steps that lead to immortality.

It is sad to think how few who seek the powers of the masters are willing to pay for them with love and thought. With a few paltry dollars and a few fine robes they honestly believe they can receive that for which Gods have died, which great souls have been crucified to attain and martyrs met their death in the arena. It is a pitiful thing, man's concept of the road to God. "It is sharper than a serpent's tooth to have a thankless child," and how many of them the gods have today!

What is the path that leads to the Initiates? It is the lifting of consciousness through this strange drama which we call life. Along the great road all beings are plodding slowly, old and young alike, all walking the same path, the road that leads to the feet of the Masters. There are many shrines along the way, many religions, many creeds, many little chapels where the seeker stops to pray and the weary to rest. But ever onward all must go until they reach the temple on the top of the lofty crags. In daily life we have our tests; the thought comes to our mind that we hate someone, but what have we to hate? Then thoughts of fear haunt us and sorrow bows us down. Then through the ages comes the realization that all things lead to good. Slowly we gain the great compassion, the great balance, the heart that is free of pain and pleasure. We have the vision of the great Truth and seek to enfold all living things within the cape of our love.

When thoughts like these come to the student, he is learning. It is that feeling of glory that brings with it the touch of pain. Everything we do carries with it a great responsibility. Those who wish to wear the robe of the Initiate must be willing to wear it over a broken heart.

With many people their greatest desire is to escape responsibility or to gain the glory of a great reward but so long as these thoughts fill the soul initiation is impossible. Until the aspirant is living the ritual he can never learn its mystery; until he can see in his own spiritual being the dying Christ on the cross he can never truly learn of initiation. It is bought with the gold of spirit and service. When he has so lived as to be worthy of it, then comes the Light. In the darkness of his own closet, far from his brother man, in the silence of his own soul the great mystery unfolds.

Thousands of figures gather round him and the Grand Master is there in his robe of Blue and Gold, the teachers of the ages gather round him; he is in the great hall of his own body through which he must pass to enter the inner room. There alone he passes through things no mortal tongue can speak; there he sees the reason for his being; the things that he must do; the greater works he is privileged to accomplish. And having learned much, his new responsibility is likewise great; having seen the work to be done he can no longer rest but must wander the world like a lost soul to labor in the endless cause. He lives for one brief moment with those things which are eternal and having glimpsed those wondrous beings, service means everything. He must help all living things to find the light that he has found. Just a silent soul alone, unfolding its wondrous mystery to its own being,—that is Initiation.

Having gone through these tests and removed the love of materiality he is given the privilege of knowing and realizing the true reason for at least part of the Plan. He goes on now, step by step, coming into the powers which were always his, not in heaven but in hell, for the place of the Initiate is not in the worlds above but in the worlds of darkness for he has consecrated his soul to the redemption of man.

We have among us today those who claim to have passed through great initiations, but do their lives show it? Are they willing to work unseen and unknown with the powers that never shine before the eyes of men? Do they work with the humility and simplicity which is the divine expression of the soul? All true Initiates point out the way by their own beings that others may follow the path to which they have dedicated their lives.

Everyone wants to be an Initiate but if they were the sun would soon go out forever from their lives. Like children, man is always wanting something and weeping for it like a child. The soul filled with uncertainty, selfishness, and materiality can never have the strength of purpose and the unity of balance, to carry the burdens of Initiation. It is a blessing then that many are not what they want to be. If it were not so, hearts would be broken that have not the strength to mend. If we could be initiated now it would do us no good, for each true, upward step must be hewn out of the solid rock of experience that each may take the path by removing from his life the personal things that stand between him and that which he seeks. We must take each cruel word and change it into a dove before we send it on its way.

When we go hence to enter into our Father's house, the greatest reward that can come to us is the privilege of laboring there. Not our will but the Master's should regulate the expression of our life.

If those who seek Initiation today could only know what it really means they would realize how false their concepts have been. What have we done that we have the right to join that little throng of God's chosen ones? If we would labor with them we must take upon our shoulders their burdens and be one of those who are responsible for the lives of men, and when we have raised our consciousness, our lives, our actions and our thoughts to this point, then we are Initiates in spirit and in truth, for the light of God's plan for man shines forth and envelopes us in its glory and its first gleam shining upon our souls show us the end to which all Initiation leads,—a lonely cross upon a hill.

ASTROLOGY

Keywords of Aries

FOR THE BENEFIT of those who wish a brief, comprehensive series of keywords, the general trend of which can be easily memorized, to assist them in judging the rising signs of individuals, we have arranged and compiled the following series which will answer practically all the needs of the elementary astrologer. The following sources have been drawn from in the preparation of this series of articles which will appear each month until the twelve signs have been analyzed:

Astrology, by William Lilly, London, 1647.

Ptolemy's Tetrabiblos, edited by J. M. Ashmand, London, 1822.

The Complete Dictionary of Astrology, James Wilson, Esq., London, 1819.

The Astrological Judgment of Disease, by Nicholas Culpeper, London, 1671.

The Celestial Science of Astrology, Ebenezer Sibly, London, 1785.

We will take the signs of the Zodiac in the order in which they come, listing under them a general compendium of known facts concerning them.

Aries, the First Sign of the Zodiac

Aries is a cardinal sign,
Fiery
Masculine
Dry
Hot
Vernal
Equinoctial
Movable
Eastern
Diurnal
Short ascension
Bitter sign
Exaltation of the sun
Detriment of Venus
Day house of Mars
Fall of Saturn

General Characteristics

Choleric
Luxuriant
Violent
Fortunate
Hoarse
Commanding
Tempestuous
Militant
Self-assertive
Pioneering
A ruler
Scientific
Explorative
Amative
Versatile
Energetic
Powerful will
Sharp
Hasty
Domineering
Combative

Physical Appearance

Usually slender
Strong and spare
Body rather dry
Piercing eyes
Long face
High cheek-bones
Black eyebrows
Rather long neck
Thick shoulders
Swarthy complexion
Red or dark brown hair
Disposition violent and intemperate
Loose-jointed and strong-boned
Aries governs the head and face
Subject to accidents

Health

Aries is subject to many forms of sudden ailments, also all things which have to do with impediments in the dynamic system. Listed below are the ones most commonly met with:

Smallpox
Eruptions on the face and body

Measles
Sunburn
Ringworm
Headaches
Shingles
Vertigo
Epilepsy
Frenzy
Temper fits
Apoplexy
Lethargy
Fevers
Forgetfulness
Convulsions
Catalepsy
Palsy
Megrims
Coma
Falling sickness
Baldness
Diseases caused by heat
Cramps through various parts of the body
Melancholia
Trembling
Toothache
Hair-lip

Aries is also susceptible to ailments as the result of early indiscretions, and it also burns up too much energy and often lives for many years on plain will power. Aries is also susceptible to ailments in the liver and kidney trouble and poor digestion on account of excitement and Aries energy which tries to do too many things at once.

Domestic Problems

Aries is not a home-loving sign and in the majority of cases is too strongly organized and energized to remain quietly at anything. Aries homes are usually more or less unhappy.

Countries Under the Influence of Aries
Great Britain
France
Germany
Switzerland
Denmark
Lesser Poland
Syria
Palestine

Cities Under Its Control
Naples
Capua
Ancona
Verona
Florence
Ferrara
Padua
Saragossa
Marseilles
Silesia
Burgundy
Utrecht
Cracow

According to Ptolemy the fixed stars in the sign of Aries have the following qualities:

Stars in the head of Aries produce influences similar to Mars and Saturn;

Those in the mouth have the qualities of Mercury and to some degree Saturn;

Those in the hinder foot of the Ram have the qualities of Mars;

While those in the tail of Aries take the qualities of Venus;

Aries, according to the ancients, is a constellation consisting of twelve stars; modern astronomy says otherwise.

Colors

Red and white.

According to Henri Cornelius Agrippa and, later, Francis Barrett, F.R.C., the following list is found under the head of Aries: Of the twelve orders of blessed spirits, Aries rules the Seraphim; of the twelve angels over the twelve signs, Malchidial is ruled by Aries; of the twelve tribes, Dan; of the twelve prophets, Malachi; of the twelve Apostles, Matthias; of the twelve months, March 20th to April 20th; of the twelve plants, the Sang; of the twelve stones, the sardonius; of the twelve principle parts of the body, the head; of the twelve degrees of the damned, the false gods.

Broken Dolls

AS YOU WATCH life through the eyes of one who has walked the path, you see spreading out before you not only a graveyard of broken hopes and shattered ideals but also a wondrous kindergarten where men, gods in the making, pass through the hours of their childhood until the Eternal Hand calls them to greater things.

Here we see the little ones, often old in years but young ever in spirit, laughing and playing each in his own free way, few of the worries and responsibilities of real life in its true sense realized or understood for man knows little of living but with care-free spirit he goes on in this way and in that, playing through the years of his youth and his manhood and passing into the Great Beyond still clasping a toy in his arms.

Off to one side, away from the laughing, playing children, there sits a little one alone for whom the world has come to an end. The little chubby cheeks are streaked with tears, a little heart is broken, and from one little life the light of the sun has gone out forever. With its face clasped between its hands it sobs its little soul away, while upon the ground before it lies a broken doll with its funny little face seamed and cracked and its sawdust body broken and twisted by the ruthless cruelty of an older child.

This is the endless story of the broken doll. It may seem at this age of the world that man does not play with toys like these but still in his heart he is ever a child; to the very day when ends his work here he is just a little one laughing with the children, playing with them, and then creeping away to weep alone over a broken toy.

The world is not filled with sinners but with thoughtless people. It is filled with those who do not realize the agony greater far than mortal mind can ever understand, the soul anguish which gnaws to the very being of a child when its toy is broken. If man could only understand how the little things we love, the little castles we build in the air, the little shrines we make and in which we place gods and goddesses of clay —if the world could only realize the soul each of the other it would not with the ruthless hand of hate and the heartless touch of selfishness tear down these little dream castles of the air; it would not leave us crying by the empty shrines made desolate by their thoughtlessness; it would not leave us heart-broken before the toy that it has shattered, the ideal it has forever slain.

Our toys are very fragile things, just one harsh word, a few unhappy seconds, and the dream of the child is shattered and its life is bent askew. All the children of men are dreamers, dreaming wondrous dreams and building in the heavens castles of rainbow colors. To many these dreams are just toys, just make-believes, and too often our quick word shatters them, and while to us they meant nothing they seemed all to some little soul who must walk the lonely way in darkness because we have torn down the fairy world which made its life sweeter.

So let us be careful of their playthings for the heart of the world bleeds too often and little souls pine away beside the toy that is shattered, which in its broken little pieces symbolizes often the shattered soul of the dreamer. Let us realie more fully that man is ever a child, living ever in the world of make-believe, and that the things which he cherishes and the ones whom he loves become gods and goddesses in truth. His life to the very grave is filled with fairy stories and forever to the soul of the mystic child the prince comes riding, forever in our souls we build little toys, and when all others go away and leave us we bring them out from their sacred closet and sitting alone with our own souls plays with the dolls of the years gone by. Again the little tin soldier comes out of his box, the fluffy little dog is there, and the old rag doll in whose simple, homely being our hearts are often hidden. Only these are no longer physical toys, they are the playthings of the mind and the soul. Instead of being of wood and painted lead the little toy soldiers who fight so true are our friends and those we love, and when friendship is broken, when man betrays his trust one to another, the soul sits alone in its closet and cries heart-broken over a shattered toy.

Let us realize that each of us in enshrined in the soul of another somewhere in the world and that when we betray our trust someone must cry over a broken doll, a soul not strong enough to stand the weight of a thing to us so trivial will know the pains and anguish of a broken heart over the toy which we have shattered. If we could only realize in our homes how love builds toys in the soul we would not tear down these gods from their shrines, we would not break the hearts of those we love by our thoughtless words and heartless deeds which to us mean so little and still fill the world of another with sorrow and sadness.

The soul of man must stay young, he must forever be a dreamer building from the subtle, unseen things toys to fill the loneliness of life. Let him build them, let him dress them as he will, let him play as he will, and deny him not his toys, for when you destroy them you leave behind a mark deep in the soul of things, a scar which the years cannot heal, which only the Masters understand who have wept for ages over broken dolls.

Man must worship something. Someone must to him seem divine, someone in whose ear he may whisper the thoughts, the emotions, and the ideals which surge through his soul. Something either of this world drawn by bonds unknown or a little cherished toy hidden in the heart,—something he must worship in the name of God. Wherever this thing is not, the life is cold.

So let us always help our brothers in the world to play more beautiful games in more beautiful ways with their toys. Let our words and actions make the rag doll more divine and in the true spirit of compassion let us play with the child that its castles may be fairer. Never, in the name of God, tear the toy from the child's arms and leave it sitting on the curbstone which borders the road of life with broken heart and shattered ideals, weeping in an anguish that our hearts can never know for a broken doll.

Ships That Pass In The Night

THERE ARE FEW who realize the power that they themselves as individuals have in molding the destinites of peoples, worlds, and gods. No man lives by himself alone, neither do our thoughts or actions affect us alone. They go on and on in a world of many mysteries and these little birds of clay which we mold fly on eternally ever closer and closer to the circling orbs of light.

The world is a great sea and the eternal, never ceasing sway of living things can be likened to the soft swishing of the ocean waves, and in too many lives this world in which we live is a stormy sea where the waves of broken hopes dash themselves to pieces upon the rocky shores of discouragement. Too many times in life we hear the moaning and sighing as of mighty winds and the night cries in the wilderness when the snowy crests of breaking waves beat against the encircling arms of the shore.

Through this stormy sea of oblivion, this endless battle and turmoil of life there silently pass thousands of little ships, the souls of living things seeking to cross this endless sea, hoping to find a peaceful harbor and there to rest in safety protected from the buffets of the storm. Too many times this world is filled with darkness, the thunderclouds fill our lives and all seems bleak and desolate. Too many times we sense the great oppression, the indescribable sense of loneliness, and the utter chill of the world. We do not see beneath this surging water the softer, sweeter and more beautiful, but lonely barks upon an endless sea with the rudder lashed and sails set, driven by every wind that blows and manned only by a crew of ghastly spectres, our ship passes silently and hopelessly through the night of cosmic oblivion.

Let us for a moment float like some mystic spectre from another world over the darkness of the seas and watch the ships that pass silently in the night. Through the darkness they come, lonely, bleak, and desolate, derelicts on the ceaseless waves of night, and they pass looking neither to the right nor to the left. We shudder, a chill comes over us, we feel the oppression of that ghostly crew of broken hopes and shattered ideals.

Many a living ship is manned only by the ghastly crews of death, set faces that cannot smile peer out from broken portholes and eyes that stare with glassy fixedness of despair gaze out from these silent ships that pass in the night. They do not know where they go. Long ago the compass of courage and ideal has been swept overboard, long before the captain has fallen a victim to the mutiny of his crew. The soft, sweet human touch, the cheery voices of the sailors as they draw on the ropes, and the song of the willing workmen,—all these are silent. Many a human bark, battered and tossed by the sea of life, waits longingly for the waves to break forever over its broken craft, there are souls crying out to their Creator to end their suffering in blissful dissolution.

These are the ships that pass in the night, these are the grim skeletons of dead hopes, these are the vessels that have for ages wandered in the darkness of the storm. One by one the noble aspirations have died, one by one the fiery desires have been chilled forever, and the hearts that once beat as other men's now dream only of lost hopes. The world is filled with these ships that must wander it seems until Judgment Day when through the darkness of the night a light shines out, there is the cheery ringing of a bell, or the starlike gleam of a lighthouse, which brings peace to these broken wanderers, rest to their shattered lives.

Far out in the darkness a tiny pillar of stone rises upward in the night on a broken crag of rock where the endless beating of the waves alone is heard, and the white crests reach upward to envelop this frail thing of man but as the lonely lighthouse stands so great souls have gone out forever from the peace and security of the shore to be broken as battered ships in order that they may keep alight the lamp for the world. The lighthouse keeper at sea is serving ships that pass in the night as the world is served by the lighthouse keepers on the rocks of life. Their gleam shines out no longer from the revolving lenses of the tower above, for in this world the lighthouse is our own being and its light shines out through the eyes, through the soft words, the generous ideals, and the great compassion which marks the lighthouse keepers on the broken seas of the world.

Still the waves break and toss and battle with each other through the eternal night of human ignorance, still the lonely vessel rocked and torn by the storm wanders o'er the sea of life, awaiting the day of liberation and the haven of peace.

A Little Episode from Life
(Continued from Page 14)

ness man with a bowler hat over his eyes and a full cut spring overcoat draped over his portly frame. He is one of the leading lights of high finance and is considered a Rockefellow in the making. He is headed for the cafeteria for the bells within and without have summoned him to lunch. He passed with a springy step, his head set straight forward on a copious neck, his nose turned slightly askew to allow the smoke of his cigar to go upwards without passing back into his nose. He passes the little figure, the notes of the accordion strike his ear but he has no time to waste, he knows but one master, the call of the inner man, and the only music that can touch his soul is the gentle cadence of sizzling bacon, and the gentle purr of a knife across a beefsteak.

As he passes from the field of vision there comes up the street from the other direction a tall, slender youth, the most conspicuous part of his attire being his light violet, striped socks and a roll-down jersey. He has a Lucky Strike under one ear and his cap is tilted well over his nose and threatens to slide off from his polished hair glistening brightly with a generous dose of brilliantine. He is whistling "Clementine" with sundry original variations, including the "Stars and Stripes Forever," and with his hands in his pockets and his chest slumped in he is headed God alone knows where, but the graveyard is undoubtedly the end of the trip. Upon his ears, also, fall the strains of the accordion but he is not interested, he has just had a break with his "steady" who'd seen him out with his "once-in-a-while."

Just then from across the corner there hove in sight one of our leading society dowagers, the heavily constructed Mrs. Gotrox, accompanied by her daughter, this season's prize for the highest bidder, who has been acclaimed the most eligible and desirable debutante in the west district. Mr. Gotrox has just made millions in his seedless pickle project.

"M'dear," says mother, "what is this peculiar squeaky noise I hear?"

"It must be that old lady over there playing the accordion," gurgled the blossoming member of the younger set.

"Oh, dear!" exclaimed the mother, who had been Cylenthe McGillicutty before her marriage, "I wish they'd pass a law against allowing beggars on the street, I'll bet she has more money than I have, every one of these old women is rolling in cash, but I'll tell you right now she'll get none of mine!" And with quite a gust of personality they sailed off, a streaming duo of ostrich plumes and real mink, headed for a well known beauty parlor where Madame was taking out wrinkles for mama and trying to add an indestructible kink to daughter's hair.

Several seconds passed and the corner seemed nearly deserted when another figure appeared, a promising young clerk from one of the downtown stores in the neighborhood. This young lady was one of those liquid types which threatened to collapse at every step. She was built on the lines of a weeping willow and from the head downward every muscular articulation expressed itself as a drizzle. As this figure came galloping by it extracted with a hairpin a small wad of gum affixed to the third molar and with a semi-hysterical gesture animated by a general disintegration of the trapizoid muscle, threatening a general collapse, she lazily tossed the gum over one shoulder, said gum landing on the head of the old lady playing the accordion.

Happening to follow its course this promising member of our younger generation twisted her mouth under one ear and bellowed forth in this fashion:

"Well, grandma, if ye hadn't been there it wouldn't 'a hit yuh! Whatter you think you're doing, parking yourself on the sidewalk, this ain't no bone orchard?" and with this elegant excerpt from the classics our flapper careened off with as much grace and dignity as four and a half inches of French heels and weak ankles would permit.

The old lady still sat playing the accordion. She had brushed away the gum and was perhaps recalling the days when she had been as young and foolish as the girl who had passed and possibly wondering if that girl's fate would be the same as hers.

One by one the people passed, the highest, the richest, and the most educated in the fair city. Here and there one would drop a nickle or dime into the cup but the majority went by. Then through the crowd another little figure appeared.

It was an old lady dressed in black. She wore a little bonnet with the ribbons tied under her chin, an old-fashioned cashmere shawl hung around her shoulders, and her plain clothes, while neat, showed the thrift which is the result of none too sufficient funds. She was the mother of a large family very likely but one after another they had gone away to their separate lives and as is usually the case none wanted her. She was alone and though the black she wore showed that her own partner had been laid away in the grave no doubt his picture rested ever in her heart. She was one of the few of an age of simple things fast disappearing from the things we know. For her it was a problem to make both ends meet but with frugal life and simple tastes she seemed like one of those who live on some little pension away from the eyes of the world.

As this old lady reached the huddled figure in the doorway playing on the squeaky accordion, she stopped and her sweet, old face grew sad and with a little black bordered handkerchief she wiped away a tear from under her glasses.

"You poor, dear soul!" she exclaimed, taking out her little pocketbook which contained only a few small coins, "I know how hard things must be for you, for the world has not been kind to me, either. Here, this is all I have to give, but, oh, how I wish that it were a hundred times more!"

The figure huddled in the doorway tried to smile but tears came into her eyes, too, for she had learned the tragedy of life. The little old lady in black went happily along, smiling through her tears at the pleasure her gift had given her, and no doubt went without the things she needed as a sacrifice for the little offering she had made. It was not the first time this had happened; the lonely woman in the doorway had witnessed it many times.

This is one of the little tragedies that is played out so many times in life. The rich and the thoughtless go their way, each living for himself, while only the poor it seems have learned to help the poor, only the suffering ones have reached the point where they know how to share one with the other.

In those darkened places where the down and outers huddle together we find more brotherhood by far than in the homes of riches. Some broken figure, aged and gray, itself standing on the brink of dissolution, will gladly share its crust with another, some life broken with sorrow will enfold another suffering one within its arms and try to bring peace to another breaking heart when its own has long since died.

Is not this in truth a tragedy, yet a divinely sweet symbol of the soul of man? Only those who have walked the silent ways know the joy of sharing, and so as we watch the beggars on the street we find that it is nearly always the poor who give to them of the little which they have which often leaves them poorer than the one they serve. Here we see again the Master's face as it shines forth from the souls of those who have but little.

If the Master came today into this world and stood on the street corner begging for the soul of men it would be the poor and the suffering alone who would feel the depth of His message. It would only be those who have not who would long to give while those who have plenty only wish to receive.

So the little old lady still plays the old accordion in the open doorway. She knows something that it takes many years to discover, and yet life is much sweeter and more beautiful when we realize how sorrow softens the heart, how poverty broadens the soul, and how true brotherhood rises among those who are down and out.

Pearly Gates Gazette

MEMBER OF THE ASSINATED PRESS — EXTRA — UNLIMITED CIRCULATION

VOL. 30000001   JUNE, 1923   No. 1000000000001

WAR IN HEAVEN THREATENS

Jupiter In Critical Condition

BAD STORMS ARE GATHERING

Conditions Very Uncertain

The Pearly Gates weather bureau announces that warm weather is expected. Several leading occult lights are due to arrive in heaven this morning and will undoubtedly bring a hot air wave with them. Low pressure area is threatening.

ADVERTISEMENTS

BARGAIN PICKUP

For Sale: A corner apartment site, three blocks east of Mercury on paved boulevard, direct route between heaven and hell. Thriving business in neighborhood, particularly South. A pickup. Will take solid gold halo in exchange, must be fourteen cara.

BUSINESS OPPORTUNITY

Investors Wanted: Young men with small capital can get rich over night in the Non Est Oil Company. Three gushers within the last two weeks. A large number of angels have gotten rich. Invest now while the stock is down. Autos leave every morning from the Cloudbeam Station, two blocks East of Pearly Gate. Barbecue meal will be served on the Milky Way. Expert hot air gushers accompany each car.

Fashion Notes

Father Time appeared with a clean shave this morning. When asked the reason for it, he said that things had been moving so fast lately that his whiskers had worn until they looker so ragged that a shave was necessary.

JUPITER MAY DIE TODAY

Doctors Give Up All Hope

Jupiter was taken seriously ill this evening. One of our leading physicians diagnosed the case as congested liver, the result of "over proteins" in the nectar and ambrosia which the god drank at a little social gathering the previous night.

FOOD EXPERT ARRIVES SUDDENLY

We also have with us Mr. Will Knock, a well-known food crank. Mr. Knock is not expected to stay long owing to the fact that he is dissatisfied with the diet.

ON OUR PRIVATE WIRE

Special Wire From Our War Correspondent on Mars

Venus was fined $10.00 this morning for parking too close to Mars during non-parking hours and for disobeying the left urn ordinance.

Special on Our Private Wire From Saturn

Saturn is to appear in court tomorrow morning on the charge of exceeding the speed limit at night with no tail light. It is suspected that he was drinking.

WANTED

Wanted: Two or three laboring men, steady, hard workers. Heathens preferred, we can't get the Christians to do the work.

FIVE HOMES BROKEN UP

War About to Be Declared

Mrs. Buzz arrived last week but was asked to leave this morning. She has already broken up the homes of five of the gods and has so many scandals on tap that a second war in heaven is imminent. She is an occult student from the planet Earth. It's funny but we have more trouble with these mystics than the Mohammedans and Zulu Islanders. The husband of Mrs. Buzz passed over several years ago but could not be found during his wife's sojourn here.

AGED MAN NEWEST ARRIVAL

Mr. Henry Jones, aged 115, arrived in heaven this morning on an eastbound cloud. When asked to what he accredited his long life he said that he had a better start than most people, he was born before germs were discovered.

PROFESSOR ARRIVES THIS MORNING

Special Wire From Jupiter

Prof. Algernon Gump, one of the leading theorists and statisticians of Earth, arrived in heaven on the Allnight Flier after a very sudden death. Prof. Gump strangled last night when he got so tangled up in scientific red tape that he couldn't breathe. He was debating the relative size of electrons.

"The Initiates of the Flame"

By

MANLY P. HALL

A comprehensive study in the Wisdom Religion as it has been perpetuated through symbolism and mythology. This work is of interest to all students of mystic and occult philosophies or Masonry. The work is beautifully illustrated with drawings to explain its principles, some by the author and others of an alchemical and mystic nature. The table of contents is as follows:

Chapter One	"The Fire Upon the Altar."
Chapter Two	"The Sacred City of Shamballah."
Chapter Three	"The Mystery of the Alchemist."
Chapter Four	"The Egyptian Initiate."
Chapter Five	"The Ark of the Covenant."
Chapter Six	"The Knights of the Holy Grail."
Chapter Seven	"The Mystery of the Pyramids."

This book is beautifully bound in full cloth with a handsome alchemical cover design stamped in gold leaf and contains about one hundred pages.

This work is not for sale but may be secured through a voluntary contribution on the part of anyone desiring to possess it. All of our work is put out for the benefit of students and not for purposes of profit and we ask your co-operation to assist us in meeting the cost of publication and distribution by your own realization of responsibility.

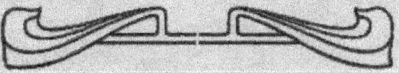

These booklets by the same author may be secured by sending to Postoffice Box 695, Los Angeles, California, care of Manly P. Hall.

Price. These publications are not for sale but may be secured through voluntary contribution to help meet the cost of publication.

The Breastplate of the High Priest

A discussion of Old Testament symbolism showing how the spiritual powers of nature reflect themselves through the spiritual centers in the human body which we know as the jewels in the breastplate of Aaron. This booklet is out of print but an attempt will be made to secure a few copies for any desiring them. Illustrated.

Buddha, the Divine Wanderer

A new application of the life of the Prince of India as it is worked out in the individual growth of every student who is in truth seeking for the Yellow Robe.

Krishna and the Battle of Kurushetra

The Song Celestial with its wonderful story of the Battle of Life interpreted for students of practical religion. The mystery of the Blue Krishna and his work with men.

The Father of the Gods

A mystic allegory based upon the mythology of the peoples of Norway and Sweden and the legend of Odin the All-Father of the Northlands.

Questions and Answers, Part One
Questions and Answers, Part Two
Questions and Answers, Part Three

In these three booklets have been gathered about fifty of the thousands of questions answered in the past work gathered together for the benefit of students.

Occult Masonry

This booklet consists of the condensed notes on a class in mystic Masonry given in Los Angeles. It covers a number of important Masonic symbols and the supply is rapidly being exhausted.

Wands and Serpents

The explanation of the serpent of Genesis and serpent-worship as it is found among the mystery religions of the world and in the Christian Bible. Illustrated.

The Analysis of the Book of Revelation

A short study in this little understood book in the Bible, five lessons in one folder as given in class work during the past year.

The Unfoldment of Man

A study of the evolution of the body and mind and the causes which bring about mental and physical growth, a practical work for practical people.

Occult Psychology

Notes of an advanced class on this subject dealing in a comprehensive way with ten of its fundamental principles as given to students of classes in Los Angeles on this very important subject.

Parsifal and the Sacred Spear

An entirely new view of Wagner's wonderful opera with its three wonderful acts as they are applied to the three grand divisions of human life, the Legend of the Holy Grail, which will interest in its interpretation both mystics and music lovers.

Faust, the Eternal Drama

This booklet is a companion to the above and forms the second of a series of opera interpretations of which more will follow. The mystic drama by Goethe is analyzed from the standpoint of its application to the problem of individual advancement and its wonderful warning explained to the reader.

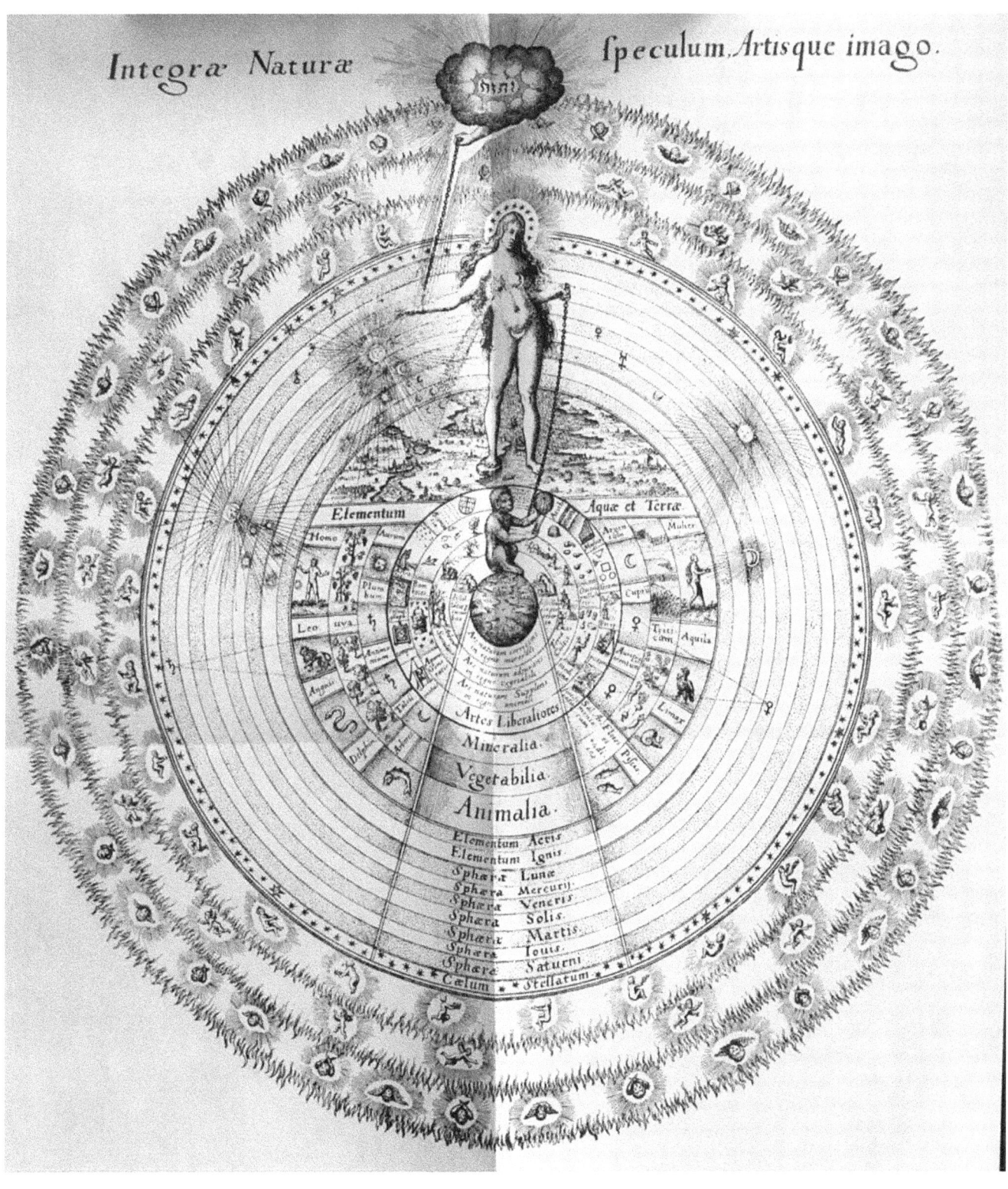

The All-Seeing Eye

Modern Problems in the Light of Ancient Wisdom

A Monthly Magazine
Written, Edited and
Compiled by
MANLY P. HALL

JULY, 1923

THIS MAGAZINE IS NOT SOLD

THE ALL-SEEING EYE

MODERN PROBLEMS IN THE LIGHT OF ANCIENT WISDOM

VOL. 1   LOS ANGELES, CALIF., JULY, 1923   No. 3

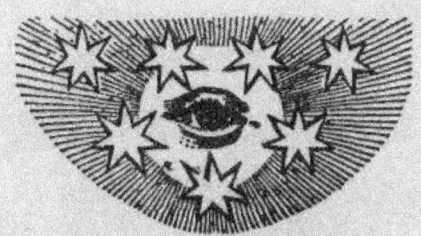

This magazine is published monthly
for the purpose of spreading the ancient Wisdom Teachings in a practical way that
students may apply to their own lives. It is written, published, and
edited by Manly P. Hall and privately published for
circulation among his students and those
interested in his work.

Those desiring to secure copies of this magazine or who wish to subscribe to it may do so by writing directly to the editor.

This magazine is published and distributed privately to those who make possible with their financial support its publication. The magazine cannot be bought and has no fixed value. Like all of the ancient teachings which it seeks to promulgate it has no comparative value but the students must support it for its own instrinsic merit.

To whom it may concern: It is quite useless to inquire concerning advertising rates or to send manuscripts for publication as this magazine cannot possibly consider either as this is a non-commercial enterprise. All letters and questions, subscriptions, etc., should be mailed to P. O. Box 695, Los Angeles, California, in care of Manly P. Hall, Editor.

The contents of this magazine are copyrighted but permission to copy may be secured through correspondence with the author.

This magazine does not represent nor promulgate any special sect or teaching but is non-sectarian in all of its viewpoints. Suggestions for its improvement will be gladly considered if presented in the proper manner.

TABLE OF CONTENTS

Poem, 'Mid Nature's Charms..................................2	Occult and Practical Eugenics..............................19
Editorial, Mental Hazards versus Hereditary Failures 3	A Letter from the Brothers of the Rose Cross, Part 3 23
The Last of the Shamen..7	What Will the Harvest Be?....................................25
The Brothers of the Shining Robe, (Chap. 2, continued) The Mirror of Eternity..............13	The Divine Masquerader..27
An Explanation of the Plate in Last Month's Magazine 18	Astrological Keywords, Sign of Taurus..........30
	The Pearly Gates Gazette....................................32

'Mid Nature's Charms

By an Inmate of Folsom Prison

As down the open road I go
   A thousand things are dear;
A boon companionship I know
   In all I see and hear.

My love is as the buxom wind,
   I taste the breath of flowers,
To me the whispering leaves are kind
   And sweet the swaying flowers.

Contented kine turn friendly eyes
   That know me as I pass,
I find a welcome in the skies,
   A calling in the grass.

A kinship deeper than of blood
   Holds me to ties of earth,
As now their source is understood
   The rankest weeds have worth.

The tendrils growing by the spring
   Tempt me to share their drink,
And 'mid the forests shadowy
   Birds tell me what they think.

I have not glimpsed the wide world o'er
   To scorn one thing as mean,
For beauty charms me all the more
   The deeper I have seen.

And I rejoice in everything
   That stirs my throbbing heart,
By myriad rampant whispering
   To lofty thoughts impart.

On mountain-tops, 'mid prairies sweep,
   And o'er the rolling sea,
These friendly comrades vigil keep
   And guide me tenderly.

EDITORIAL

Mental Hazards vs. Hereditary Failures

SINCE the beginning of time man has leaned. It seems part of his nature to drape himself upon something or someone. In the beginning he leaned on the Lord, then he leaned on his relatives, and after many ages of evolution he finally learned to balance himself gracefully against his own spinal column.

The world is so large that it would seem man could live in his own little plot without implicating others in the various phases of his growth. But this he is not able to do and all through the ages he lives not either for himself, by himself, or with himself but is eternally involving others in the complexities of his expression. He creates a very personal God to look after him and an even more personal Devil to blame for all the misfortunes of his life. In other words he surrounds himself with a series of self-created and mental hazards and scares himself to death with bugaboos of his own making. These bugaboos are manyfold in their expression, differing with the stages of development reached by the temperament creating them, and the more highly evolved the individual, the more spiritual and wonderful, complex and intricate, seemingly, is the bugaboo that he creates, until finally when he becomes proficient it is very difficult to differentiate between nature herself and man-made hazards which sometimes are so perfect that they will deceive the elect.

Of all the mental hazards which people serve, that strange, weird figure known as the Past is probably the greatest. Somewhere concealed in the family closet is this grinning skeleton which is the dowry bestowed by ancestry upon ensuing generations. A person without a past nowadays is like a servant without a reference, and little by little man is making ever worse pasts out of promising presents and unawakened futures. This grinning and rattling skeleton is now pedigreed and distinguished by being termed the Family Tree, and azure shields on gold backgrounds, et cetera, or a fistful of watercrest, form the family coat of arms. Very few people will admit that they haven't got one of these peculiar creatures snuggled away in the family vault where every few minutes it points bony fingers at the next generation and whispers that not living creatures but mental concoctions of diseased intellects are to rule each generation of the world.

In spite of the fact that we are living in a democratic age, most of our families are nourishing somewhere in their conservatories a family tree with the same love and sincerity that one of our tenement inhabitants might guard the solitary rubber plant on the window sill. In the majority of cases this family tree is a weird and wonderful piece of horticulture and like many of the Burbank variety carries more than one kind of fruit on a single stem. Often we find lemons and prunes growing side by side with some luscious, rosy-cheeked apple, all nourished upon the single trunk of that family tree. Only in the human variety the luscious apple was Uncle Joshua who made five millions out of shoe-eyelets while the lemon is Aunt Samanthy who married below her social position when she eloped with the gardener.

So the family tree grows on and on until at the very peak of this rather eccentric plant with its exotic fragrance, John Doe is born as a glorious orchid bringing with him into the world of affairs a strange combination of mystic-heterogeneties. According to proud and doting parents he is something as follows: He was born bald just like his great grandfather who was scalped by the Cherokee Indians; his bleared eyes came from his mother's side of the house where his great grandmother's sister-in-law went blind at the tender age of 103; he has a peculiar shaped face, has John Doe—his jaw is a little on one side—he inherited that peculiarity from his uncle who had his own jaw smashed while fighting Moorish pirates. His big mouth he inherited from his grandmother who talked a great deal, while his high cheek bones came from his great granduncle's brother who married an Indian squaw. From the very start in life John was heavy the same as his father's cousin, while he learned profanity at a tender age the same as his great granduncle's nephew who fought in the Civil War. He inherited the color of his hair from his mother, the shape of his teeth from his godfather; the size of his ears from the minister who baptised him and his blurred complexion from his eleventh cousin. In other words when we gaze upon John Doe we behold Joseph's coat of many colors and a grand composite coadunation of hectic botany. And there he nestles amid the branches of the family tree, predestined and foreordained since the beginning of the world to be bowlegged because his grandfather rode horseback.

After he has been raised in this environment for a few years his own little mind starts working, and he soon joins that great line of mystic shadow-shapes that bow with humble reverence before the moulding scarecrow of antiquity. And in a short time he really believes that his grandsires have measured the possibilities of his worth and that he will never be anything because an unkind fate placed him in a generation of failures and because his family crest boasts only ne'er-do-wells. He soon believes that the mean traits of his temperament are perfectly natural and desirable because that temperament belongs with the heraldry of his house and soon he is listed as just another little nut hanging on the family tree.

We very often hear this as we go through life: "No, I can't help it. I realize I have a mean disposition but I inherited it from my mother. You should have seen the way she used to bend rolling pins and lead pipes around papa's fourth cervical. It's an inherited trait and there's not much use in trying to do anything with it." This mental frame is the incubator which hatches forth one after another the mental hazards and pedigreed non-entities which rule our lives after we once abdicate in their favor.

It is for no other reason than this: At the present time there are many people wandering through life on reputations or who are considered great, strong, and noble because their aunt's sister had a husband who wore epaulets. Then, of course, we must not forget the titles which come down with the family tree. Anyone who has had that experience socially knows what it means to be acquainted with a count or a duke or a lord somebody and with what zealous care these titles are resilvered and nickeled for the express benefit of each new generation, when in many cases the inheritance consists of a title, scrofula, and bad bills.

Take the average individual and show him his weak points and he will lead you into the conservatory and there protected by a wonderful glass domicile stands the hereditary elm, and he will in a perfectly serious tone and an earnestness excruciating explain to you exactly which branch was cracked when he came along. You tell him he is a liar, he will admit it freely but will explain with perfect gravity that he can't help it, and he will point out a raisin dangling on the family tree that was a liar also and who wished his failing upon him about three hundred years before the death of Cromwell. If you tell him he is dissipated he will immediately reach into the foliage of said tree and pull you out a wild cherry that came over in the Mayflower from whom he inherited his rakish temperament. If you tell him he is sour he will point to the glorious yellow lemon on the family crest and explain to you that there was someone in his heredity responsible for it. If he is a failure he will point out certain qualities in the prune that grows amid the shadows of the self-perpetuating elm whose mental qualities were productive of failure in the nth generation.

Slowly there dawns upon our minds the realization of a fundamental truth. The family tree is the greatest of all excuses for humanity's faults and people who are too weak, too silly, and too hopelessly lacking in backbone to do anything themselves are continually blaming their ancestry for their own inherent weaknesses. It is very often the case that people who do not have family trees, or rather who do not know about them, are often far more successful than the offspring from generations, or shall we say degenerations, of admirals, marshals, and Lord Whatnots. The fact slowly impresses itself upon our consciousness that failures are individual, self-sustained combinations of intricate mechanisms that would never have been successes under any other conditions.

The only cause of failure in a family tree is the mental hazard of this lonely elm upon which hangs suspended anywhere from one to an hundred generations of deceased ancestors who have gone to their happy rest and are not in any way worried over the work of implanting their qualities in their already suffering descendents. There is nothing on the family tree but fossilized concepts given power by those who believe in them. If these past generations were alive they might cause success or failure but as dead they can only affect dead ones and those who allow the dead to run their lives are themselves listed with the deceased.

Any living creature may be, if he so acts and lives, the first success in his family regardless of the wizened appearance of the family crest or the drooping attributes of miscellaneous progenitors. It is also true that those who do not strive to live up to their best can in a few short hours disgrace the noblest heraldry that the world has ever known. Successes in this world are the ones who do things, who labor to master environments if they be evil or to be worthy of them if they be good, realizing that all great things rise out of effort. Therefore, the worse the family tree the greater the opportunity of the individual to shine out as an illustrious denial of his inherited debits.

Then we have another type. They are the ones who while unhampered by ancestry and unpolluted by blue blood have gradually become failures through inherent qualities and mental reactions during their own lives. This type we generally list under the style of "Type B". Their slogan is, "If you'd been through what I've been through you wouldn't be anything either," or with variations something like this, "If I hadn't married so and so, I wouldn't be what I am now," or else, "I never had a chance." There are several sub-varieties of this type as follows, "I always have had tough luck." Also, "If your family treated you the way mine treated me and cheated you out of everything you had you wouldn't talk either." And then the grand closing hymn, "It's my hard lfe, dearie, that's done it!" These are sour apples grown and developed upon their own tree without the overshadowing presence of heredity, for such examples as these need no ancestry to produce failure, they are self-containing.

There are a large number of people who do not seem to realize that the harder you are thrown down the higher you bounce, but they spend the last sixty-five years of life in a spiritual wheel-chair because they slipped on a banana-peel when they were young. Once having made a mistake and having had a beware label hung on the heredity elm alongside of them, they feel that they are ruined forever and ever, amen, and believe it is their God-appointed duty to spend the remaining scores of their lives putting the capping-stone on the general ruin.

People who live in the past and like Lot's wife look back eternally upon the things they did in '64 or the scrape they got mixed up in in '83 will never get anywhere mentally, physically, or spiritually. The thing for these people to do is to remember the lesson, forget the incident and keep plugging, realizing that if they had never made a mistake they could never enjoy the privilege of doing better.

Then there is another type, "Grade C," who believe that they have been elected by the Most High and chosen by the Divine One to be the eternal brunt of His ill humor. There are thousands who honestly express themselves as believing that the Lord had a grouchy fit on when He made them and that He has been down on them ever since. They go through life manifesting the incarnated essence of concentrated gloom, dissolution, and despair, for no other reason on earth than that they firmly believe God has it in for them, therefore what's the use in trying, anyhow? It is difficult to imagine what an awful feeling it must be to have God down on you and to know that the All-loving, all-wise, and kind Father has sent seventy-seven deputations of demons with matrimonial problems, financial worries, kidney trouble, sour stomach, gloomy religion, and general indisposition to prod you continually with pitchforks of incessant catastrophe for no other reason at all than that you happen to be a blonde when the Lord likes brunettes. Yes, this exhibit is quite common and those people who believe that stomach trouble is the vengeance of the Lord for missing church and that falling arches have been sent to man to teach him contrition of spirit or simplicity of soul are in a class all by themselves.

In other words, a large percentage of our population are failures but lamentably few of them believe that they have personally done anything to deserve it. They are all suffering from hereditary ailments, counting either their family tree or their God as the source. There are few who are strong enough to stand up before the world and honestly say that they are the one and only cause of their shortcomings, that regardless of heredity or environment they can be successful when they will live in such a way that it is possible for them to secure balance.

A family tree is a pedigreed non-entity which only affects those who believe in it. Past mistakes are only the seed grounds of future successes and the idea of God's wrath which He showers upon us as brimstone and sackcloth is the greatest, most honored, and revered bunkum that the human race lists in its category of superstitions.

Man is not a failure until he makes himself one, as no granduncle can do it for him. So long as he goes through life with a prickly disposition because his grandfather owned a cactus farm he will be listed with the world's genuine failures, self-ordained and self-perpetuating. Great souls rise over adversity and use it as a stepping stone to heights above, while weak backbones bend beneath the load, blaming the Lord for the weight of the material which He has given them to build their temple.

So let us go out with Paris Green and a sprayer and set to work on the family tree, effectively destroying the insects, bugs, grubs, et cetera, that are nestling in its branches and used by mortals as excuses for buglike tendencies and wormlike consciousness in their daily lives.

If there is any person, creed, or religion that in your haste or thoughtlessness you look down upon or dislike, it is there that you must look for the help and development that you need. It is the plan of the Great Ones to show those on our plane of existence the great doctrine of universal brotherhood, they often teach this by sending the truths and knowledge that we need to us through those whom we dislike, and this great thought may be safely kept in mind in all stages of human development.

A doctrine that is based upon a personality dies with that personality while a teaching based upon principle is eternal.

The veil of form that conceals the face of God can only be cut by the sword of enlightened spirit.

Truth cannot be bought or sold but it is the birthright of all who will live in harmony with it.

The emnation body functions by means of air while the physical body develops through food. The more one eats the less one breathes; the less air, the more waste there is in the body. Science states that the average individual breathes one-third as much air as he should and eats about three times as much as he should. The result is disintegration and crystallization and general shortening of life.

Evil is misplaced energy, it is the right thing in the wrong place. Whenever energy is misdirected it tears down something, be this misdirection mental, spiritual, or physical. Laziness and ignorance are the causes of misapplication of energy and we know that misdirected energy is the cause of all our misfortunes.

The secret of youth is oxygenation and the secret of death is carboniation. Misdirected and wasted energy destroys all things.

The Last of the Shamen

Dedicated to the Memory of a Dying People

THE majority of people know little if anything of the American Indian, of his ideals, his hopes, and his fears, for there are few indeed who can pierce the stoic attitude of these people who while they are fast dying still preserve in the majority of cases the dignity and self-control which mark the ancient races.

I was raised in an Indian country and from early childhood mingled more or less with this strange, broken people, now scattered remnants of what was once the most powerful of all races. There is something very wonderful and fascinating in the study of the Indian and I must say that I have always liked them. An invisible cord, a mystic bond, drew me even in my childhood to these wandering nomads and I spent many years in the study of them. I lived not far from one of the greatest of the American Indian reservations and have been with them many times, and maybe I am just a little liked by them too. I have seen young braves dashing madly on half broken bronchos and Indian ponies down the main street of the town, covered from head to foot with yellow ochre or green and blue aniline dye, shouting and screaming their warcries in truly terrible yet wonderfully fascinating ways. I have stood beside tall, blanketed figures in the years that are past as in the drugstores they spent the money gained from horse selling and cattle raising for various colored pigments with which to smear their being. I have stood on the street corner where the squaws sat, surrounded by pottery and bead work fashioned by their skillful fingers, crying out the value of their wares or cooing cradle songs to the little papooses fastened by thongs to their beds of wood.

They are now but a broken people, these red men of the plains, and few there are who care much about them, few there are who concern themselves as to the fate of the Indian. Nor can you blame them for everyone does not know the beauty, the sweetness, and the deep mysticism of their ancient but now broken ideals. Every race, like every individual, plays its part in the great plan and its work done vanishes from the light of men. In his soul the Indian knows that the path of his race is run, and while his heart is sad still the voice within whispers and the old brave knows that the Great Spirit is calling his children home from the corners of creation, and calmly and serenly the aged warrior, philosopher, or stateman gathers the folds of his blanket around him and walks along that apparently endless way that leads to Manitou the Mighty.

Of course, I did not always feel as I do now for I did not always understand the Red Man as I did after I met Uncle Joe. It was in a small town in the western states, where the main event of the day was the passing of the Southern Pacific, that I met probably the strangest Indian in America, yes, in the world. He always reminded me of that wonderful character created by Eugene Sue in "The Wandering Jew," for it honestly seemed that this Indian had lived forever. Nobody knew where Uncle Joe came from but some of the oldtimers remarked that they guessed God made him with the country, nor did they realize how true those words were. Everybody agreed that he was over a hundred but nobody seemed to know just how much over and he never answered personal questions, and when you asked him he would only grunt and wrap his blanket more closely about his face. There were very few people who were friendly with Uncle Joe for he was a strange, lonely wanderer who belonged hundreds of years back when the Red Man was in his glory. He still wore the picturesque garb of his people but he was very different from the Indian, and although his face was wrinkled and copper colored his heart was of pure gold.

He was no fool either, was Uncle Joe, nor was he lacking in education, for he spoke better English than the white men who scorned him. It seemed he had travelled widely, also, for he could tell you of distant countries and he spoke a dozen or more foreign languages. A polished gentleman in temperament and nature, he seemed a strange misfit among a rabble of half breeds. Some said he was a great chief, others that he was the medicine man for a once mighty people, while the eternally suspicious ones whispered that he was a secret agent for the government. But when it came right down to it, all admitted that they did not know anything about Uncle Joe.

Every few weeks he would mount his little Indian pony and head out all alone into the broken and rocky desert filled with broken mesas and shapeless crags which lay to the south of the town. Everyone used to wonder where he went and try to follow him. They would get just so far, however, each time and then he would vanish as though the earth had swallowed him up and no one ever found the secret which Uncle Joe guarded somewhere out among the painted rocks.

I lived in the little town many months studying Indians and listening to the dinner bell when the trains pulled in, and my love and admiration for the strange wandering Red Man must have been felt by Uncle Joe for he became very friendly with me and we had many talks on the future of the Red Man, his history, his government, and his philosophy. Uncle Joe was no ordinary Indian, as I have said before, but a real scientist and philosopher whose knowledge and shrewdness of mind won my admiration from our first meeting.

I became in the course of about three years his closest companion for I was with him nearly all the time except when he would go out into the desert, then he would say,

"I go now into the hills. Some day I shall take you with me but not now." In a short time he would return and then for many weeks we would be together again. So the time passed and I learned much of the history of the Red Man, his secret customs, his religion, and his great ideals. Uncle Joe would sigh as he told me of the dead ambitions of his people and now and then a tear would steal softly down his cheek as he spoke of the way of the Great Spirit and of the gods who had come to care for and instruct his people.

One day as the third year of our acquaintance was drawing to a close, Uncle Joe laid his hand on my shoulder and his great black eyes seemed to look into my very soul,

"I am going out into the desert," he said, "and I shall never come back again, for my gods have called me and my father's fathers have whispered to me in the night. In all the years that have passed I have never taken anyone with me on this trip, but today my gods have spoken and said that one at least of the coming race should know the secret of my dying people. So if you will go with me out into the desert you may, and there you will know the reason why Uncle Joe has been here all these years and why no man has ever followed him."

I jumped at the opportunity for I knew that there was some great secret that the old Indian had been guarding all these lonely years, and so the next morning we started out together on two little pinto ponies in the direction of the broken ground which lay to the South.

As we rode along Uncle Joe told me some wonderful things about the Indians, some of them I am not allowed to tell but others I may relate. He told me that among the Red Men was a mystic body who for thousands of years had kept the records of these wandering people. Little was known concerning them, they were hidden from even the Indians themselves, for they were a small body appointed by the Great Spirit to labor with his people. This little band of Sacred Ones had come out from the silent East where the rising sun rose, they came from a wondrous city of shining lights that had vanished forever beneath the waters of the mighty ocean. They were the priests of Malkedek, the priest kings of the ancient Red Men, arrayed in robes of birds' feathers and shining gold, possessors of the wealth of emperors and the wisdom of gods. These strange masters had brought out of the silent East the knowledge of the Great Spirit and had formed the Red Man into seven great nations like the planets in the heavens. For thousands of years these wise men had labored with the Indian who before that time had been a straying, savage race, dwelling on the outskirts of a more ancient civilization. They had brought with them along the path of the sunbeam the great serpent of wisdom and had guarded the Red Man's destiny all through the years of his development. But now the Red Man's work was done, the Manu was calling his people, and the Great Spirit had given to his sons the work of gathering in his broken tribes like the harvester gathers in his wheat.

I listened while the old man spoke. It was all very wonderful to me to hear such words as these from the mouth of one whom the world called a savage, yet I realized, alas, more plainly than ever that the world has little power to judge who its philosophers are.

We had been riding some time and slowly the broken stones rose up about us, bearing the marks of water on their roughhewn sides, showing that once a mighty ocean had carved them by its ebb and flow. But now all was dry and dead and here and there the whitened bones of some animal showed that, alas, water was but a memory of the past. We were on a tiny trail that wound in and out among the reddish rocks and shifting sands.

Suddenly before us rose a mighty pinnacle of sandstone and the twisting trail seemed to end at its base. The aged Indian stopped, raised his hand, and muttered a few words in his strange, guttural language, at the same time making the mark of the cross upon his forehead. As he did so the rocks dissolved and a gateway appeared in the mighty sandstone mountain, and motioning me to enter the mystic arch Uncle Joe followed me and darkness surrounded us, for as we entered the rocky door closed behind us leaving no mark upon the outer wall.

"For many hundreds of years," whispered my companion, "this rocky cavern has remained unknown to the white man and it always will for in it is buried the lost people, and there are few who know the mysteries of the Red Man. Even the young brave growing up has forgotten and will never think again of the power of his sires."

I remained spellbound at the strange miracle for I had never believed in supernatural things up to that time, but as we rode slowly along in the gloom a strange feeling of awe and reverence came over me for my companion.

"Who are you" I asked, "who have these strange powers and know so much of these ancient people?" My guide made no answer but we continued on through the gloom until we finally came out into the light on a beautiful little plateau way up on the side of a mighty mesa.

Here the Indian dismounted and I followed suit and we stood together overlooking a grand expanse of rolling and broken country which stretched out to the distant mountains a mass of brown and yellow sand in strange relief against the glorious blue of the summer sky.

The old Indian waved his hand,

"Behold the land of the Red Men, now a broken desert. Water alone made this a fertile land and the waters of life pouring out from the heart of the Great Spirit alone made the Red Men a great race. No longer the waters come forth for the work of the Red Man is done and soon he will be as dead and broken as the desert which stretches before you. But come, my son, child of another people, you are the first white man who has ever lived to enter the presence of the Red Man's god."

Taking me by the hand Uncle Joe led me to a small opening in the side of the cliff, just a narrow slit which led in to unknown depths. I passed in and the Indian followed me, and after going some hundred feet into the mountain the crevice broadened out and became a great room dimly lighted by a blazing fire of mighty logs. Of living inmates there was no sign but the whole room wos filled with ghastly figures. In a great circle sat a row of mummies robed from head to foot in the grandeur of the Red Man, preserved against decay in that subtle atmosphere by some force unknown. Twelve of them sat crosslegged upon the floor and in the center of this ghastly circle was a great throne before which burned the fire of never-consuming grandeur. The great throne was empty and seemed of solid gold with a glorious sunglobe and the thunder bird carved upon its back.

The aged man pointed around the ghastly circle,

"These, my son, are the Chiefs of the Red Men. They were the last of the line of priest kings who dwelt here and who came out of the land of the sky-blue waters. One by one they have passed beyond to the land of their ancestors. Each time one of these Great Ones died the hand of Manitou was cut off from a race of the Red Men. One after another they have been carried here and in the heart of this mountain of red sandstone they lay, mute testimony of faithfulness to the end. They were the Order of Malkedek, the Priest Sachems of the roving nomads of the world. Here you see all that is left of them, my son, their spirits have returned to the Great Father for their work is done. Their children cry in the wilderness for the Manu has called them and one by one they join that silent throng, passing over to the Blessed Isle. No longer can the hand of the gods guide them for their work is done; one by one they are gathered in and taken over to another shore where some day they will come forth again a mighty people."

The old Indian leaned heavily on my arm as he was talking and slowly we went out again into the sunshine of the day. The Red Man sat down upon the ground on the edge of the cliff and there we talked for many hours, and he told me the glories of his dying people and begged that some day I would tell the world of the wonderful labors of his race. Slowly the shades of evening fell and the short purple twilight that divides the day from the desert night hung over the plains and prairies and the broken desert which stretched out before us. The Evening Star rose—a glorious light in the heavens—and the whole world seemed to rest save where here and there the howl of a coyote broke the eternal silence.

The old Indian pointed unto the gathering clouds, whispering, "Look!"

As I did so a great procession seemed to form out of the mist and crossing the sky in endless train they vanished where the last dull gleams marked the setting sun.

"They are the dying race," whispered my companion, "and I am one of them. Each night as I sit alone or wander in the desert I can see my people passing slowly by—one after the other. Long since I have buried my race and there out in the desert a few broken sticks alone mark their resting place. No longer does the smoke rise from their peaceful tents, no longer do the white wigwams dot the plain, never again shall the Red Man hunt the bison, no more shall he rise at sunrise on the mountain peak to worship the Great Spirit. See them, my son, see them? Chief and priest, brave and squaw, are passing on in an endless file to the home of the gods. Just a few short years and they will be no more. The hand of the gods feeds them no longer, their work is done, why should they stay? Remember, my son, they go not like slinking coyotes in the night, like cowards crawling away from the field of battle, they go like kings and emperors, for they know that their work is done. They go not as failures to the chastisement of their gods but as those who have finished, claiming their rewards. The white man will never know the Red Man for the white race has made him a stranger in the land of his birth, a nameless vagabond in the beatiful world created for him. But it is well. For as today the Red Man sinks away into the eternal night so shall the white man, when his day is done, drop silently to rest."

All the while he was speaking the endless procession swept across the sky. Mighty chieftains in robes of wampum and war bonnets of eagle feathers, braves on desert ponies, squaws and children, medicine men with the heads of buffalos, and priests with their feathered staffs, —a ghostly file of spectres passed on in triumphant march, all with heads up, eyes to the front, and with a dignity and regal grandeur which bespoke a strange pathos, yet a sweet and masterly understanding.

The old Indian beside me gazed longingly at the passing throng and pointed upward to the stars,

"Look, my son, my peoples' campfires are burning in the heavens!"

I followed his finger with my eyes and there unrolled to me in the sky millions of little campfires stretched out as far as the eye could see, millions of little tepees flowing in the ethers, and the dull murmur as of reverent prayer.

"That, my son," whispered the old Indian, "is the bivouac of the dead. I can see them every night and as the shades of evening fall the braves dash across the sky hunting the buffalo or float in their beautiful canoes down the rivers of stars. Still again through the night there comes to me the plaintive wail of the moonlute as the Indian youth plays his love tunes, the smoke of the signals on the hills, and the sound of the ancient war drum. Once again the great braves gather from all their peoples to listen to the words of their Chieftains. It is all gone, now, my son, but still it lives in the world of spirit, and there it is eternal. And I am old for I have lived since the Red Man was born, I was with him in the days of his youth, I was with him in the years of his glory, and one by one I have laid their wise to rest. From the mighty land of the Sioux, from the tribes of the Algonquians, from the Muskhogean and the wandering Iroquois, even to the distant Shoshoneans, I am known. Each time that one of the Great Ones have died, it is I who in the silence of the night have walked from mountain top to mountain top with his body in my arms. I have brought him here to the cave of the sandstone mountain in whose darkness my secret shall be locked forever, and never until the time when Manitou the Mighty shall roll away these mountains shall the twelve priests of Malkedek be found, for no white man shall desecrate them, no curious eyes shall pierce this darkness, no heathen laugh shall awaken their slumbers, no vandalizing grave-robbers shall in the name of science disturb their resting-place. They may search through the seven stars but they will never find the secret of the Red Man for as he passes silently into the Great Beyond he carries with him the truths of his creation.

"The years draw nigh when the end is at hand. I know, for I am the Spirit of the Red Man. None know where I came from for I came not—I am. None know where I shall go for I go not—I am. Each of my red brothers who is laid to rest knows me, I feel his going, and a drop of my own soul joins with his, a cloudy phantom of the night. One by one they pass away, their young braves live other lives, and the Red Man is forgotten. At last the twelve have come, for in the silence of the night I brought the last. My people shall wander for a little while with man but their spirit is gone, gone back across the great waters to the Father, to wait until the appointed day when they shall come forth again on other wheels and in another race. The spirit of the white man rules the Red Man now and we bow before another god. It is well, for all things work for the Great Spirit and the Father of Fathers whose home is by the Great Waters where He watches the tiny grains of sand that dash upon the seashore. But the Order of Malkedek is no more. A few scattered seekers there are among my people but they wander among strange gods for in this day is sealed forever the Order of the Kings."

The tears were rolling down my cheeks as he told his pathetic story and yet it is a grand story, the story which is written in the soul of every Red Man unless his lonely heart has found rest under the banner of the white king.

At last I spoke:

"You say you have lived through all the ages of the Red Man?"

The old warrior nodded his head:

"I have lived with them and, my son, I die with them for they are my chosen people. I came to them with the glory of the rising sun, as it rises a ball of fire from the silent waters. I rode across the heavens with them as their great orb of day brought with it peace and power; I fought with them through the storms of winter and loved with them through the calm of summer; and now that the sun of the Red Man is sinking and the last of the vanishing race is being led silently to rest, I go with them. For the sun will rise some day in a distant land and there I shall be once more the Spirit of the Sunrise as now I am the over-brooding Angel of the Night. This, my son, is the message of the Red Man, a wondrous people who in the years that are past and now covered with the sands ruled the world, whose libraries and universities were the glory of creation, whose scientists were the marvels of the world, whose domed temples and mystic arches rose to the skies in every land of earth.

"Listen—a voice calls from within. It is the voice of the ages, for the pyramid builder speaks through me this night, the Pharaohs of Egypt are still alive in my blood, the phantom of the Manu, he, too, is with me, and in my soul is the heart of the dying Montezuma. Amid the Andes, through the mystic caverns of the Sierra Madres, among the broken everglades that border the shores of Okechobee, along the silent Nile where the great stone faces gaze peacefully through the night, I wander and I am one with them. Yes, I am the Spirit of the Red Man. You ask who I am, that has been asked before. Once I answered, "I am the Morning Star," later I answered, "I am the Star that shines with the glory of the Sun," still later as my people sank to rest I was the Evening Star who whispered of an eternal peace. But now it is all different, for now I am the Spirit of the Night and you may call me Silent Tongue for I speak and there are none who hear my words. I am the last of the Shamen, the last of the priest-kings who came out of the lost Atlantis, I am the last who was ordained in the Temple of the Rising Sun, I am the last to bear the mark of the serpent."

As he spoke he dropped his blanket and tore

away the shirt which he wore and there upon his heart and twined upward across his chest was a strange serpent tatooed in vivid pigments upon his breast. The upturned head of the serpent coiled around his neck while its little beady eyes and forked tongue seemed to end where the upper cervical vertebrae join the skull.

"That is the mark of Malkedek," he whispered, "a mark no living man knows from one end of the world to the other. It is the mark of Quetzalcoatl, the mark of the feathered serpent who is dead forever. I am the last living thing to bear that mark which was placed there four million years ago."

I looked at the Indian for several seconds as if doubting his words, but one look into those terrible eyes of living fire and I realized I was not gazing at a man but a god.

"Wait a few minutes," he whispered, rising, "then come back into the cave, for there are other things that I would that you should know." And he left me gazing out at that endless procession of figures that still crossed the skies silently as the stars in their course. I waited for several seconds and then a voice whispered to me to rise and enter the cave.

As I did so I gave a startled cry. In the great throne surrounded by the twelve dead sat the aged Indian we knew as Uncle Joe! He was robed from head to foot in the garb of the Red Man, covered with jeweled ornaments and the finest wampum, his bronze body shone in the flickering light of an endless fire, and his war bonnet of eagle feathers reached nearly to the floor even from the height of the throne-chair. On his forehead was a cross of living gold and from his breast the snake gleamed forth in many colored lights while the feathered staff he carried as a sceptre swayed slightly as his arms moved.

"My son, the last of the Red Men, the last of the priests, has been called to rest. They were my kingdom and now I am an emperor of the dead. You shall see me no more for I go to the Land of the Setting Sun, the Manitou has called me and I obey. But, remember, my son, there is no death. I go on to other works, to other lands, for I am the Spirit of the Red Man and I can never die but will live on forever to guard the destinies of my people, who while their race is broken still live and will continue their endless procession until the day when the All-Father shall call home even Manitou the Mighty. Somewhere in the bonds of the infinite we shall meet again, you and I, for you, too, are chosen of your gods. When your race is drawn silently into the unknown I shall ask the Manitou the privilege of being there that I may greet another people coming home. Behold the Order of Malkedek, the sacred brotherhood of the Red Men, the priest-kings of Atlantis, for they are now in session for the last time! The fire that has burned for ages will soon go out and with it vanishes the last of the Red Men. No more the world shall see me, for on this throne I sit awaiting the last of my people. Though years may pass before they gather, I shall be sitting here, surrounded by the dead, the emperor of a dying race."

"So as you go out into the world and people ask you what has happened to Uncle Joe, just tell them he is waiting, waiting through the hours of the night, waiting with the jury of the dead, waiting for the last log to burn and his people to come home. In the ages that are past I said that I would become strong and worthy to be given charge of the Red Man. In many worlds and for many ages I have filled that trust, even until today. So here I shall wait in the cave for it is not long, already my spirit is calling me from somewhere over the distant hills, and even as I speak another Red Man's soul passes me on the way to rest. I wait as sometime you must wait for the last whisper of the dying, and here I remain until the last one goes when I shall seal the book of my works and return to my Maker. Goodbye, you have heard my words. Never seek me again for no man shall know where I have gone. But remember that my spirit waits in the darkness of this cave for the last of my people in the Mountain of Red Sandstone. And when they come I shall gather them lovingly to rest, and then with the spirit of the twelve priests of Malkedek I shall go before my Creator with the glory of a million emperors, the power of kings, and the light of the Rising Sun and the Serpent of Wisdom,—I whom the world knows only as Uncle Joe, the last of a dying race, the last of the Red Men."

The Brothers of the Shining Robe

CHAPTER TWO—Continued

The Mirror of Eternity

As I gazed at the light of the star which seemed a great way off in the deep haze of the magic mirror it twisted and turned and twinkled and there arose from the broken, confused mass of swirling clouds twelve mighty mountain tops that seemed to rival in height the lofty Himalayas in the heart of whose hills I now stood gazing into the deathless mirror of eternity.

As I watched I saw the spark divide itself like a wondrous, bursting rocket and one tiny gleam rested on the top of each of the twelve lofty mountains where it glowed and shone like a ruby. Again the question flashed into my mind and once more it seemed that the Hindu read my thoughts, for he answered in his soft, musical voice strangely stilled and quieted:

"Those are the mountains of the twelve Fates. Far up on the crags and crests of their lofty heights in the sacred caves of the holy men live the twelve Compassionate Brothers of humanity, and to each of them is drawn part of that tiny spark which now you see. Hark! my son, for they are calling you in the soundless depths of your soul. They bid you follow them and climb those same rocky crags as it has been written by the hand of Brahma. Of all the world you have been chosen for the gods know and man must obey."

Again I turned my eyes to the mirror and as I looked closely into its deep blue ether I saw lonely figures standing amid the glaciers that crowned like silver locks the peaks of the hills, twelve lonely forms from whose hearts gleamed forth the tiny stars like promises of the gods to all mankind. In strange contrast were these little lights of purest gold from the dull glow which rose upward from the base to break the darkness of eternal night that concealed forever the foot of these lofty hills. Far below were the flames of hate and that weird, broken world which my guide had told me was the land of the Lonely Ones.

A strange hush came over my being and I realized for the first time in a dull sort of way that there were things in life that before I had never known or understood, and in the depthless haze of that mystic frame, held between the golden fingers of the gods, a new world had been unfolded to me—a world invisible to mortal men, the mystic world of the soul. Still, I am ashamed to say that I understood but little of that scene, and it was more with curiosity than reverence that I passed through that night which I shall remember to the last moment of eternity. But then the Compassionate One within myself was still unawakened and it was only in the years that followed that my soul, mellowed and deepened by experience, fully realized the privilege that was mine that night when I stood in the Temple of the Caves with the ancient Hindu Master.

Slowly the scene in the great void changed and there unfolded before my eyes a broken, rock-strewn coast where dashing waves broke with a mournful sound along the winding seashore. Somewhere in my dreams I had heard that sighing and the broken crashes of the surf had sounded out from the depths of my own heart. But now I was seeing for the first time the wilderness and the desolation that I often had felt. The dashing waves broke along a shoreline, high strewn with the wreckage of scattered ships. As far as the eye could see the dashing and never-ceasing waters cast broken crafts upon the rocky shore where they were ground to pieces by the endless tide.

As I watched in the mirror a file of lonely figures, their white robes blown by the gale, came like phantoms from the darkness and walked silently along the shore. They picked up the wreckage and seeming to whisper soft words to the broken timbers, they held them above their heads where the water-soaked and shattered wrecks were turned, it seemed, into wondrous birds that flew away with sweet songs or hovered around the heads of the lonely figures. There were twelve of these silent forms who passed like specters through the night, and finally walking out on the surface of the waves, which were stilled as they passed over them, followed by the shadowy file of birds created from the broken wreckage, they vanished in the gloom of a limitless horizon.

The mirror cleared again. All that remained was the deep blue haze, as boundless as eternity itself. I turned eagerly to my companion for a more complete explanation of the strange phenomena. In the gloom of the temple he seemed to gleam and glow with a strange light and his robe appeared to be of shimmery gold and opal.

"What does this all mean?" I asked in amazement, staring at the great eyes of the Initiate.

"My son," answered the old man in the same sweet voice, "this rock strewn shore is life, these broken crafts of wreckage are the souls of men, while the white-robed figures represent the tiny band of servers who have dedicated themselves and their lives to the salvation and redemption of their fellowmen, and with the love and power which is theirs they turn the broken wreckage into birds that with the life and truth which they have given may fly upward to the sun. Although you realize it not, you are one of this band. As they have sworn, so have you dedicated yourself to the salvation and regeneration of your brothers. You must be one who is to salvage the wreckage of despair and redeem the broken crafts of life. Although you know not your destiny, soon you will understand."

"You say that I have sworn and dedicated my life to some mystic end of which I know nothing?" I asked in amazement.

"Yes, my son," answered the white-robed Brahman, "and yet is this not true of all? Are not all living things working to an ultimate they can never comprehend? Yes, indeed, for none but Brahma know the ways of Brahma, yet all must serve Him and walk the path that leads to Him. And only when beyond the shades of Nirvana man is one with Brahma will he know the end for which he came into being or the works for which his Master and Creator has ordained him. From childhood to youth, from youth to manhood, from manhood to old age, from old age to dissolution—this is the path of those who know not Brahma. But for those who have seen the light of His shining face the path is from life immortal to life immortal, with only this shell of not-being for a moment and then eternity forever. My son, mysterious are the ways of Brahma and yet those there are who have seen His face, who have listened to the words that dropped like pearls from the lips of the Creator, to rest like beads of dew on the lotus blossoms of the soul."

The old Hindu's eyes seemed to pierce the wall into the endless eternity of not-being and he whispered to me,

"My son, may it be that you shall see the face of Brahma, that the shining light of His eyes shall rest upon you, that the lips of compassion shall speak to you. For when you have seen as I have seen, nought else is there to see, for what can human eyes reveal to man after he has beheld his Creator? For Brahma is all in all, to all, for all. If you hunger and have seen the eyes of Brahma you are fed; if you are cold and his face has been unveiled you are warmed; if you are unclothed but have been enfolded in His light you are garbed as the prince of men; if you are weary and have slept in His arms you have had rest; if you are lonely yet have felt His presence then indeed are the multitudes with you; if you are ignorant and have been within His power then is wisdom yours; if you are sad and have seen Him then are you glad with the sadness of the divine. My son, seek ye for no thing but Brahma for all else is maya, illusion. When you have found Him you have found all; when you have not found Him you have nothing. Behold! all the love in the world is from the heart of Brahma; all the peace in the world is from the rest of Brahma; all truth is the word of Brahma; all light is the glory of His smile.

My son, many long years have I lived in the darkness of this cave and yet I am ever in the light for I have seen Brahma. Though I am weak and old I am young eternally for the life of Brahma brings back the youth that is gone. The world knows me as the mouthpiece of the gods, a master of men; but I ask no glory for it cannot come to me from the plaudits of the world. All that I ask is to be one with my Creator. Walk you the way that I have walked until you too shall reach the footstool of Brahma, for behold His ways are good and His compassion is everlasting. He alone can open the eyes that are blind and the hearts that are cold. Serve Brahma and live, serve men and die. Labor for Brahma and have peace, labor for man and have misery. Treasure up the things of the world and lose them, treasure up the pearls of Brahma and they are yours forever.

In the days when these hills were not, Brahma was; in the days when these mountains shall be no more, still Brahma is. For all that is is Brahma, all that can be pours from His lotus lips. When you are one with Brahma you are one with eternity; when you are one with men you are measured by time. If you will live as Brahma would then alone shall you be free from the wheel of birth and death and rest in Nirvana as one with that which is, yet is not, yet ever shall be. My son, I speak the words of Brahma, in the name of Brahma, for the glory of Brahma, for there is no other Father, no other God. Be glad to serve Him for He is just; be glad to glorify Him for He will ornament you with the jewels of immortality. Oh, that men might know Brahma and live! But come, look again, and I will show you how you have dedicated your being to Brahma and how again you are to annoint yourself upon His altar in the name of the living God, Om the Unknowable!"

Again I gazed into the mystic mirror and this time a new scene appeared there. It seemed a great pin-wheel of light which twisting and unrolling slowly became a great spiral. The spiral took shape and a great scroll appeared and on its mystic pages I saw a history unroll and a voice within whispered that it was mine. My guide spoke again, "This is the memory of the Eternal One. That golden star who now knows himself as William Edmundson."

Slowly the scroll ceased to spin and a scene unfolded itself in the mystic haze of eternity. It was an ancient plane which stretched out to be lost in the blue sky. Far in the distance there rose great twisting towers of snake-like spirals which gleamed and glowed amid mighty domes and minarets that marked a city of the plains. It was a glorious sight, a shimmering city of many colored lights like some mirage of the desert.

"Behold the City of the Golden Gates!" murmured the Oriental as he laid one hand on my shoulder.

It seemed that I was passing across the mighty plains until at last with the rapidity of lightning I floated through its gilded gates and entered a strange, many-sided room, lighted by lamps of virgin oil in niches on the wall. But I was no longer myself as I know myself today. I was an old, gray-haired, bent man robed in blue and gold carrying in my hand a cross which I raised upward to shadowy forms that gazed down from above, great spectres that whispered of the days when gods walked with men.

The Oriental spoke again,

"Here in the sacred temple of the Lost Island you took your vows to the Compassionate Ones, you took your oath that your being was dedicated to the realization of a great ideal. Today you are fulfilling your vows and in the name of the gods I warn you,—stay not the wheels of the Infinite."

The scene grew dark and blinding flashes of lightning and thunder broke upon the air and a hideous roar swept over my senses.

"The sinking of the Lost Island," murmured the voice beside my ear.

(To be continued)

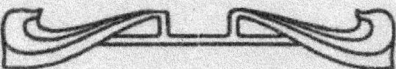

There are two forms of clairvoyance: positive in the brain, negative in the solar plexus. Concentration upon the solar plexus is a step backward in evolution for the white races. The priests of Chaldea are said to have lived a thousand years in one body, but there is no doubt that they had learned how to make better use of their time, for the average individual wouldn't do any more in a thousand years than he does now if he had the chance of living.

The man who cannot see God in his brother will never find him anywhere else.

The prayer most acceptable unto the Lord is the daily life in accordance with the plan of being.

A quick temper is one of the greatest curses from which a student can suffer. If an occultist carries a chip on his shoulder the laws of nature will knock it off.

Just Lonely

FEW people realize the absolute loneliness which fills the heart of a large percentage of children. The little ones who come into the world are indeed strangers in a strange land, and the vehicles which they are seeking to build have not yet the power and consciousness that come in later life or should come. Indeed, in many cases we go through life without ever breaking down the wall of loneliness.

There is a great obligation confronting parents for most of them forget their own childhood, and, interested in other things, absorbed in their own lives, they seem to be unaware of the soul agony which so often fills the heart of a child that is eternally seeking for love and protection.

While we hear the little one playing with the children it seems to be happy, and yet often with the laughter and the smile the discerning eye sees a pathetic little look that tells of a lonely soul. As the years go by there is often built around the child a wall which not even the parent can pierce, for in many homes the parents know less about their children than the stranger on the street, for the comradeship, the understanding, the mutual love is lost, because the lonely child has forgotten how to make a confidant of them.

This generation is producing millions of lonely little souls to whom home means nothing but a shelter for the body because self-centered and thoughtless parents have come to believe that bcause the child is young it does not feel. How many lives are broken, how many romances fall to pieces, because the child has been so lonely that it sought just someone to talk to, someone to make a confidant of, when at home a stone wall seemed built around it.

A large number of children instead of loving and confiding in their parents either despise them or merely treat them with respect and regard in accordance with social obligations, and in the majority of cases it is because the parent has failed to plant the seeds of love and trust in the heart of the child.

This condition is becoming more acute every day, for the world is filled with young people who are divided from the bonds of home by lack of mutual understanding. This is often the result of the fact that during the years of childhood and youth when things were needed the parents were not there, when there was work to do that the child might be what it should be they shirked their duties and the child lost confidence.

There is nothing sadder in all the world than to find a little child who has lost confidence in its parents, and yet at the present time there are few homes where a child can have real confidence, for a sweet temperament cannot be raised on forgetfulness and the average child feels that it is in the way at home, so it goes out and one of two things is the result. Either its little heart is chilled forever and it becomes self-centered, secretive, and often dishonest, or in its hunger for love it suffers all its life.

At this day and age of the world there are no more unhappy creatures in all the universe than children. Instead of being welcomed and their years of youth watched and guided, they are regarded from the very beginning as a nuisance and as something which stands between the parents and the gay pleasures of life. So slowly the child drifts into other company, mentally if not physically, and oftentimes it picks very poor associates, not because of criminal instinct or of malicious intent, but it went astray just because it was lonely.

This condition faces us as a problem far greater than we generally understand. Many youths go into the business world or leave home because there was no companionship there for them. Many young girls have married at immature ages to escape the loneliness of home and to find someone whom they thought would be a friend. Too often this choice is unwise but in nearly every case it is the result of the fact that there is no love and compassion and brotherhood in the home.

The answer to the problem is this. The father and mother should not be the boss of the children. Children are not servants or slaves and when treated as such and ordered around like puppets, they either sulk away determined some day to make a break or else their spirits are crushed and they become useless chips of driftwood on the sea of life. No one likes a boss, children no more than the rest, and children who fear parents will never love them. Brotherhood must be born in the home where parents and children are tied together by the bond of mutual sympathy and understanding. Kindly and wisely like brothers, parents must love and labor with their children. For many a little one has gone away to weep alone when a scar has been made in the soul that will last to the end of time over the thoughtless cruelty of the parent or an unjust accusation.

It is harshness and fear which make dishonest children and promote lying, stealing, and even worse habits. It is the lack of the feeling of brotherhood between parent and child that makes young children keep secrets which may injure them all their lives, whereas if confidence has been built the wiser and more mature thoughts of the parent will save years of suffering. But the privilege of the parent to help the child is lost when that privilege is abused.

So we find thousands of children who are just lonely, who while they are properly fed and clothed are merely strangers boarding at home. This condition is the basis of a generation of lonely souls, broken and misunderstood, who crawl away to melancholia or else sell their souls for the sake of a kind word. There are few who realize the power that a parent has and there are still fewer who realize how that power is abused today, when there is coming into the world a generation of lonely children, great souls who will never be understood and always blamed for the lack of those very virtues which the parents should have stimulated.

As you read this article there are many of you who will recognize how your own lives have been twisted and changed by loneliness in childhood and the fact that you never were understood, and this should be a divine incentive within the soul of every parent that when young hearts come to them they shall be understood and not be just little strangers in a strange land —lonely and forgotten.

"THE SACRED MAGIC OF THE QABBALLAH"
The Science of the Divine Names.
By
Manly P. Hall

In this work the study of numbers and the Hebrew alphabet is taken up in a way never before undertaken. No system of numerology or cabalism is promulgated but a few underlying principles are given here useful to all students of mystic, occult and cabbalistic philosophy. The work is divided into three parts as listed below:

Part One .... The Key to the Sacred Wisdom.

A Study of the flaming letters of the Hebrew alphabet, the creation of the Sacred Name, the mystey of the vowel points and the unwritten books of Moses.

Part Two .... The Origin and Mystery of Numbers.

Under this heading are grouped the natural laws as they are expressed in numbers from 1 to 10, and the application of these laws to the problems of daily living.

Part Three .... The Power of Invocation and
The Science of the Sacred Names.

In this part of the work transcendental magic is completely unveiled and the ancient rituals of calling up spirits is exposed and the true meaning of transcendentalism and the finding of the lost Word is presented to the student, including the invocation of Christ. A most unique and unusual document containing over fifty pages, neatly bound in an art cardboard cover. This work should be in the library of all occult students, not to be believed but to be considered.

As is the case with our other publications you must fix your own price for the work, not to cover your share of the responsibility but that the entire work may go on and you and others may be in a position to receive the work which we are putting out.

This month's issue also contains a rare occult plate taken from the writings of Robert Fludd, the English Rosicrucian and alchemist. The original is dated 1619.

The description of this plate will appear in next month's magazine.

Explanation of Last Month's Plate

THE folder plate which appeared in last month's issue of "The All-Seeing Eye" was reproduced from the rare work on "Occult Cosmogony" published in 1619 by Robert Fludd, the English mystic and alchemist. It represents a speculative explanation of the phenomena of nature and of life, and while space makes it impossible for us to give a complete interpretation of it, the student who will study and analyze it in the light of the principles of mysticism and occultism will find it an endless source of information, and through the study of it may gain tremendous analogical powers.

Briefly considered, the plate is threefold, spiritual, intellectual, and physical, as can be seen by the three grand divisions into which the globe is divided. The cloud at the top represents the Spirit of God, and, as the word or name Jehovah signifies, it represents the form-building power of God or that part which manifests in matter. The cloud represents the body of the Celestial Being whose vehicle is a globe and who materializes necessary organs from that globe, as is shown in the hand which appears in the plate.

In the center of the plate is the Earth which is connected to the superior creature floating in the cloud by means of the female figure which represents the Spirit of Nature, the Divine Mother of created things. The stars represent the celestial hierarchies in the brain of nature while the lunar crescents symbolize the spirit of fecundity. The figure is standing with one foot upon the water and the other upon the land for she represents the two lower elements of earth and water. She is chained 'twixt heaven and earth, dominion wielding, while the little monkey sitting on the globe represents the Adamic man in his coat of skins and the compass with which he is measuring symbolizes material limitations.

All the kingdoms of nature are symbolized with their respective elements, qualities, powers, arts, sciences, et cetera, in the inner of the three worlds, while in the central sphere we have the solar system with its suns and powers. This is symbolic of the solar and macrocosmic man of our solar system, while outside of this sphere, consisting of the planetary orbits, we find the stellar worlds which are the symbols of the other created universes of our chain. At this point the second sphere ends and we find the three rings of fire flames, which are symbolical of the three grand creative principles and the powers of the three worlds of nature. The inner circle of flames represents the form-building powers; the second row, the mind-building powers; the third or outer row, the spirit-unfolding powers.

Examination will show that the little figures in these rings of flames differ. In the inner ring they have no wings and are material; in the second row they have bodies and wings and are therefore partly human, partly divine; in the outer circle they have wings but no bodies, symbolizing the fact that they are no longer connected with material things.

The whole plate is symbolical of the human body, the creation of a germ plasm, and the unfoldment of a universe, and each student will gain from the study of it just exactly what he has within himself. The only way in which a student can judge his own advancement is by taking such a plate as this and opening it before him, sit down and say, "What does this mean to me, and how will it help me to live better, think better, and more completely carry on the duties and responsibilities of life?" If the student will then apply his own knowledge to the various parts which he can comprehend, he will find explanations of things which before he never understood. That is the reason for symbolism; it forces the student to express himself. For that reason we are not going into detail as to the full meaning of the plate, but the basic principles set down will enable the individual, if he will study it, meditate upon it, and apply the knowledge gained from daily experience, to use these ancient pictures as concentrating points by means of which he may measure his own limitations and breadth of knowledge.

Practically the entire scheme of human evolution is shown in the picture as the Divine Life passed through the manyfold expressions of Nature, however, will be able to read the mystery it contains.

In this magazine you will find another rare plate taken from the same source, which shows the creation of the universe and the coming of the elements. In next month's magazine we shall have a few words to say concerning it, but the purpose of placing these illustrations before you is not to explain them but to enable you to explain them yourselves.

Occult Eugenics

Reprinted and Re-edited with notes and corrections from our classes of 1922.

OCCULTISM is a very unusual study. Many people enter into it in the hope of being transported into mystic worlds where hooded figures and strange lights flit through somber ruins. They believe that they will gain strange powers and great riches and find a world of happiness over night. This is very far from the truth, and the student will find as he goes along that occultism is not a doctrine of miracles but of Cause and Effect, not of shortcuts but of slow, ever-increasing development, not of romance and glamour, but of serious study and self-improvement; it means not only to delve into forgotten lore, but to consider with uncommon common sense life and its many problems.

To the brave student it offers the great incentive of justice and a sure reward. To the coward and those who seek to shirk the duties of life it stands a looming mystery, a great giant between them and the easy road to happiness and success for which they seek. Good or evil, depending upon the eyes that see it and the hands that apply it, but, standing in spite of all, the Mystery School remains unmoved from the first great dawn of creation to the last falling shadows of a dissolving universe. It offers no incentive other than truth, no reward other than a greater power to help your fellowmen.

The occultist must take his occultism into his life, his works, and his ideals. One place alone is the source of the joys and sorrows of the world, and from the half-closed lips of that looming mystery which man knows as the Occult Wisdom there comes forth these words, "The Strength of a people depends upon the harmony, unity, and virtue of its homes."

The great problem of Eugenics faces the world at the present time as it never has before, because under it is listed the study of causes and the improvement of causes, and the world is slowly coming to the realization that everything we know as an effect is the result of unknown and unstudied causes. Man with his ever higher ideals now realizes that the day has come when it is in his power to mold the world into what he wishes it to be, greater and more glorious than ever before, if he will mold causations and develop them as he should.

Man is beginning to realize that he cannot grow roses on a thistle plant, neither can wisdom thrive on ignorance, but that by the natural law of attraction each plant that we know bears fruit according to its kind, and under the head of Eugenics man is studying to build only those conditions and causes which will produce constructive, elevating effects. Eugenics not only holds good in the building of physical forms but also in political, scientific, social, and religious body and soul building.

We are in every case the causes that will produce the effects, mental and physical, which shall mold the great Tomorrows as Yesterday is molding us, and it is our duty to our God, our brother, and ourselves to study and live by the knowledge we have gained more in harmony with the divine plan for man.

There are listed below twenty-five condensed statements for the consideration of students of Eugenics in its various forms. The proof of these statements can easily be found by anyone who will spend even a short time in the consideration of living problems. It is suggested that the student take them one at a time and see just to what extent they are true in the surroundings of his life. If he wishes to be an occultist, a mystic or even a healthy heathen, he should not only consider them but if he agrees with them practice them in his own life and among those with whom he comes in contact.

First. The intellectual, spiritual, and evolutionary progress of a race depends upon the ability of higher evolved egos to find proper vehicles of physical expression among the homes and parents of that race. At the present time they are needed in the world as never before but they can only come where they will find harmony and purity, knowledge and love. When these conditions express themselves as causes in our race the effect will be power, growth, and balanced genius.

Second. In this world like attracts like and the same is true of the ego seeking incarnation. It will come where it can receive the growth needed for its own spiritual extension. Therefore, ignorance draws ignorance, wisdom draws wisdom, squabbling draws squabbling, and the little ones drawn to the home of man today will sometime rule our world with the same powers which attracted them and with which we are surrounding their young lives.

Third. Inharmony in a home where a highly developed ego is striving to gather its new body for manifestation here invariably results in one of two things. Either the ego, the spirit, will withdraw from that family because it cannot stand the vibratory rates or else it will have the finer side of its nature and its usefulness here impeded or dwarfed. In both cases the thoughtless parents are guilty in the eyes of the spiritual law of murder in the first degree.

Fourth. There is a very mistaken idea in the minds of many parents concerning the faculties of a child, mental and spiritual. During its younger life and approximately up to the age of majority, it is completely under the mental and spiritual supervision of the parent who is responsible to God and man for the qualities which are implanted in the offspring.

Fifth. A child is born clairvoyant and remains so varying lengths of time under different conditions, usually until the soft spot in the crown of the head closes. This makes it possible for the child to feel things and see things which the parent does not realize. Children know what their parents are thinking and doing even when they are apart. Therefore, it does no good to kiss the child goodnight very sweetly, tell it to love everybody and be good, and then go downstairs and have squabbles and disagreements such as occur in many homes, and believe that the child does not know and will not be affected by it.

Sixth. By example as well as by precept must children be trained. If you tell a child to do a thing and you do something different you must not be amazed that the child follows your example. We cannot lie to children and then expect them to be truthful. It is often a wonder how children have as much respect for their parents as they do, and it shows that the little one has in many cases a higher sense of justice than the parent. No parent has a right to blame a child and punish it for a fault the parent has himself, until first of all he has sought to correct it in his own being.

Seventh. Not ignorance but a thorough understanding of nature's plan is the basis of all virtue, and the parent who has not given its child an understanding of life's problems has failed in its most sacred duty and lost its greatest opportunity for self-development.

Eighth. In the Orient there is a rule followed that should teach the western world a wonderful lesson. Life there is divided into three great divisions. In the first third of life the ego is guarded and taught by its parents the duties of life; in the second third the grown person raises his family and takes care of his parents, he also earns the funds to take care of his life and those who depend upon him; and in the last third he in his turn is taken care of by his children and allowed to study and meditate. This system cannot be applied in full in this country, it seems, but it has many good points to be considered.

Ninth. A parent should remember that children don't "jest grow" but require attention all the way through childhood. In America at the present time no attention at all is paid to the average child, and it runs wild until it disconcerts the entire neighborhood, and then the father and mother finding that the child is impossible try to spank good manners into it with failure as the usual result. At least seventy-five percent of parents use this system at the present time, then these same people wonder why no one likes their children and why the landlords prefer lap dogs in their apartments to the young hopefuls, or rather hopeless generation of today.

Tenth. While on the study of Eugenics, which means to be better born, or to have a more harmonious beginning, there are other children which we should consider as well as our visible families. Many millions of lives are evolving and depending upon us about which the average individual knows absolutely nothing. It has been estimated that inside the physical body of man alone there are living, developing, and evolving seven hundred and eighty-nine quintillion monads, each one of them a complete being made up of millions, yes billions, of still smaller beings. These depend upon the superior development of the human ego for wise and humane care. When we through thoughtlessness, indolence, or ignorance fail to properly supply and intelligently preserve these parts of ourselves we break one of the most important laws of natural Eugenics.

Eleventh. When we read the story in the Bible of the Last Supper, do we ever stop to think how it is being repeated every day and minute of our lives? Do you remember how the Master gave his disciples the bread and said, "This is my body broken for you?" Let us remember that the Christ Spirit, the principle of life, is in all these cells and that thousands, millions, of living things die daily that man may live. In the running down of the body many tiny forms must give up their vehicles of expression. The food that we eat is the tiny shell that our younger brothers have taken hours, weeks and years to build. We owe these little lives a great debt of gratitude and we have no right to abuse their confidence in us and injure them by misapplying the principles of nature.

Twelfth. The smallest of lives has a God-given right to a chance of development and greater expression in the world of forms. Those who aid in the giving of these opportunities help each in his own way the development of the Plan, and as we help others to express themselves we gain greater ability to manifest our own latent qualities.

Thirteenth. One of the greatest mistakes that a parent can make is to overlook the health of a child or exert an undue influence over its growth on account of their own ideas concerning sickness and spirituality. While it is often possible through the power of will for the parent to master inharmony within, and while many believe that sickness is only a concept of the mind, this idea cannot be safely applied in dealing with children. Parents are directly or indirectly responsible for ninety per cent. of sickness among children, and large doses of common sense should be administered to the mother and father instead of drugging the child.

Fourteenth. A large percentage of the aches and pains of the human race come through the stomach and that which goes into it—sometimes through that which cannot get out of it. The adult must learn to take care of himself, but with the child the parents must use a different course and teach their children how to live in a clean, practical way.

Fifteenth. It is the duty of every adult in the United States and in all other parts of the world to spend enough time in the study of self to learn how to prevent the causes of disease which later wreck his body, if he does not learn in younger life how to use common sense in taking care of himself. Moreover, people who do not know these things can never hope to bring into the world or to raise healthy children.

Sixteenth. No one has the right to call himself a student of any line of higher philosophy, science or religion, who does not understand the fundamental construction of his own being, mental, physical, and spiritual, and any teaching that promises spirituality, growth, or broadened consciousness that does not include these principles is not listed among the Wisdom Religions.

Seventeenth. It is said by those in position to know that a large percentage of adults in the so-called civilized countries have the brain development of fifteen-year-old children, in many it is much lower. This is undoubtedly the result of the fact that the ego coming into this world is forced to build its physical vehicles, including the brain, from the quality of material furnished by the parents. Therefore, it is up to the parents to build better bodies that the next generation may be greater mentally, spiritually and physically than the present one, for the children of today are the law-makers, teachers, and citizens of tomorrow. In this way each generation is largely responsible for the next and many people at the present time are laying up terrible Karmic debts.

Eighteenth. It would seem that the world should know these simple principles of life and many people consider that work of this kind is too elementary for "spiritual students," yet the very persons who say this, and in fact nearly all of the occult students, while standing apparently on the tops of the mountains, are daily breaking practically every law in nature, and as they break them they tell the world they have become so great that they no longer need them.

Nineteenth. If you will read the daily papers you will find that during the summer months great numbers of children die. Few persons realize how many babies pass out before they reach their first birthday. People pray to God to spare their children and say the Lord took the little ones from them, when in reality they kill them through ignorance, indolence, or indifference, and this at an age of the world when all the needed information is within the reach of everyone. There is no need for such ignorance save that people do not care enough about life to learn how to live, and it is necssary for them to keep on dying to find out.

Twentieth. It is very important that we understand that the ego coming into life is not born full fledged, but through a gradual process in which one by one the vehicles of consciousness take hold, until youth reaches the age of majority when it comes into control of its vehicles. The danger points in the life of a child gather around the fourteenth year when the fire or emotion body begins to be felt. It is then that uncurbed by thought the child is most subject to those mistakes which have ruined the lives of millions. It is during these periods that the greatest responsibility rests upon the parents, and it seems that at this time there are few willing to take the responsibility of giving the incoming egos the proper start in life.

Twenty-first. It is well for us to understand that occult Eugenics not only teaches that man must produce better bodies, but that he must give birth to better thoughts, emotions, and actions. These are children of our own being for which we are just as responsible as for physical, visible children. With his evil thoughts man is breeding demons that will later pave his way with hardships and his world with suffering. In truth the children of his consciousness must be better born.

Twenty-second. Education is a very important consideration and this must take a great place in the mind of the parent, for in order to educate children in the practical things of life the parents themselves must first have knowledge of them. When we come to consider that less than one in ten of American children receives a complete education, we are confronted with another very important matter that rests in the hands, directly and indirectly, of every adult in this country.

Twenty-third. It is also of importance to remember that education consists of drawing out the latent qualities within the child rather than in cramming the mind, which in later life will be forced to forget many of the things it has learned in order to be practical.

Twenty-fourth. Parents should remember that they both have responsibilities in the rearing of their children. In the majority of cases at the present time each is trying to shift the responsibility onto the other. Another curse is now springing into families at a deadly rate of speed and this is the old story of the favorite child. In almost every home you will find children who are tolerated as necessary evils while another child is pushed forward and all attention heaped upon it. A condition of this kind shows that the moral and spiritual development of such parents is far below the average scale for animals and they are a disgrace to the human race. The unbalanced and in many cases criminal actions of parents, if continued, will bring the destruction of our civilization.

Twenty-fifth. Young children are like parrots, they are the greatest mimics in the world. They only understand that which they can see, and somewhere either in their home or among their acquaintances will be found all the mean traits which they demonstrate. They act and live and talk the way they see the old folks do, so when little Johnny comes out in the yard and swears like a trooper, loses his temper, stamps around, and throws tin cans at the cat, it is merely a reflection of what he has seen someone else do. In other words, the baby and the youngster are the thermometer showing the temperature, mental, physical, and spiritual, of the parents, and the most powerful way of teaching a child is by example.

This may sound as though it were a terrible rehash of antiquated precepts. It is. The entire civilization of the world for millions of years has depended upon the understanding of these principles. Our farmers have spent years in developing extra fine hogs and in learning how to produce the greatest amount of corn to an acre. In every line of business and enterprise man is being taught efficiency except in the line which gives him the right to live.

The work must be gone over again and again because ninety-nine out of a hundred people, if they know these things, show no symptoms of their knowledge. God must judge us by results. Read the daily newspapers and see if the world has passed the need of studying the practical problem of natural Eugenics.

Occultism does not tell man what to study or to what creed he should subscribe, but it takes him out and showing him things as they are tells him that his duty is to improve himself and his world in the best way that presents itself to him.

"By their works shall ye know them," unfolding consciousness of man which becomes his guide in the distant places and makes possible his ascent into the dome-shaped skull which is indeed the temple of the gods.

A Letter From the Brothers of the Rose Cross

The Magical Mountain of the Moon
(Continued)

IN the May and June numbers of this magazine we considered in part the symbolism of this remarkable letter said to come from the secret order of the Rosicrucians. It is a well known fact that these Adepts and Initiates were modern adaptations of the ancient Hermetic mystics who flourished during the 16th, 17th and 18th centuries in Central Europe as alchemists and philosophers by fire.

If you will turn again to the plate in the May magazine we shall consider briefly a further study of its symbolism. In the upper corners of the picture we find the Sun and the Moon. These have been used for many ages, in fact hundreds of thousands of years, as symbols of spirit and matter or God and nature. The Sun represents the fiery Father while the Moon represents the earthy and liquid Mother of all things, and as all products are the result of the combination of two or more elements it was said that the Philosopher's Stone, the divine achievement of alchemy, was formed out of the Sun and the Moon by blending their elements in the philosopher's Mercury. We may call this the union of spirit and matter through the link of mind or the focusing point.

There is a mountain that rises out of the darkness of ignorance. This mountain is built out of regenerated life substances raised out of the muck and wire of cosmic oblivion. The black circle shown here represents the elemental and chaotic worlds which are inhabited by the lower, destructive passions and desires, or, in other words, this is the land called by the ancients Egypt, the land of darkness, or the oblivion into which the spirit flees in order to escape destruction at the hands of degeneracy. Darkness is not necessarily malignant, it is merely a shroud or a garment which conceals and protects light, but in it and through it are the evil and destructive passion centers, thought creations, and astral larvae, so well described by Paracelsus and other followers of the alchemical schools. It is out of this valley of death that the Magical Mountain rises as the supreme accomplishment of the alchemist. This black circle at its base is called the region of fantasy because it is the world of ever-changing things, of grotesque ideals, and spiritual unrealities. It is the world of deception that surrounds and conceals forever the mountain of truth. Only one power known to man is capable of piercing the veil of Maya, and that is the faculty of discrimination. One of the most important steps in the unfolding of an Adept is the development of the faculty of discriminative thought. Anyone can think fantastic thoughts which are not logical and reasonable. We can dream fantastic dreams created out of the fiilaments of diseased imagination, we can live fantastic lives surrounded by the fantasies of the unreal, and the test of the student is his ability to discriminate between unreal possibilities and actual realities. Therefore, the path to light leads through the veil of darkness where the student faces the problem of discriminating between the powers of life and the false lights of passion creation.

The dragons, serpents, and beasts that people this world of darkness represent the animal qualities, beastial passions, and perverted energies which live and thrive only in darkness, but are scattered forever with the coming of the true light. Every thought and action of man creates astral entities and powers, which, if destructive in nature, take strange and horrible forms and people the region of oblivion with hosts of demoniacal shapes which are nothing more or less than the perverted activities of ignorant people.

Within this circle is a circle of light illuminated by the light of nature. This represents the area of activities illuminated out of darkness by the light or candle of human consciousness, nourished by the tallow or oil in the spinal canal, which when raised out of the cube of matter radiates the illuminating qualities which bring cosmos out of chaos and keep the demons forever away from the germ of life and light concealed within the sacred box or chest of form.

All the mysteries of nature are solved by the light of nature, but those mysteries which are not of nature but are of God can be solved only by the light of God.

The figure of the man blindfolded groping in darkness while within the circle of light represents the consciousness of individuals who believe themselves to be in the area of darkness when in reality darkness is only light to which their organs of vision, mental, spiritual and physical, do not respond. Therefore, the ignorant wander in darkness while surrounded by light because of the blindfold of conscious limitation which surrounds them. In searching for the light they grope out into the darkness, failing to realize that the light is in the center and not outside. But this they do not know until they have sought for it in the ring of darkness. This represents the power of reason searching for the answer to the riddle of being.

On the other side stands the Angel of the Flaming Sword, who faces the light of nature and with the flaming brand in her hand points to the Magical Mountain. This flaming sword is, of course, the upturned spiritual consciousness of man which alone can show him as his guide and instructor the path that leads through the dangers to the foot of the lofty mountain. The cord she carries in her hand is the spinal cord up which he will climb in search of those wondrous grapes that grow in the land of Canaan. The figure with wings represents the

At the base of the picture is the dragon with its tail in its mouth, the divine symbol of alchemical mastery. This symbol shows that all the broken threads of life have been gathered and their ends tied together in the endless band of never-broken consciousness. It means that the spirit spinal serpent has raised itself upward and fastened its tail and head together, completing the vital currents of the body and mastering the previous waste of vital energy by closing the circuit of its expression.

Inside of this ring is the seated figure of the philosopher counting and enjoying his great treasures which are the pearls of truth and of spirit and not material jewels. He represents the one who seated in the center of a purified, diamond-like organism, is surrounded by the jewels of unfolded centers of consciousness which are beyond the price of kings and are the inheritance of gods.

The entire plate represents the human body. The mountain represents the head, the lighted candles on the chest are symbolical of the heart, while the dragon represents the generative system which is the keynote to the regeneration of its forces and the purification of its centers.

Thus the whole picture is an alchemical essay on human, mental, physical, and spiritual redemption which if studied and understood by students of the spiritual sciences will give them a great key to the Rosicrucian alchemical school. All of the Brothers of the Rose Cross were symbolists and their truths have been perpetuated only in symbolism. Each one of us takes the part of Christian Rosenkreuz wandering in search of the answer to the riddle of being. Like him we are buried, that is our spiritual consciousness is buried, and finally raised from the dead, when the two phases of our being, the red lion and the white eagle, fire and water, unite, and from their mystic blending is born the Philosopher's Stone which is hidden away in a mystic cave at the very top of the Magical Mountain of the Moon.

The end

What Will the Harvest Be?

AS we gaze out at the seeds, (mostly wild oats), which the present generation is sewing so thoughtlessly we cannot help but think of those immortal words which have sounded down through many generations, "What will the harvest be?" As we look out into the world it seems that we are producing a generation of anaemics, hardly able to drag one foot after the other, who when they reach such a mature age as, say, eighteen, are broken down wrecks of dissipation who wander aimlessly in ever smaller circles around untimely graves.

Let us classify a few of the specimens of modern manhood and womanhood that are to be the law-makers, the parents, the scientists of the next generation, and ask ourselves again, "What will the harvest be?"

As we gaze out in search of true timber for the building of worlds it seems that we are gazing on the valley of dried bones referred to by the Bible prophet, for there is little material for the building of minds and bodies. Children with old and sunken faces and haggard eyes alone confront us, who while they have not lived long have ruined their opportunity for usefulness in the world of affairs. There is little in common between the humanity of today and the ideals of the human race. A large percentage of our population are morons and over fifty per cent. seem close to savage ignorance; the finer qualities are fast vanishing from our midst and it seems that real thinking is becoming an impossibility. Responsibility and the realization of life's duties seem unknown, and those who pass through years of learning forget before they pass out of the portals of the schoolroom whatever useful things they may have learned. Five years after graduation, or even less, about all that the average boy or girl can remember is the football yell and the school dance. Everything else is merely a muddy blur stored away somewhere in an emaciated and under-nourished comprehension.

To speak in words of eloquence and refinement, we are producing as fine a generation of hollow-headed idiots as the world has known in many a day, and the few thinkers that do storm the tide of human indolence are getting ashamed of themselves and crawl away alone to escape the laughter and the jeering of those who know nothing. It disqualifies a man or woman at this day and age of the world to be a philosopher, while those who disqualify them can find no earthly reason for their own being. The thoughts of man are so far from heaven at the present time and his spiritual ego is so divided from its own true position that to find the centers of consciousness in the world today it is necessary to dress in asbestos.

Now let us analyze this year's crop of dashing anaemics, which to tell the truth have been badly frosted and rather worm-eaten. Of course there are a few exceptions which prove every rule, but generally speaking we can diagnose the young man of this generation something as follows:

He is tall, or if not tall at least slender in frame, finance, and brains. Taking a possible hundred per cent. as perfect we shall find the general averages listed as follows: In health he is about forty per cent. human; his lung capacity is about twenty-five per cent. of what it ought to be; his stomach is in convulsions sixty per cent. of the time; his eligibility to think sensible thoughts is about ten per cent. out of a possible hundred; his ability to smoke bum tobacco is ninety-nine per cent. perfect or better; in dancing he is very efficient, but in arithmetic not so good; he knows every burlesque show in town but couldn't possibly find the public library: his ability to make money, one per cent.; his ability to make dates the other ninety-nine per cent. He is beloved by everyone who doesn't ask him to do something for them and if all goes well and in accordance with harmony and the plan of his being he should have, say, nine love affairs a year and be out of work about eighty per cent. of the time. He is usually slightly round-shouldered, possibly knock-need, he is very important to himself, but absolutely useless furniture to everybody else. He usually gets married before he gets a job and then has a job trying to stay married, as he doesn't know anything and thinks less he does nothing but wonder why his romance won't last and his best girl goes off with a handsomer man.

In other words if we plant this type and wait for the harvest we are not even likely to find a weed when the gathering time draws near, for there is not enough within the average gallant of our generation to cause even a commotion, much less a harvest. Leaving this angle of the problem to bury itself, if it has the strength, we will pass on and consider "Exhibit B," or, as Kipling would call it, "the female of the species," and diagnose the case from that angle.

Taking the general score of one hundred per cent., as before, to represent the perfect, let us briefly consider, list, and label the attributes, accomplishments, and eccentricities of the "species feminalis." General physical health considered first may generally be termed zero; spinal curvature common; weak lungs common; anaemia common; general lassitude prevailing. Each one of these ailments will be found in from fifty to sixty out of every hundred; in other words, if put to a hard day's work said rare specimens would last until they get started and then would call a halt for lunch. Intellectuality, doubtful in ninety-nine per cent. of cases; have never heard of Nathanial Hawthorne nor Samuel Coleridge, but will look in next month's "Snappy Stories" and see if they have written for it. Memory is good but varied, and usually turned into certain channels, most of them useless. Geography, mathematics and history, one hundred per cent. imperfect. Occasionally an eccentric education in art and music, especially in landscape gardening, exterior stucco working, and general external decorations where some proficiency is shown occasionally. Memory of dates, scandals, and vacations, perfect; exceptionally fine in remembering names of motion picture stars. Chewing gum one hundred per cent. perfect, never sound a flat note. Cooking a lost art except for cooking up trouble; domestic sciences, nil; mending, darning, etc., ditto. Usually proficient in dancing except when feet hurt; can wear five-inch heels without staggering; good appetite, especially for shrimps, sardines, and Granada olives. Common sense, nil; ambition, zero (movie ambitions excepted); average length of life, thirty; number of marriages averaging from three to twenty; strongest asset, pugnacious temperament of her own; plenty of energy to hold up one end of a scrap, sometimes both ends, said scrap usually of a domestic nature, but not sufficient energy to do anything useful.

These form the leading features and hopeful prospects of our human race. Politeness, courtesy, simplicity, all of these sweeter and finer sentiments have been discarded for lack of time. Fineness of quality, love of study, art, and science, and all these things which tend to elevate are forgotten. Elevators do not seem to be needed for most of the pool rooms are downstairs and the dance halls are on the main floor.

So with a cigarette snuggled under one ear, a squashed Fedora hat over one eye, his nose squinted to one side, and his eyes half-closed with a drooping expression which is enhanced by a gracefully receding chin, we find him embellished with a high white collar and blare tie, big feet, and a small consciousness, perambulating towards the nearest dance hall or nth class movie with his steady swinging on his arm. So far as she is concerned, at this day and age of the world we are not surprised at anything. She may be smoking a meerschaum or a Virginia cheroot or chewing tobacco, no one knows. But with a swing like a tar and a general makeup resembling an ex-prize fighter she swaggers along. And these two are about to unite for the general betterment of creation to go through life together, sans brains, sans sense, sans everything, sans end. (With apologies to Omar).

And if these are to be planted in the great half-acre of the world's works we ask you again to figure out on the pure principles of mathematics—"What will the harvest be?"

There are three things which, if considered and lived, will make the day of mastery closer for the individual who discovers their mystic truth. First, we must use the powers that we have in the best and most constructive way possible for it is only those who show ability who will be given greater responsibilities. Second, we must look for greater opportunities to be be given the power to fill thme. Third, you must improve yourself every day so that when the appointed time comes you will be a credit to your work and to your God.

The Divine Masquerader

THERE are many people in the world at at the present time who are not what they seem to be. There are those who appear to be poor but who conceal under the veil of poverty riches unnumbered. There are others who seem to be well supplied with the things of this world, but who in reality when the last great moment comes have little either in this world or the worlds to come. There are those who seem to be honest but who have evolved the subtle spirit of dishonesty. There are some who claim to be spiritual, but whose lives tell only of sordid things. Then there are others who claim nothing who are listed with the saviors of mankind. In truth, the world is not always as it looks to be, but it is always what it makes itself.

Now, in the universe there is a power which we can accurately describe as the great Unknown. This power is the sublime and supreme mystery, and for the sake of clearness we have named it the Divine Masquerader, for in truth that is just what it is, a strange and mystic one who masks Himself under a thousand disguises, is known in a million different ways, yet is ever the same.

One of the great incentives in life is man's eternal search for something, a strange and unknown power, which he realizes is valued beyond the gains of earth. He only knows this power as the Masquerader, that mystic spirit of uncertainty, for none know where He will come next or how he will appear when he does come, but consciously or unconsciously all growth depends upon Him. For thousands of years this divine trickster has been masking under the guise of simple things. He is always with us yet remains unknown because he loses his personality and is unseen behind the part He plays. Shakespeare was right when he said that the world is a stage, for the Divine Masquerader is the greatest actor of all; He lives and is the very part that He plays. The old symbols of comedy and tragedy were the smiling face and the downcast face, and these faces are the masks of life.

Behind the mask of an ever-changing personality there is hidden a soul which is ever the same. The great centers of spiritual consciousness expressing through this endless kaleidoscope of ever-changing manifestation are animated by the powers of a single mind, the life is always the same, but the mask is ever-changing.

There is a certain Mr. Raffles, a mysterious individual, and he has a price upon his head for he becomes the servant of all who discover him. The alchemists symbolized him as the gold in the heart of the dross surrounding its precious center with a disguise of worthless stone. Just so with the Masquerader, for he conceals the greatest prize beneath the homeliest mask and every minute he is before your eyes donning a disguise which will bring him into your environment.

The Divine Masquerader cannot live without a form, but he changes this form perpetually. He is eternally whispering to you, but his disguise is too subtle for you to penetrate. What is the motive behind the actions of this strange being; why does He hide His light eternally from the eyes of man? He is not trying to conceal himself, but in reality uses His disguise that He may mingle with you and labor for you in ways that you can understand. This is the motive of the disguise that coming down from the great Divine, He may reveal himself in simple things and labor where you can understand and know Him.

He disguises Himself in a way that will bring Him close to the heart of everyone, but as the average seeker after the light looks for the great, the wierd, and the unusual rather than the simple and the practical, we seldom rcognize the Masquerader who is as one of us in our daily walks of life. We should realize, however, that in the circle of our daily happenings there are many things that are not what they seem to be, for behind appearances is this jaunty spirit of concealment who has put on a domino to appear to you as something that you know. If your daily labor is with a pick and shovel, somewhere among those working with you the Masquerader will be hiding. If you are of the houses of riches and the homes of plenty, somewhere among them He will be concealed. His disguise is always perfect, but man overlooks the simple and the direct and seeks the great and the spectacular. If the Master Jesus should come to the world today, who would recognize Him? We would receive Him if He descended in a cloud of glory surrounded by a host of angels, but who would know Him if He walked the earth in rags?

Everyone has seen the Masquerader today, but few have known him and fewer still have claimed the reward. This mysterious individual is the keyhole that leads to an understanding of how the door of life should be opened. Everyone has met and shaken hands with this Divine One who is not what he seems. Tomorrow you will meet Him again and He will seem to be different, but ever He is the same. All the way through life there is never a moment when He will leave you, but with only the Masquerader as a companion most people feel alone.

While we judge things only by what they appear to be, the Masquerader will never be found, but when man learns to judge things for what they are and what is within them, then this mystic stranger will be unveiled by the one who has become master of personalities. No one knows through whom this Masquerader will work next. It may be you. Everyone of you may tomorrow become unconsciously the dwelling place of this Divine One traveling incognito.

The Initiates of our world are never known for they go through the world living like the people they seek to serve, shrouding thir divine powers in robes of clay.

The spirit of the Masquerader is always close to the hearts of men, it is the unknown quantity, the missing power, but in truth it is all there is to live for. The problem that confronts man is to know this stranger when he sees Him, to realize that opportunity comes masquerading every day, that truth and light and knowledge and greater understanding come to us in strange disguises every hour and moment of our lives. When those come up to us who need our aid we think little of them, for they are poor and have nothing to give. We do not see the Masquerader concealed there, the unknown One behind the mask, but at that moment there comes to us an opportunity to do something worthy, and opportunity is the Divine Masquerader who will serve all who discover Him.

The Masquerader plays as our enemies, He shines out from those we dislike for He is the opportunity of reconciliation. He shines out to us from all with whom we come in contact, and we must wander the earth in rags until we find Opportunity. He is so subtle in his workings and so perplexing that we are often in doubt whether to accept Him or reject Him. One minute he inhabits us and a second later the soul of another.

Growth is the divine result of opportunity and is hidden behind every hard knock of life. The spirit of growth is disguised as a problem or a disappointment which wrecks and tears our soul. He is like the spirit of temptation that seeks to lead us astray and still prays that He may fail. For growth is the divine good which man gains from trouble; disappointment and failure are the gloom masks behind which the true actor is concealed. When we tear these masks from the spirits of negation there is nothing behind but Opportunity; when we tear away the mask of the devil we find God underneath, for the devil is just another disguise of the Masquerader. When some one robs us, cheats us out of everything we have, it seems a terrible injustice, but tear away the mask and Opportunity is all that is really there, for tests like these are opportunities to do something great and to rise above our grief. When we lie on the bed of sickness, tear away the mask from disease and we find just Opportunity, for the Divine Masquerader gazes down upon all these things. When someone tears us down and leaves us broken at the feet of our life work, tear away the mask and we find again the same smiling face of opportunity.

The Masquerader hides Himself under the discouraging, disheartening experiences of life. They are the masks and shams with which He is trying to help us to greater works. He is giving us the opportunity to master Him and every time we win a battle with Him we unmask the spirit of perversion and find the face of God smiling up from every disappointment. Over the battlefield with its shot and shell floats the spirit of opportunity, even Death itself when unmasked is the spirit of infinite growth. As the last sail of the ship vanishes beneath the waves nothing seems to remain but destruction, but even there is Opportunity.

All life conceals behind its strange and mystic workings just one great principle—the opportunity for growth. We are here to learn and our knowledge is of greater value than happiness unless we can be happy with the knowledge of work well done. Every disappointment, every problem, every hard knock of life, is given to man that he may grow, and in truth each one of them is Opportunity in disguise. Most people cannot agree with this concept. Few can see in those who injure them the face of Opportunity. There is in every life a place where there seems to be no redeeming feature; we know that failure must dwell there for Opportunity could not so disillusion us. Yet unveil the problem and you will find the same sweet spirit there. Every enmity is an opportunity for friendship, every sorrow is an opportunity to rise to greater heights. We call Him failure but he is in truth the maker of success; we call Him discouragement but without Him the great achievement is impossible. Always found where you do not want Him, always pointing out the difficult things, confronting us with problems which seem more than we can handle, He is neither popular nor desired, and yet He is the creator of gods.

There is but one spirit, the spirit of good, the spirit of God. Everything is an opportunity to lift or be lifted. No two people can meet but what opportunity is with them. In every life there are three or four great opportunities, and most lives are not successful because people have not learned to recognize them. People cry out to God, saying, "Oh, Lord, give me this or give me that and please, Lord, give me something!" But those who are wise know that the only thing they have a right to ask is the thing they have so often refused—opportunity. People want the fruits without the works necessary to produce them; they do not want a chance to work, they wish the rewards first; they want success upon a silver platter. They do not realize that God's greatest gifts to man are the powers of negation and opposition which stimulate the soul to greater effort.

If opportunity came and gently tapped us on the shoulder and said "Kind sir, I am Opportunity, and I am going to give you a chance to be great," he could not even wake us up, we would merely roll over on the other side and sleep calmly until fate gave us a rap. But the Lord of Creation with His divine wisdom has decreed that man must go out and look for opportunity as the farmer looks for woodchucks. You may have to smoke him out or choke him out, set a trap for him or maybe crawl into the hole and drag him out by the tail. The world is failing, not because it does not gain results, but because it does not recognize opportunity and seek to make use of it. The loss of an opportunity is a damning failure—the only failure in all the universe. Fools can follow where wise men lead, many can make good when someone else has shown them the opportunity, but the only success is when we discover it ourselves.

The world finds what it looks for and there are many looking for Opportunity but it is usually an opportunity to evade work, and to find a soft snap is too often considered the acme of wisdom. The world is a genius when it comes to digging up skeletons and a wonder in analyzing reputations, and there are experts of all kinds on unnecessary lines. But if people would only take out their high-powered magnifying glasses, put on their checkered suits and turn Sherlock Holmes to detect Opportunity they would find a new world opening before them.

Remember, when you are laboring to unfold and bring opportunity to others, that you are then the Masquerader yourself and your duty is to remain unknown, to become the Spirit of Good forever concealed behind the mask of the Masquerader. Therefore, if you are working with friends whose profession is that of digging ditches do not go down in a tall silk hat and spats and deliver a doxology for you will only lose all opportunity to be of service. You must disguise yourself and your concepts as the Masquerader, you must have your mask and become a master of makeup, and be able to help people where they are and not where you are.

When people lose themselves in the parts they are playing, they are no longer acting but are living many lives in one. As surely as every living thing is to you an Opportunity so you are the Masquerader to all other things. Our duty is to learn to play many parts. The Divine Masquerader knows all parts and just steps from one to another, that He may serve people where they are by disguising Himself as one of them.

Let us realize that the great Master is the one who can do the most good to others without himself being seen. So let each of us play this wonderful game of the Masquerader, slipping into other lives unknown, so far as personality is concerned, just to help someone along the way and then to vanish again as the Spirit of Opportunity, to receive and to give in the Name of the Divine Masquerader.

ASTROLOGICAL KEYWORDS

IN last month's edition we considered a few of the outstanding characteristics of the sign of Aries and we shall now consider Taurus, the second sign of the Zodiac, known to the ancients as Aphis of the celestial Bull. Students of Astrology should remember that these signs were named after animals or symbols which demonstrated the characteristics of the sign, and that by studying the creature or the symbol they may secure a very good understanding of the general temperament of the sign.

Briefly considered, we may analyze the keywords as follows:

Taurus, the second sign of the Zodiac:

    Vernal
    Cold
    Dry
    Earthy
    Melancholy
    Domestic
    Nocturnal
    Southern
    Fixed
    Succedent
    Unfortunate
    Fourfooted
    Commanding
    Hoarse
    Short Ascension
    Night House of Venus
    Exaltation of the Moon
    Fruitful sign
    Detriment of Mars.

General Characteristics:

Taurus is a very peculiar sign in general characteristics. We find certain phases of it slow, unsympathetic, and cold, while if well placed it is artistic, emotional, vital, sympathetic, and excitable. If provoked becomes malicious.

    Strong Will Power
    Tremendous Determination
    Hard to rule
    Can be coaxed but never forced
    Usually rather material

Physical Appearance:

    Broad forehead
    Rather curly hair
    Square face
    Usually dark
    Handsome
    Fairly short, well set stature
    Large eyes
    Full mouth
    Governs neck and throat
    Prominent face
    Strong shouldered
    Often short fingers

If Venus is well posited in Taurus it adds great beauty and balance to the figure and harmonious, symmetrical development to the form. If a malefic afflicts Taurus is often defomed around the head and shoulders.

Health:

Taurus is often afflicted with poor health, both in her own region of the throat and in the opposing sign Scorpio, which governs the animal energy centers.

Nervousness, muscular ailments, and often trouble in the liver and kidneys is noted, sometimes stomach trouble. Anaemia is sometimes present and Taurus is subject to sprains, strains, and twists of the body.

The following are the most prevalent diseases:
    Consumption
    Scrofula
    Croup
    Melancholia
    Quinsey
    Sore throat
    Nervousness
    Emotional ailments

Troubles in basilar processes of the spine and through Scorpio regions.

Domestic Problems:

Taurus, under proper conditions and unless afflicted, is an earthy, home-loving sign and usually settles down after a certain time of youthful wandering. Astrologers agree that Taurus is usually successful in domestic problems.

Countries Under Influence of Taurus:
- Ireland
- Great Poland
- White Russia
- Holland
- Lesser Asia
- Archipelagoes
- Cypress
- Lorraine
- Switzerland
- The Campania

Cities Under Its Domain:
- Mantua
- Leipsig
- Parma
- Nantz
- Franconia
- Sens
- Blythynia

Colors:
- Green
- Citrin
- Red

According to Ptolemy the stars in the abscission of the sign of Taurus resemble in their temperament the influence of Venus and in some degree that of Saturn. The Pleiades are like the Moon and Mars; Aldebaran, the eye of the Bull, takes the quality of Mars; the other stars resemble Saturn and partly Mercury. Those at the top of the horns take the qualities of Mars.

According to Henry Cornelius Agrippa, Taurus governs the Cherubim; is ruled by the angel Asmodel; of the twelve tribes of Israel, Ruben; of the twelve prophets, Haggai; of the twelve apostles, Thaddeus; of the twelve plants, upright and vervain; of the twelve stones, the cornelian; of the twelve degrees of the damned, it is said to rule the lying spirit.

The Indian Snake Charmer

FEW travellers have ever been to India who have not been fascinated by the street-jugglers and snake charmers of the East. You will see these old delapidated-looking individuals, covered with very little clothing and a great deal of dirt, sitting crosslegged on the ground, while before them is a little native basket containing an Indian cobra.

The fakir plays upon a three-note flute or reed and as the strange sounds come from it the snake sticks its head out of the basket and slowly rises upward lifting nearly one-half of its body off the ground. There it sits coiled up, its puffed head swaying back and forth to the tune of the snake-charmer and it seems hypnotized by the notes that he plays until he can handle it or do anything he desires with it.

There is a great secret of interest to the occultist and the mystic concealed under the story of the snake-charmer, for all of these ancient rituals and ideas have sacred origins and in the light of the Ancient Wisdom let us analyze the occult meaning of snake-charming.

In India the spinal spirit fire is called Kundalini and is symbolized as a serpent. According to the ancients, in the undeveloped man this snake lies coiled in the basket of the solar plexus. It is from this point that it is raised up the spinal canal through the spinal nerves by means of the development of the neophyte. This spinal spirit fire is the force which carries with it the power of spiritual sight and illumination. The three-pipe flute or the reed with three openings symbolizes the three keynotes of spiritual growth, namely thought, emotion, and action. When man plays proper harmonies upon his three bodies, the flute of Krishna, then Kundalini, the sleeping serpent, rises out of its basket and ascends through the blossoms on the spinal column awakening them with its power. In India today this is called snake-charming and its mystic message is perpetuated by the fakirs on the street who themselves know nothing of its inner significance.

Pearly Gates Gazette

MEMBER OF ASSASSINATED PRESS   EXTRA   UNLIMITED CIRCULATIOO

VOL. 30000001   JULY, 1923   No. 1000000000002

KING TUT NOW RESTING QUIETLY

Political Campaign Is Very Heated

COMPLETE RECOVERY OF KING TUT EXPECTED

His Majesty, King Tutankhamen, is reported to be improving and the Doctors hope for a complete recovery, which is most comforting to his large circle of friends and relatives. King Tut is suffering from neuritis and a complete nervous breakdown, as the result of the continual strain which the Pharaoh has been passing through during the last few weeks. The King is a very sensitive man and having remained a recluse for over two thousand years, his sudden jump to fame was too much for his delicate constitution. During King Tut's illness he was attended by a number of his favorite wives, one of whom could not be present owing to her absence on a short trip to Earth.

NOTED PSYCHOLOGIST ARRIVES FROM EARTH

Prof. Alexander Blitherskyt, well known psychologist from the planet Earth, sneaked into heaven on a slow freight early this a.m. The Professor had great difficulty in getting here, owing to the fact that he lacked the price of a ticket. He will deliver a lecture at the Skydome Auditorium this evening explaining his thrilling experience and how to get to heaven without the necessary railroad fare.

Prof. Blitherskyt is an authority on free traveling, and states that a fundamental study of modern psychology will produce a talented freight-car tareveler. We may say by way of detail that Prof. Blitherskyt arrived by clinging to a rail on the underside of the refrigerator car that was bringing Apollo his winter supply of cold storage eggs.

MADAME BLASE ADDRESSES CLUB

Low-cut diadems and King Tut haloes are the height of fashion this spring among the upper set. Wings of elephant-breath buff and biege are the rage in smart circles. Madame Blase made these statements while addressing heaven's Five Hundred at the Satellite Evening Club here today. Madame also states that henna will be used among the angels of the younger set. It was also stated that male angels will wear Barney Google derbies and robes cut on Sparkplug lines this spring. At the bachelor angel symposium it was stated that full beards will be in fashion during the summer months.

PEARLY GATES WEATHER BUREAU

Monthly Bulletin

Moderate winds and possibly a few showers. If it doesn't rain it will remain clear while if the winds fails to materialize we may expect calms.

BARGAIN PICKUPS

King Ptah-resu-aneb-f desires to sell, trade or exchange a complete second-hand mummy out tfiat very low price. His object is to realize something on it before scientists steal the entire tomb. Will take a good second-hand pair of non-skid retreaded wings or exchange for a Ford car with inter-planetary attachments. Must have extra tires and be six-cylinder. Ptah-resu-aneb-f, 1313 Pharaoh Row, East Heaven.

PEARLY GATES CITY COUNCIL FIGHT IS ON

In the recent election for President of the Pearly Gates City Council the standpatters and the Progressives very nearly came to blows. The Pearly Gates Sewerage System and street paving contracts formed the hub of the discussion. The Progressives were adamant in their opposition while the standpatters stood for taxing sun-power. The First and Eighth wards were with the Progressives nearly to a man, and there is no doubt that the suffrage vote settled the question. The Progressives stood for free cloud dispensation, while the standpatters are in favor of municipal management of all storms; they also believe that all angels should carry license plates and be equipped with stop-light signals. The Progressive's candidate, Mr. Gusto Bang, was elected by a slim majority. Plans are already on foot for the next election, which will be held in the year 982,000,000.

WANTED

A number of angels to sell roadmaps and encyclopedias in outlying districts and residential section of heaven; exclusive territories granted. We can also use a number of snappy story magazine salesmen; routes assigned. Also, one or two good salesmen from the Earth to dispense vacuum cleaners, electric irons, washing machines, energetic angels need apply. See I. Catchem and U. Cheatum, Importers, 1414 Ether Avenue, three blocks from carline. Open Saturday evenings.

SPECIAL ANNOUNCEMENT!
Just Off the Press—

"The Ways of the Lonely Ones"
When the Sons of Compassion Speak
By MANLY P. HALL

This is the latest work of this author and approaches the problem of spiritual enfoldment and growth in a manner both new and unusual.

The book contains six allegorical stories dealing with the spiritual development and initiation of mystical characters EACH ONE OF WHICH CAN BE PLACED IN THE LIFE OF THE STUDENTS OF THE WISDOM TEACHINGS. THE READER IS THE HERO OF EACH OF THE MYTHS, and concealed under the fables are many of the very deepest principles of occultism.

The book contains the following chapters:

The Maker of Gods.
This deals with the regeneration of matter and the transmutation of bodies.

The Master of the Blue Cape.
In this chapter the mystic meaning of the elixer of life and the philosophers' stone is given to the reader. Also the inner meaning of Alchemy.

The Face of The Christ.
The mystery of the last supper and the great problem of the second coming of the Christ is taken up from the occult standpoint, and presented in an understandable way.

The Guardian of the Light.
The duties and labors of one who seeks to be given charge of the Divine Wisdom are set forth in this chapter. Also the price of the Mystic Truth.

The One Who Turned Back.
This is the allegory of one who reached the gate of Liberation and renounced freedom to return again into the world. A study in Mystic Initiation.

The Glory of the Lord.
What happens to those who seek to enter the presence of the Lord without purifying themselves according to His laws? Read what happened to one, in the Tabernacle of the Jews.

The book is well printed on good paper and bound in boards stamped in blue. It contains sixty-four pages closely written.

This work like all of these publications is presented to the public without fixed price, leaving it to your own higher sentiments to show you your part in the work we are carrying.

The edition of this book is limited, so if you are interested send at once enclosing the contribution that you wish to make, not to pay just for the book but to help the work along, and you will receive your copy in the return mail.

Address all orders to Manly P. Hall, P. O. Box 695, Los Angeles, Cal.

These booklets by the same author may be secured by sending to Postoffice Box 695, Los Angeles, California, care of Manly P. Hall.

Price. These publications are not for sale but may be secured through voluntary contribution to help meet the cost of publication.

The Breastplate of the High Priest

A discussion of Old Testament symbolism showing how the spiritual powers of nature reflect themselves through the spiritual centers in the human body which we know as the jewels in the breastplate of Aaron. This booklet is out of print but an attempt will be made to secure a few copies for any desiring them. Illustrated.

Buddha, the Divine Wanderer

A new application of the life of the Prince of India as it is worked out in the individual growth of every student who is in truth seeking for the Yellow Robe.

Krishna and the Battle of Kurushetra

The Song Celestial with its wonderful story of the Battle of Life interpreted for students of practical religion. The mystery of the Blue Krishna and his work with men.

The Father of the Gods

A mystic allegory based upon the mythology of the peoples of Norway and Sweden and the legend of Odin the All-Father of the Northlands.

Questions and Answers, Part One
Questions and Answers, Part Two
Questions and Answers, Part Three

In these three booklets have been gathered about fifty of the thousands of questions answered in the past work gathered together for the benefit of students.

Occult Masonry

This booklet consists of the condensed notes on a class in mystic Masonry given in Los Angeles. It covers a number of important Masonic symbols and the supply is rapidly being exhausted.

Wands and Serpents

The explanation of the serpent of Genesis and serpent-worship as it is found among the mystery religions of the world and in the Christian Bible. Illustrated.

The Analysis of the Book of Revelation

A short study in this little understood book in the Bible, five lessons in one folder as given in class work during the past year.

The Unfoldment of Man

A study of the evolution of the body and mind and the causes which bring about mental and physical growth, a practical work for practical people.

Occult Psychology

Notes of an advanced class on this subject dealing in a comprehensive way with ten of its fundamental principles as given to students of classes in Los Angeles on this very important subject.

Parsifal and the Sacred Spear

An entirely new view of Wagner's wonderful opera with its three wonderful acts as they are applied to the three grand divisions of human life, the Legend of the Holy Grail, which will interest in its interpretation both mystics and music lovers.

Faust, the Eternal Drama

This booklet is a companion to the above and forms the second of a series of opera interpretations of which more will follow. The mystic drama by Goethe is analyzed from the standpoint of its application to the problem of individual advancement and its wonderful warning explained to the reader.

DE MACROCOSMI PRINCIPIIS. 41

Ut in mundi primordio, ubi tenebræ cujusque cœli cum partibus lucidis, quas viscositas spirituum in illis conclusorum, informationisque avidorum amplexa est, luctabantur in unica eademque massa, in regionem elementarem contracta.

The All-Seeing Eye

Modern Problems in the Light of Ancient Wisdom

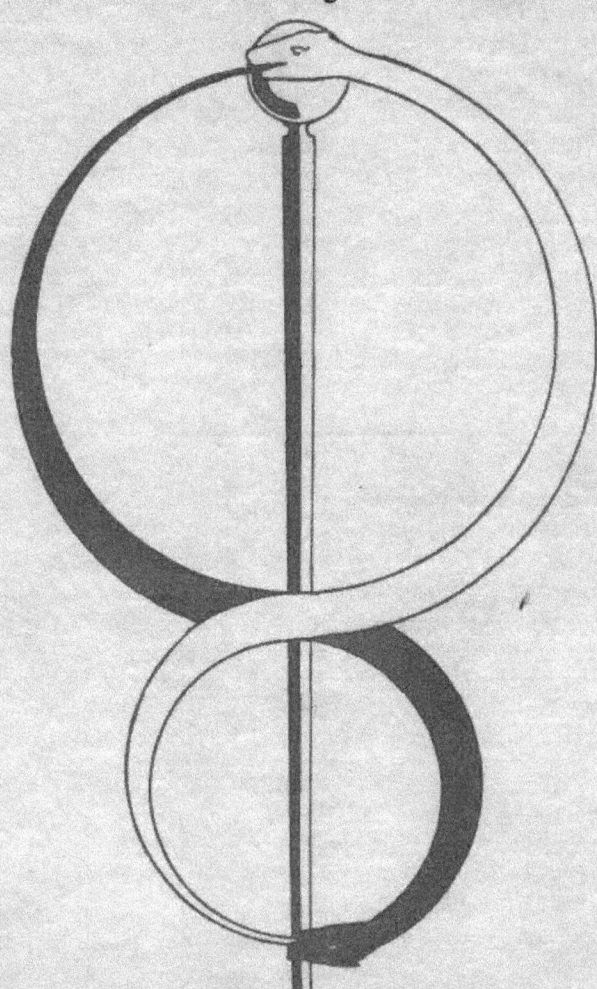

A Monthly Magazine
Written, Edited and
Compiled by
MANLY P. HALL

SEPTEMBER, 1923

THIS MAGAZINE IS NOT SOLD

"The Initiates of the Flame"
By MANLY P. HALL

A comprehensive study in the Wisdom Religion as it has been perpetuated through symbolism and mythology. This work is of interest to all students of mystic and occult philosophies or Masonry. The work is beautifully illustrated with drawings to explain its principles, some by the author and others of an alchemical and mystic nature. The table of contents is as follows:

- Chapter One — "The Fire Upon the Altar."
- Chapter Two — "The Sacred City of Shamballah."
- Chapter Three — "The Mystery of the Alchemist."
- Chapter Four — "The Egyptian Initiate."
- Chapter Five — "The Ark of the Covenant."
- Chapter Six — "The Knights of the Holy Grail."
- Chapter Seven — "The Mystery of the Pyramids."

This book is beautifully bound in full cloth with a handsome alchemical cover design stamped in gold leaf and contains about one hundred pages.

This work is not for sale but may be secured through a voluntary contribution on the part of anyone desiring to possess it. All of our work is put out for the benefit of students and not for purposes of profit and we ask your co-operation to assist us in meeting the cost of publication and distribution by your own realization of responsibility.

"The Lost Keys of Masonry"
By MANLY P. HALL

In this work an attempt has been made to dig from the ruins of Speculative Masonry the lost keys to the operative craft. In it the three degrees of the Blue Lodge are taken up separately, their requirements explained and the real meaning of the Masonic allegory given out for the benefit of Masons and Masonic students. The book contains a preface by a well-known Los Angeles Mason.

The following headings are discussed in the work:

- Prologue, the Masonic allegory, "In the Fields of Chaos."
- Chapter One—"The Candidate."
- Chapter Two—"The Entered Apprentice."
- Chapter Three—"The Fellow Craft."
- Chapter Four—"The Master Mason."
- Chapter Five—"The Qualifications of a True Mason."
- Epilogue—"In the Temple of Cosmos."

The entire presented in a sensible, comprehensive manner which can be understood by those not otherwise acquainted with the subject.

The book is handsomely illustrated with a four-color plate of the human body showing the position of the three Masonic Lodges on the cosmic man, also other pictures in black and white. The book is handsomely bound in solid cover with three-color cover design.

The work contains about eighty pages printed in two colors with a very fine quality of art paper.

Like all of our other works this book is only securable through the free-will offering of those desiring to secure it. Each person is placed upon his own honor and only reminded that the perpetuation of the work depends upon the cheerful co-operation of the workers.

THE ALL-SEEING EYE

MODERN PROBLEMS IN THE LIGHT OF ANCIENT WISDOM

VOL. 1   LOS ANGELES, CALIF., SEPTEMBER, 1923   No. 5

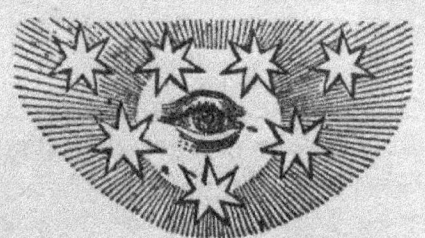

This magazine is published monthly for the purpose of spreading the ancient Wisdom Teachings in a practical way that students may apply to their own lives. It is written, published, and edited by Manly P. Hall and privately published for circulation among his students and those interested in his work.

Those desiring to secure copies of this magazine or who wish to subscribe to it may do so by writing directly to the editor.

This magazine is published and distributed privately to those who make possible with their financial support its publication. The magazine cannot be bought and has no fixed value. Like all of the ancient teachings which it seeks to promulgate it has no comparative value but the students must support it for its own instrinsic merit.

To whom it may concern: It is quite useless to inquire concerning advertising rates or to send manuscripts for publication as this magazine cannot possibly consider either as this is a non-commercial enterprise. All letters and questions, subscriptions, etc., should be mailed to P. O. Box 695, Los Angeles, California, in care of Manly P. Hall, Editor.

The contents of this magazine are copyrighted but permission to copy may be secured through correspondence with the author.

This magazine does not represent nor promulgate any special sect or teaching but is non-sectarian in all of its viewpoints. Suggestions for its improvement will be gladly considered if presented in the proper manner.

TABLE OF CONTENTS

EDITORIAL
- Ten Rules of Religious Etiquette 3
- Spiritual Hobos—A Romance in Phychologics 4
- Poem 2
- Question and Answer Department 12
- Prometheus the Eternal Sufferer 15

OCCULT FICTION
- Brothers of the Shining Robe, Chapter Three, The Divine Presence (Continued) 13
- The Ave Maria 9
- A Knight of the Holy Grail 26

SPECIAL ARTICLES
- Impractical Occultists 22
- Explanation of Last Month's Plate 18

ORIENTAL OCCULTISM
- Discourse on the Eight Perfections 19

ASTROLOGY
- The Keywords of Cancer 30

PEARLY GATES GAZETTE 32

The Song of Life

Listening for the footsteps of the Master,
    Watching for the glory of his smile,
Praying for the strength that comes with knowing
    As we struggle on alone each weary mile.
Seeking in the throngs that surge about us,
    Waiting as the years roll slowly by,
Sighing as the burdens grow so heavy—
    It seems 'twould be better not to try.

Groaning as we see our brothers happy—
    While our hearts grow weary with their load—
Wondering why some paths are strewn with roses
    And only tears we find upon the road.
Wondering why the price of truth is sorrow,
    Wondering at the bruises and the strife—
Can we really be the winners in a battle
    Where only death can pay the price of life?

Why are those who live the lives of hatred
    The guides that show the way to perfect love?
And why are those who live below in darkness
    The ones that lead us to the light above?
And as we hear the jeers of those about us
    Can we smile and bravely lay aside each fear?
And through the gloomy mask of every sorrow
    Can we see the light and feel the presence near?

And with the strength that comes alone with knowing
    Can we gladden other's footsteps with our song?
Can we see that every sorrow that we suffer
    Is but the payment for some distant wrong?
Then sing the song of life as on we struggle
    And learn from those around us every day?
Behind each Brother's form there stands a Master—
    Shall we serve him or shall we turn away?

EDITORIAL

Ten Rules of Religious Etiquette

1. Do not attend the meetings because you have an antipathy against the hall and do not like to associate with the class of people who sit around you. This is a proof of your ultra-refinement.

2. If you come be sure to attend irregularly and under no condition tell anyone about the meeting or bring anyone with you. This indicates that you are exclusive and belong in the upper set.

3. Be sure that you acquire all our books but never read them. Ask the questions in class that are answered in them. This demonstrates your mental superiority beyond all doubt.

4. In securing our books and magazines never consider the contents—always estimate their value upon the price of the paper. This is a sure sign of business shrewdness and erudition.

5. Always lock up our publications where no one else can find them or read them. This proves that you understand their esoteric value. To advertise them would be decidedly plebeian and would lessen your superiority over others.

6. Always kick about the way things are being done—the chairs, gas-stoves, music, and so forth. This is very refreshing and proves your aristocracy.

7. Never put anything in the collection plate. Always give someone else that opportunity for soul growth. This shows spirituality and brotherhood.

8. Workers should never get along well together—each one should be jealous of all the others. This shows professional temperament and helps to simplify the teacher's work, at the same time setting an illustrious example.

9. Do not spend much time studying. It isn't being done in the better circles. You should make the meeting hall a rendezvous to circulate all the latest scandals. You should also be filled with advice which you should give freely especially on subjects about which you know nothing. This shows your occult leanings and family breeding. Every member of the student body should follow all the others and see what they do. This is deep brotherly interest.

10. If anybody should get up and do anything useful—oppose him in every way possible, crying out that he is trying to boss and run the whole show. If there is a mass movement in any direction gather up yourself and depart, telling everyone you meet that the work is being run by a clique. This is decidedly refreshing and relieves the monotony which might otherwise cause the work to stagnate.

All of these points help to simplify matters and are of vast encouragement to all concerned and if followed religiously will produce perfect results.

I Thank You.

Spiritual Hobos
A Romance in Psychologics

IT IS, alas, too true that few individuals care to be reminded of the hollows, furrows, ravines and gullies in their mental, physical and spiritual make-ups! Compliments are always in demand and a suave disposition never fails to draw around it bevies of friends and admirers who will bask in the honeyed sentiments like flies in a sugar bowl. People love to foster the fond idea that somebody else believes them to be something which they honestly know they are not.

Most of our occult students will many times declare themselves to be braced in all the weak spots, strong and courageous, ready to listen to the truth, whole truth and everything but the truth! But rarely do they demonstrate any great amount of joy when reality does strike against them or seek admittance into their consciousness. Most students tell us that they want to know their weak points, where their spiritual bunions are located and what constitutes the leading detractions of their temperaments but if we happen to intimate even for a second that they are suffering from any slight imperfection they immediately leave us—thoroughly convinced that we lack polish, grace and refinement, and are most hopelessly deficient in spiritual sentiments. While if we "gush" prettily over them, address them as "old students," "advanced souls," ad infinitum, they are then in a condition where most any living creature can separate them from their rent money, salary, and more than likely their family.

In other and shorter words, they like to be patted on the back, are willing slaves to anyone who will weave fanciful dramas around them for their own glorification—even though they really know that they possess none of the attributes in question—but if for a moment we infer that the average seeker-after-the-occult is a hobo, a bum, a tramp, a nonentity, a vagabond, vandal and vampire, for some absolutely unknown reason he passes us on the street next day without recognition though he may realize that he is all of the things described, plus more known only to himself.

But let us, just for the sake of the principle involved, be truthful for once and spite the devil, admitting that at the present time the majority of seekers after things spiritual are not only looking in the wrong direction for the truth but positively ignore it when they do see it. They continue gliding through life talking themselves into believing that they are personifications of the Eternal Seeker when in reality they are nothing but omnipotent, omnipresent, omniscient (never omniactive) Incarnations of Specific Worthlessness.

These may not seem pleasant thoughts, in fact we may be called cruel, cold and unjust, but with the pure eye of logic, the brain of reason and the steady hand of the surgeon let us anatomize what we discover when we start carving modern super-spiritual cadaver and see how it sums up:

As we cast the searchlight of common sense upon the problems of modern religion and examine the fruits of philosophical endeavor, listening with rapt attention to the weird discourses which pour forth as bubbling brooks and dashing cataracts of modern Platonic reasoning, a great pessimism grips our soul and the icy fingers of doubt strangle out our tiny germ of hope as we seek to synthesize such hopelessly impossible brain-storms!

So at last we are forced to the conclusion that most of our so-called Thinkers are neither spiritual, philosophical, intelligent nor studious but are merely brain convolution contortionists twisting their dua-mater and pia-mater into bowknots and figure-eights and then—ye gods!—inviting others to join them in their mental gymnastics. In other words instead of being statisticians, economical reformers, teachers and logicians they are merely straining the cerebral vesticles and painfully spraining the mind. When we realize this we are confronted with a great problem—what is thought? And how should its wonderful power be used to express a maximum of intelligent result?

The answer to the problem is, *man must learn to think in harmony with nature and natural law.* When he seeks to battle against his own intellectuality, to deny the existence of things which he daily and hourly contacts, or seeks with sheer force of will to change the direction of the universe or reverse the poles he is merely wasting power and energy on an absolutely hopeless, helpless and non-productive series of concepts which would be comic if they were not divinely sad.

The average person does not know how to think and never will until he individually evolves the mental faculties and powers to do it with. And the first step towards this is to cease imitating the ideas of others, learn to reason out and master the problems of your own existence and being responsible to yourself instead of rushing to another fool for help—whereupon each clasps the other and both sink! The average person who believes himself to be philosophical, spiritual and ethical is merely a rambling intellectual hobo, helpless and harmless, whose every thought and action he has begged, borrowed or stolen from somebody else. Those who think other people's thoughts, lean on other people's shoulders and do not labor mentally, physically and spiritually for the things they want are tramps, imposters and human fungi as sure as there are such things in nature.

Taking the modern occult student as an example of spiritual unfoldment and moral culture, we usually find him to be merely a religious vagabond wandering from cult to creed, sleeping in intellectual box-cars, under pseudo-theological haystacks and persistently avoiding the woodpile of labor with a highly evolved efficiency that is positively uncanny. Students of the Wisdom Teachings little realize how like beggars they can become if they continue to wander from pillar to post knocking at each farmhouse door, hoping that fortune will present herself but inwardly praying that the bull-dog of adversity will not advance to the rear of their immediate environment.

There is a great Kingdom of the Unemployed and there is also that aristocratic fraternity known as Gentlemen of the Great Outdoors and, alas, it is but too true said institutions do many things not in accordance with the ethical statutes of our beautiful country. But let us not add infamy to insult or further scandalize their already dubious reputations by listing with them our modern spiritual students. For, 'tis sad to relate, these Gentlemen of the Open Road and non-eventuating pilgrims are never half as guilty of mental or physical vagrancy as that band of new thought and spiritual students are addicted to intellectual grafting and sem-conscientious knavery!

None of us will ever forget Tattered Tom or milord the Baron Rags and other blue-blood members of the slipshod aristocracy for they are in a class unapproachable and inimicable—the very acme of active indolence. As they promenade along the tar-paved boulevard resembling animated scarecrows or bi-pedular ashcans they manifest and express in every movement of their being a nobility greater far than a scion of the House of Navarre. They are sublimely humorous, pathetically ridiculous, and always bring poetically to our minds a picture of injured innocence and over-worked ennui.

Along they go with smiles on their faces, whistling merry tunes, while clothed in a bundle of rags and tatters! Gentlemen of leisure whose motto is: "Don't work when there's anything else to do!" (Latest psychological axiom.) You have all heard them as they gently knock at the backdoor, after making sure that the Airdale is chained, and with fringed hat in hand deliver a touching elegy with a seriousness and masterful eloquence worthy of a trained tragedian:

"Please, lady, I'm a poor man, down and out and too sick to work, I'm tryin' to get money enough to make the next city where I have a brother in business. I come from a good family, mum,—I'm not a tramp or anything like that. I'm just suffering from pecuniary embarrassment—a slight financial shortage—I wonder if it would be possible for you to give me a piece of pie or some of your husband's old clothes?"

This is a noble art—the art of begging—a cultured science which has been evolved through generations of practice, the developing of sympathetic voices, said looking eyes and cherubimic expressions that shine out with celestial radiance from beneath several days' growth of whiskers!

When poor people enter this profession and the down-and-outers promenade along the dusty road of life in someone else's clothes we call them tramps. But when they rise upward to more ethical circles of philosophical, spiritual and scientific things we then call them mystics, psychologists, philosophers, eccentric geniuses, advanced thinkers and deep students of the occult. If you will just take the average modernist in religion, however, and analyze him carefully you will find a weird and wondrous composite combination of borrowed plumage. Like Aesop of the ancient Fables, in examining said rare specimen, we find an ugly duckling with one glorious peacock plume rising from the rear. Such a sight as would give a naturalist or poultry fancier epileptic convulsions unless he knew for a certainty that the glorious tuft was not an inherent product of the bird!

Mentally, physically, never to mention spiritually, not one thing our occult student wears fits him. Surely he represents the Ex-president of the ancient and honorable Order of Whatnots! His hat is too big and nestles grotesquely over ears that pivot and turn outward by the weight. Of course it is no longer a delapidated derby or gently atrophying tall silk but just a philosophical concept and shortcut to heaven he has begged off the Jones family down the street. His borrowed alchemy hangs loosely from his shoulders, gathered in by the safety-pin of someone else's ethics. His pant-legs of affirmation and denial were made for a man three times his size, consequently fit him too much, but still he is wearing them—and what makes it infinitely worse is they are not mates for he sneaked them out of Smith's backyard while Mrs. Smith was paying the iceman. His shoes, one a patent-leather the other a goulash, leave strange footprints on the sands behind, which footprints are the measure of his soul. For they are not his own either but have been begged, borrowed or stolen from some oracle along the meandering line of his pilgrimage.

Thus he stands before you. Nothing more, nothing less than an intellectual vagabond and spiritual lounge-lizard. (Or shall we say chameleon? For as this little lizard changes his color to suit his background so the "mystic" changes his creeds to suit his needs.) Like the ordinary tramp he hates work worse than poison, hates water like a cat, but is hoping against hope that he will get to heaven somehow if he can borrow enough old clothes to make it or can hop an empty freight going in that direction.

In other words, our nondescript student of religion is eternally searching for something easy that he can secure without labor and lives ardently hopeful of finding a way to enjoy the harvest that his industrious brother creatures have stored up. Students do not mean to do this but it seems an innate faculty of the human mind to seek to avoid exertion. The lower in man cries out for rest while the higher spiritual powers seek to express more incessant activity. There are hobos on the physical plane of nature who claim to have been tired for fifty years and to be suffering from strange ailments which obstruct the vital energies, when the real cause of their ailment is chronic laziness. The same may be said of our spiritual seekers for most of them are wasting away with some mystic lassitude which is nothing more nor less than a pure lack of a desire to do anything.

Sciences which seek to promote mental exertion and individual advancement become less and less popular all the time while intellectual and spiritual soothing syrups and teething rings are in ever more constant demand. Spiritual narcotics which will prevent human beings from feeling the pains of daily life are called blessings but in reality are the greatest curses of the human race. If students could only realize that when they search for others who will answer for them the problems of their own lives with formulas and recipes which eliminate individual expression making it possible to glide en masse to the Eternal Footstool, or who will rent them pseudo-evolutionary roller skates to shorten the path—they are only being hoodwinked and deceived! And always by those who have themselves fallen slaves to their own or their brothers' absurdities.

There is no way of reaching the true position the human race is ordained to fill without individually standing upon our own feet and learning mentally, physically and spiritually to earn legitimately and honestly whatsoever quality we are seeking mastery over. There must be an equal effort expended and an honest foundation laid for everything which we want or else man is, in the sight of nature, a thief and a robber. Those people who fondly believe that their duty ceases with the getting of things or that they can make slick transactions in religion or turn rather clever intellectual deals to their own profit have a great awakening before them, an awakening filled with sorrow and unhappiness because they have failed to realize that the Universe is governed by just, non-commercialized non-favoritism which as a great abstract Intelligence governs impartially all of Its creations, rewarding each according to its works.

There is no greater crime in the world than to promise or to intimate that we can make another spiritual, intelligent or prosperous, for it is absolutely impossible to do so. And those who charge exorbitant prices for shortcuts to heaven are charging for something which they do not possess and are assessing work that only the ego of an individual alone is capable of carrying on. In other words, Mr. Jones is paying Mr. Smith for the privilege of saving his own soul. Persons who graft in such a way as this should be treated in the same manner that the Government treats oil sharks who sell shares in non-entited wells and the like. They are mental, physical and spiritual criminals and those who patronize them are merely demonstrating a super-abundance of vacuum in the cranial cavity. But the demand will always produce the supply and as long as there are people to be fooled there will always be those pleased to do it for them.

It is perfectly legitimate to instruct man in the ways he should go (providing that the party of the first part knows what way anything should go) but to promise results is beyond the privilege of God himself. Instead of giving a spiritual tramp a meal in every case he should be ushered into the back yard where stands the menacing wood-pile and told that if he will chop two cords his lunch is ready. At such a moment as this the physical hobo disintegrates while his spiritual correlate dissolves into a dank cloud of irridescent dew—nose cracked, insulted and with every quill in his temperament standing on end.

We may not believe it this way but when work is mentioned the seekers after eternal wisdom rise, one after another, and magically vanish effervesing streams of many-colored indignation—this at the bare suggestion of earning their daily bread! If he is suffering from a gouty toe or a gastronomic reaction and you tell him to watch his diet and stop eating roast goose or breaded veal cutlets he will immediately rise, a towering pillar of righteous wrath, and tell you that you are neither spiritual, ethical nor philosophical. Said student will then head for some temple of solace where he will wade through a long concentration, take an aphromatic pill or ten grains of sugar-coated sentiment and then go out to eat fried bricks and ten-penny nails a la carte until the closing of the last act when the nail he could not digest is used to hold down his coffin lid.

If you hint to the student of ancient wisdom that bathing is an inducement to health you are ordinary, materialistic, and lack Oriental ideality. But there is not one "occultist" in a million who has studied the plumbing system of Pompeii while engaged in his ancient researches. If you tell him he has a mean disposition, you are a low-brow, a mishap, an inferior and several other things he cannot remember but which nevertheless apply to the problem on hand. However if you will prove to him conclusively and beyond all shadow of doubt that his spavin can be cured by some supernatural agency which requires no temperance or moderation in his own life, then indeed you are gifted of the gods. He will then peel forth the last shekel and think nothing of working at a dollar a day for fifteen years to pay you for a Latin formula or a Sanskrit delineation punctuated in Hebrew, when for a five-cent bar of Ivory soap he could be a healthy man for seventy-five years—that is, of course, if he adds to the soap the necessary exertion for applying.

There are also people—strange creatures of demented reasoning!—who will condescend to study the occult if you will guarantee them illumination, unity with the Absolute, mastery and initiation, not to mention such trivial things as the seventh sense and the ability to rove on other planets or pick daisies on the Milky Way at the completion of a two-week course. If you have a dashing personality they may even wait four weeks for their spiritual insight especially if the language you clothe the supernatural sciences in is sufficiently set with the rubies of eloquence and like the sages of old you are an orator with a silver tongue.

But when you advise said persons that mastery requires from one to three hundred and fifty million years of hard work, low pay and tough luck, he immediately tells you that you lack inspiration, that you know nothing of heaven and its mysteries, that your aura radiates bone-set tea, and that by good right you should be burned in effigy on the public square. If you warn him that his eternal salvation depends upon his own works he is discouraged, disconcerted and perplexed for he knows he has never done anything worthy and can never get far on individual merit. But just whisper mysteriously in his ear a state secret all about a new way of leaning on the Lord whereby you may slip in for nothing he is thenceforth a subject of exuberant reaction, for our average student has no intention whatsoever of giving up anything he likes but will always do the thing he wants to even if it is being miserable—and some are never happy unless they are completely miserable.

To enjoy hard work at this day and age is to invite investigation from the psychopathic ward and if such a case could be found a symposium of international scientists would come into session to diagnose the extraordinary phenomenom. A person who glories in labor and in contact with the hard knocks of the world are about as rare as a total eclipse of Gloombridge or Uncle Si's three-headed calf and are to be listed with the scientific marvels of the age—especially if found among spiritual students.

So they go, praying for the day when someone will build an environment for them wherein they may be ideally happy or that a great Master will come to clean up the world—a work we ought to be doing every day—or that a great Light will descend from the heavens—when we ought to be out lighting our own way. They are longing for someone else to heal them of something they have no business to have, and while they have a mean disposition and a cussedly bad temper they long to find a way to conceal it by plastering it deep down under a thick layer of beauty mud which comes under the heading of convincing personality cosmetics.

So Tattered Tom and Frenzied Freddy—address unknown, vocation unthinkable—wander from door to door asking for pie, overalls and old shoes and like the foolish virgins of old begging of the wise ones oil for their lamps instead of standing up like the men and women they claim to be, kicking out their mean dispositions, cleaning out their self infected body and taking a good long stretch. Perhaps some day they may learn to look somebody straight in the eye and say, "There is nothing in the world equal to a life filled with works, worries, trials and troubles for it has given me the experience and strength to rise above misfortune, stand on my own feet and proclaim my inherent right to be one of the elect!"

The price of knowledge and spirituality is the proper use of the powers which man has and seventy-five squadrons of angels, three hundred battalions of gods, fifty-seven varieties of divas, two hundred and eighty-seven regiments of psychological infantry and fifteen or twenty spiritual big guns are not enough to stand forth and say "boo" to the powers of nature much less claim the responsibility of easing an individual into heaven. Sixty-five million chariots drawn by cherumbim will never be able to get our big toe over if we continue to tramp around in the name of religion, vampirizing and vandalizing everyone with whom we come in contact.

Each is foreordained and predestined from before the time the universe was formed to figure his way out of and work his way out of the undesirable qualities of nature. When he sits back asleep at the switch or trusts someone else to carry him all is lost.

Never with such concepts as these will the spirit of man find rest in the lands beyond the River Styx. (He would surely drown in said river if someone didn't swim in after him.) But it seems that each leans on everything else perfectly content to let someone who can think for them, and someone who can work for them.

Instead of building the faculties, powers and qualities within themselves which entitle them to stand upon their own feet with well fitting garments of their own making earned by the sweat of their brows, they now stand as divine incarnations of the cosmic spirit Celestial Hobo—tagged out in a little bit of everything belonging to everybody else. If by any chance the people who loaned them their robes should ask them back the average mystic will stand shivering at the gates of the Great Unknown as one by one his pet concepts fly home until nothing remains but a dismal failure personifying the true inherent qualities which the student himself has evolved by his own lack of active labor.

The Ave Maria

THIS is the story of a spark buried deep in the heart of a dying flame, one of those tragic little legends which bring close to our soul the realization of nature's subtle working. Few realize that the shell of clay shrouds a deathless spark, and yet if the world thought they would know that this is the truth. Something hidden far within, unseen and unknown, cries eternally to be admitted and realized by its prison walls. Man must not judge his brother creature by the form alone for behind rough exteriors of this world there is ofttimes hidden a finer, sweeter and more beautiful spirit than we would ever dream could exist there. Often from the shadow of a broken, discordant body there shines forth a gleam of celestial radiance.

There is a strange pathos under the thoughtlessness of the world. All have felt an inner urge, a great desire to realize some hidden ideal, and man often soars heavenward upon the pinions of inspiration—only to have the ever human crush the vision with the stony fingers of crystalization. And how often the spirit in the world of forms chafes to be free from the living corpse that holds it to the sordid things! Nature is like a string of wondrous beads; all are connected by a single thread of living gold and a tiny spark of divine life shines out between all the beads that have an end.

It is hard to realize that the tools will grow dull with age and as time slowly crushes the instrument we wonder why the glorious dreams that fill our soul are no longer shaped to realities. We try ever to be young; even when the unseen Reaper gathers us to the Great Unknown still the divine spirit of youth within looks forward with eagerness to creation's endless adventure.

* * * *

It is in a little town in the old country, with its cobblestone streets, its simple folk and honest simplicity, that our story is laid. In the center of the town stood the great cathedral with tiny buildings gathered under the protection of its massive form; its grand Gothic arches rise to shadows of an endless night which hangs forever amid its lofty rafters and mysterious hallways, only but dimly lighted by the sunbeams which struggle in through the panes of many colored glass.

A dull hush filled the building and its cold, lifeless air reminded one of the vaults of emperors and the mauseleums of kings where endless rows of marble tombs stand like phantoms in the dim uncertain light. At one end of the massive building where the altar place stood, guarded by tiny gleaming candles which sent flickering shadows on the dark stained walls, the mighty organ rises— a weird mystery of tubes and pipes, a mighty sentinel guarding the holy place of God. It is an ancient church and for many ages worshipers have knelt upon its marble floor, deep rutted by the footsteps of the pious.

Suddenly the silence was broken by footfalls which sounded hollowly in the great blank silence of the place of worship. A little figure walked slowly down through the gloomy arches to the foot of the ancient altar. It was an old man, his back bent with age, and his long white hair hanging in ringlets over his shoulders. Reaching the foot of the altar steps he stopped and gazed lovingly up to the monster organ half concealed in the gloom of the nave. A thin streamlet of tears coursed down the old man's cheeks and a sob echoed through the ancient hallways. And then slowly the glorious spiritual face turned away from the organ and with his arms hanging at his sides the old man walked away. Day after day he came there just for a few moments and then crept away again to his little home on the outskirts of the town.

Sometimes there were others in the mighty cathedral, kneeling in prayer upon the worn flagstones. Their eyes grew misty also as they watched the old man for they knew the sacred tragedy of his life. The white haired figure was the organist who since the days of his youth had lent the voice of angels to the pipes of wood. Everyone knew the sad story of his life for in that little town there were no secrets and all lived like one great family with compassion and tenderness each to the other. The good housewives sighed when they told the story of how one day as he was playing his beloved "Ave Maria" the old man's fingers had fallen from the keys—paralyzed—and the mighty organ was silent in the midst of its melody. They knew that he had played his organ for the last time for his dead fingers could never again move lightly across the keys.

The little story was the tragedy of the village and all hearts went out to him as day after day the lonely old man entered the ancient cathedral and gazed up at the lofty instrument which had been his friend for threescore years and ten.

Although his fingers were stilled forever the soul of the musician was still alive. For years the mighty man-made thing with its harmony celestial had been the comrade and companion of a lonely life and up in the little balcony where the keyboard stood the organist had left his heart. In the days of sorrow when all others had deserted him, through the nights of anguish which always fill the heart of a dreamer, he had climbed the little stairway and the people outside had heard wondrous symphonies swell forth, melodies born of sadness and the shattered soul of one the world could never understand. Through pain and pleasure, through youth and manhood, and even as the snow of age gathered upon his brow, the old musician had played, loved by all and loving all but understood by none save the old organ in the great cathedral.

New fingers now played its ancient keys, another master gave it life, but still the heart of the old musician dreamed of his beloved instrument and prayed that once more he might touch its aged keys before eternity shrouded him with the endless past. So each day he came and humbly offered his little prayer that once more his dead fingers might play the living harmonies which filled his soul.

The spirit of man never grows old but through the ripening years of experience just learns to feel more, to be greater and closer to the divine. The life within does not age though the frame is bent; the same glorious harmonies filled the musician's soul but the fingers of clay no longer heeded the genius of the master's mind. But still with simple faith he prayed for the joy of one last communion and the feeling of its possibility comforted his aching heart.

So the years passed, the step of the musician grew tottering and broken, the very stones were worn by his footsteps and the Angel of Death hovered near him as the chill of eternal winter crept ever closer to his heart. But still he came each day to gaze upon the thing he loved, to pray, to hope and to remember.

It was late one afternoon and the setting sun was sending its last rays through the towering windows adorned with their many colored pictures of the Master's life. The old organist had entered the church and was standing as he had so often in the past at the base of the mighty organ gazing up at the gloomy shadows which partly concealed the rows of ancient tubes. In a hushed voice he spoke as to a living thing:

"Oh, friend of my youth! oh comforter of my old age! inspiration in the moments of glory! silent comrade in times of sorrow!—my pilgrimage is nearing its end. Will I ever play again upon your ivory keys the melodies that fill my soul but which these poor hands can bring forth no more? Still great ideals thrill through me and the music as of angel's voices sounds ever in my ears. Ofttimes in the shades of night I hear strange songs and melodies and had I now the fingers the world would know many wondrous things. But, alas, it is all over—all but a dream of the deathless past! You were my life, my all, and somewhere among your ancient tubes and pipes my heart will always be for I love you now as in the days of old. Oh why must the soul of man remain in darkness when the clay is broken? My time here is not long for in the shadows of the night I hear voices from a mystic land unseen; the world of spirit surrounds me and I understand it better as the world of men grows fainter every day. Only one thing I ask before I go—once more I would play your ivory keys! once more to give life to your soulless being!"

Obeying an impulse which he could not understand the old organist slowly climbed the narrow stairs which led to the keyboard of the organ, and sitting down upon the ancient stool gazed lovingly at the form so darkened by age. The setting sun sent one lonely beam through the tinted panes lighting the face of the aged man with its halo of silver locks in a glory divine. The great inspiration filled the musician's soul, the youth so far behind flooded back again as wondrous rythyms swayed his being and all the glory of the music he loved so well thrilled through him. Instinctively he sought to raise his arms and place his fingers upon the keyboard then he realized, alas, that his youth was but a dream and with a broken sob the old man's head sank upon the organ. The ancient keys were wet with his tears as the last shades of the glorious sun shown dimly through the painted glass. . . .

As the good folks of the city sat round their fires there suddenly broke upon their ears a sound—the voice of the mighty organ in the great cathedral pouring forth in a welling fountain of symphony and harmony! They stopped to listen—there was but one in all the world who could play such divine chords and he was paralyzed! Those who dwelt near the cathedral whispered that never before had such thunderous tones, such mellow notes, such divine sound issued from that organ. It seemed alive and each recognized the melody that sounded forth. In the years gone by they had heard it when the old musician was in his prime. Each knew that it was the one he loved so well, the harmony that had soothed him so many times in sorrow and inspired him in peace—the Ave Maria.

A few came out of their homes and reverently crossed the open square to the portals of the church. The very building seemed to rock and in awe and trembling they crossed themselves for a strange presence was in that cathedral, a hush, a mystic power which they could not comprehend. One by one they gathered and knelt upon the rutted floor. Still the harmony poured forth in welling cadences from behind the little curtain which marked the keyboard of the organ. One, a little bolder than the rest, slowly climbed the steps and gazed with reverence into the alcove where the organ stood. Then he raised his hands to his face and with a cry rushed down the stairs and fell in prayer at the foot of the organ. A few moments passed and then from among those gathered a good man of the town came forth—a sturdy Christian of honest principles beloved by all—the blacksmith of the town. Hat in hand he slowly climbed the little stairs and entered the alcove from which the other had fled. He too gave a gasp and knelt in prayer.

On the floor in the gloom lay the body of the organist, his white face turned upward to the half shade of the descending night in which loomed the organ pipes. His beautiful spiritual face was lighted with a divine peace and his whole being seemed at rest. But this was not the miracle. Two hands were playing the organ—two wondrous dexterous hands which flew nimbly from key to

(Continued on page 21)

QUESTION AND ANSWER DEPARTMENT

Is man a free agent or under the control of outside entities?

Ans. Nothing but God is a free agent and even He must comply with the laws of creation. So called free-will is the power of choice and the greater the range of possibilities the greater the power of choice. The one who can choose between three things is freer than the one who must choose between two. Only in perfect knowledge comes the greatest expression of the power of choice. Man's evolution is being assisted by outside intelligences but he must himself make all the important decisions of his life.

What is death and what causes it?

Ans. Death is the phenomena of the separation of a life from a body. It is caused either through a shock or an accident or disease which makes the body incapable of functioning whereupon the life withdraws itself and, the center of power having left the body because it can no longer use it the shell disintegrates.

Does the Bible contradict Reincarnation?

Ans. The Bible contradicts nothing but is a neutral work and means exactly what the reader gathers from it as do all the works of the wise. Persecution and tyranny has been based upon the Bible, it has been used as a tool for bigotry and crystalization, and it is also the divine guide to the illuminated seeker. It does not contradict Reincarnation but seems to be based upon the idea of the law of Rebirth being an accepted fact.

What is success?

Ans. Success is the adjustment of the individual to the plan of his work here. This plan is the result of his previous actions. Whenever he begins a new work or pays off back debts he is walking the path of success regardless of his financial condition or his comfort. His future experiences are going to depend upon his present action and noble, honest efforts are the basis of future success. A success is one who meets and masters every unpleasant condition and obstacle, planting flowers where thistles grew before.

What is law?

Ans. Law is the Plan through which God, man and the Universe were differentiated, are maintained and will later be resolved into the infinite, plus individualization.

Is there anything above Law?

Ans. Those who are above law are above breaking it. We mean by breaking it an attempt to oppose its dictates. NO ONE HAS EVER BROKEN A LAW, THE LAW HAS BROKEN THEM. To obey nature's laws is to make them your greatest friend; to attempt to evade them is to make them your bitter enemies. Man is walking between two lines; These parallel lines are the laws of being and as long as we keep on the road we do not know that they exist. When we lose our true center we strike against these walls saying we have broken a law because we suffer.

What is God's plan for man?

Ans. Harmonious adjustments with ever rarer and finer planes of consciousness. The so-called Master is one who has made adjustments with planes where the average individual has no consciousness. The degree of the Initiate's unfoldment depends upon the fineness of his adjustments.

Can consciousness be lost?

Ans. Consciousness can be lost when the vehicle connected with the plane where consciousness is becomes crystalized through age, abuse or atrophy. Consciousness upon any plane of nature depends upon a body properly functioning and attuned to the substances of that plane.

Why are we always in doubt as to what is right and wrong?

Ans. Because our scale of morals is ever changing and the thing that is right today is wrong tomorrow for we are ever growing and demanding finer things. The highest that we know is the only thing that is ever right.

Brothers of the Shining Robe

CHAPTER THREE
The Divine Presence

My trip back to England after I left the Temple of the Caves in Northern India and my Master of the Shining Robe was without event so there is little use in describing it. The long ocean trip, then the railway with its stuffy little compartments and finally back again to the scenes of my earlier life. I was not, however, the same individual in many ways, for a great ideal had been given to me —that of giving to the world the wonderful truths and inspirations that had been given to me in India.

My estates and position gave me considerable opportunity, and added to this a strange eloquence came to me after my return to England, so I sought to instruct a few of the Western world on the problems which had been unfolded to me. The way, however, was beset with difficulties. Only those who have sought to educate the human mind can realize the hopelessness of the task. Day in and day out I hammered at the wall of conventionality and popular opinion which religiously and scientifically paralyzed thought. In many cases I met opposition and in still more an absolute thoughtlessness with no desire to change the condition. But still I kept at the task that I felt had been given to me, attempting to warn mankind of the great cataclysms, pestilences and sorrows which hung over them as the reward for their foolishness, selfishness and indolence. I gathered a few thinkers around me and also some who opposed my every move and who seemed to glory in each opportunity to tear down and destroy my selfless efforts.

One person especially appointed himself as my annihilator. Through press, pulpit and rostrum I was assailed, both personally by this individual and through others whose instigations were based upon his maliciousness. He was a scientist of the old school, one of those narrow minded individuals occasionally met with who in the spirit of the Inquisition fights tooth and nail for the perpetuation of antedeluvian concepts. For many months he railed against my very being, pointing me out as a scourge to the race, for no earthly reason whatsoever except an honest difference of opinion. Insult after insult he heaped upon me, spitting out his venom between clenched teeth, and finally challenging me to publicly meet him and prove my impossible theories.

The thought terrified me for the man in question was one of the greatest, most noted scientists that Europe had ever produced, a graduate from a dozen colleges and universities, indefatigable in his researches and unapproachable in his scientific reasoning. He had broken a dozen scientists and philosophers who had sought to question his statements. A colossal mentality and an unbreakable will with a convincing power of eloquence listed him as one of the materialistic marvels of his age. Although I realized the truth of my statements, the idea of my attempting to debate him upon his own ground seemed ridiculous for though what I said might ring true in the caves of the Himalayas —how would it sound before a group of physical scientists who did not believe anything which they could not see, weigh and measure? I was minded to refuse but something within my being whispered "No." So with much hesitation and many qualms I accepted his ultimatum and arrangements were settled that on a certain Friday evening I was to debate and discuss with him the continuity of human consciousness, mental evolution and the existence of the sacred schools of wisdom in the heart of the unknown East.

As the hours drew closer a peculiar sickening sensation made itself felt in the pit of my stomach and my knees wabbled in a rather undignified manner as I got into my cab and headed for the gloomy walls of a certain local club where scientists and bookworms were accustomed to gather. I felt pretty sure of what my opponent was going to say but I had no idea whatsoever of how I was going to answer his attack in a manner convincing to materialists. So with fear and trepidation and a mental hope that my opponent would be kind, which I greatly doubted, I entered the club and mingled with the group of London philosophers and scientists who composed it. The professor with whom I was going to debate was introduced to me and I met my rabid disqualifier for the first time.

He was a short portly gentlemen in a nice fitting, black Prince Albert and striped trousers. His two steely gray eyes, divided by a very hooked nose, shone out from beneath brows of Darwinian proportion. He was very much bespectacled and heavily bewhiskered and his gold pince nez insisted on sliding down his nose at the critical moment. When we were introduced he looked me over with the air of a physician examining a specimen, answered "Humph!," and turning on his heel walked away his hands clasped beneath his coat-tails. (The reader will of course realize that this put me entirely at my ease.) I felt like a tiny Lilliputian entirely surrounded by a mountain range of massive brows, weighty intellects and overwhelming pomposity and I also not a little feared the raging lions and tigers which intuition told me lived in the fastnesses of these mountains.

Slowly the exponents of worldly wisdom gathered and seating themselves in the massive leather arm-chairs whispered together in awful tones from the midst of clouds of tobacco smoke. Of course I imagined that they were talking about me—probably sympathizing with my dying cause.

As I seated myself beside the professor on the small rostrum some fourscore pairs of spectacles reflected a dazzling light in my face and I seemed gazing out on a blank void edged with gleaming stars. As these exponents of learning, lost arts, and buried sciences, gazed analytically at my shrinking figure which grew smaller as the moments passed, the professor rose, and carefully arranging his notes, placed his spectacles once more, (fitting on an extra lens), cleared his throat, balanced one elbow on the reading desk and gazed benignly over the top of his glasses at the assembled group.

"Ahem!—It is indeed a pleasure to address you for a few moments on this problem. There is nothing more interesting than the analysis of psychomo, blood clots on the brain in various forms of non-violent insanity and mental unbalance such as my opponent suffers from."

He then began quoting eminent authorities on the problem and misquoting me profusely. As the moments passed the professor's ire rose. He heaped infamy upon insult in endless procession, grew red around the collar band and puffed excitedly. Most of his verbose outbreaks centralized upon the first point, namely, that I was dangerously insane, completely irresponsible, and that my only possible use in the world was to die in order that scientists might have the privilege of performing a postmortem autopsy upon my cerebral vesticles purely in the interest of research. (At this point the professor's glasses fell off and he rearranged his notes.)

"Friends and fellow scientists, the theory of mental evolution is tommyrot, pure and simple; the outpouring of a demented imagination perpetuated only through lunatics such as the one sitting beside me now. I will defy him to prove that anything proceeds protoplasm or follows disintegration or incineration!"

The professor then continued to explain life as being something coming from nothing through a series of scientific deductions and returning from whence it came through another series of physiological inductions. He proved (to his own satisfaction) that neither God nor spirit, life, or any energy outside of matter, was necessary in the perpetuation and procreation of specie, but that a full and complete knowledge of this indispensable fact was the basic outpouring of modern, unapproachable science. (Hearty applause at this point.)

The professor bowed and slipped one thumb under his vest flap exposing a massive gold watch-chain draped artistically across an astonishing expanse of white waistcoat.

It appeared that the professor was quite a religious man for he quoted Scripture glibly and with evident gusto to discredit the doctrine of physical rebirth taught in the East and which I had been promulgating in my studies. He quoted various scientific authorities in profusion and finally wound up by presenting me with a series of questions which he demanded that I answer if I expected even a moment's recognition from the infallible sciences of which he was the omnipresent incarnation.

Handing me the slip of paper containing the questions, typewritten in mathematical precision, he sat down—a whirlwind of personality and the most perfect example of self-conceit that it has ever been my privilege to gaze upon.

I was broken. I had no oratorial harangue to come back with and I felt that my knowledge—although I knew it was true—based upon only an improbable story of apparently impossible happenings would carry no weight among this band of thoughtless thinkers and second hand mental gymnasts.

I rose to my feet. A deep hush and a rather blank atmosphere surrounded me—not half so empty however as my own mind which seemed incapable of any expression. What I was going to say I had no idea of and the slip of paper in my hand seemed a living coal which I longed to drop.

I was the most miserable thing on the face of the earth, none excepted, and a chuckle from the professor showed that he realized this fact. (Of course it was a very low, refined chuckle.)

I had been standing some thirty seconds, which seemed like as many years, trying to gather some word or thought from the ethers which swirled in my brain—when suddenly a hand was placed upon my shoulder, and a voice whispered in my ear,

"Have courage, you are not alone."

I must have started violently although it appeared that no one noticed me. The voice was that of the Master I had left in Thibet and his hand rested upon my shoulder as it had that fatal night in the Temple of the Caves. In some mysterious way I seemed to see him there, standing behind me, his robe flowing in silver and opal, and with a great courage which seemed born of divine inspiration I opened my mouth and started to speak—words that I did not understand myself but which flowed in an endless stream with a power and eloquence unquestionable.

(To be continued.)

Prometheus the Eternal Sufferer

THE seer gazing out into the endless ages of the past sees a phantom file of Mighty Ones passing like spectres through the eons of the past; mighty powers in world creation these silent shadowy Unknown Ones pass down the endless corridors of time. Living, suffering and dying the Divine Illuminators serve a world that knows them not.

Once there was a seeker who sought to learn the meaning of life with its compound riddle but for him the great compassion, the realization of truth and the knowledge of nature's sublime laws were still shrouded in the Great Uncertainty. So one night he was taken far away from the haunts of men by a guide he could not see and a strange story was unfolded to him which made life different than it had ever been before.

This searcher after knowledge wandered over many mountains and through the deep blue of an endless sky on wings of unknown power. Guided by some subtle force he was carried to the base of a mighty mountain which rose broken and twisted by nature's upheavals. It was a gloomy mountain whose lava-blackened rocks and lofty sides were seamed and broken as they reached up to touch the blue above. Slowly the student was carried up the mountain through the shades of evening and as he ascended one lonely pinnacle rose above the rest like the mighty needle of the Matterhorn.

As he neared the ragged crest a strange sight met his vision and he gave a gasp of astonishment. There stretched upon the bare stones was a human body—unprotected by even a single garment from the icy blasts of snow! The form writhed and struggled in mortal agony as it feebly sought with the puny strength of man to loosen its bonds of steel which seemed cast by the gods themselves. The figure was chained to a great rock by four shackles held down by steel stakes driven deep into the stone; the arms and legs were spread and the tortured figure was literally crucified upon the gigantic granite boulder.

As the student drew near he shuddered for the rock was red with the blood of the agonized captive and a mighty vulture—greater far than any bird known to earth—clawed and tore at the side of the chained man! The student turned aside his head, the sight was too terrible and he could not stand it, but a power greater than his own forced his gaze back to the figure chained to the living cross of granite. As he stood there his eyes held by he knew not what, a low moan escaped from the lips of the sufferer and two great eyes wet with tears of anguish and suffering turned toward the man who had come from earth. No word the chained being uttered, no plea for help, but the agony of his soul poured out from those great eyes of sorrow, reaching to the very depth of the seeker's soul.

"Who are you?" asked the one of earth, gazing at the massive brow bordered with locks of golden hair.

"I—" gasped the Crucified One, "I am Prometheus—Friend of Man."

"Why are you chained to this rock?"

"Because," murmured the chained victim, while the vulture still gnawed at the gaping hole in his side—"Because I rebelled against Jupiter, Lord of Heaven. Not because I loved Him less but because the woes of mankind pained me more. When the gods decreed that man must die I stole the Sacred Fire from heaven and brought it down to earth that man might live. For this I have been chained to the rock where I must remain forever unless a champion is found on earth who can break the fetters that bind me."

The student, sick at heart and in agony unutterable, turned away and passed silently down the mountain side back again to the land of men from whence he had come.

But each day a great sadness gnawed at his soul, even as the talons of the mighty bird clawed at the entrails of Prometheus. Through nights he prayed, through days he labored, until a great ideal was born within his soul. He would liberate the Friend of Man from that awful rock which formed his cross!

One night—after years of waiting—as he knelt in his little room a shining form appeared to tell him of the wondrous truths which he had sought. In a ray of light the shining figure stood and holding out his arms said,

"Come I will teach you how to liberate the dying Prometheus."

The candidate rose and passed with his shining companion into the darkness of a great unknown. As they went along, the guide of many colored lights spoke—saying:

"In the days when the world was young Great Souls suffered that man might live. A divine essence descended from heaven against the will of the gods bringing with it the light of Truth. This Essence took up its home in the body of man bringing with it the fire of the gods; and from this fire is born the mystic essence which feeds the mind that man may think; it has given him the flame of energy but has brought also the flame of war and the torch that burns the home, it is the birth of the passions, the lusts and the greeds; and now the Friend of Man is chained to the rock while the lower animal desires and passions of humanity feed of the life which he brought with so much suffering to illuminate man.

"Know you, oh son of man! you are the black stone. Within you is chained Prometheus the Light-Bringer—a divine intelligence—the friend of mortal things. But the perversions of man and the crystalization and degeneracy of his life have chained this World Saviour and the god of life is now crucified upon the cross of matter there to remain until man shall kill the vulture which gnaws at his vitals. Our lives—while we seem to live them for ourselves alone—are far more important than we think, for it is our duty to release the Saviour from the darkness of His cross which our own actions have chained him to.

"For what has man done with the fire that came down from heaven? Has he burned it upon the altars of his gods? Has he returned it again to the divine from whence it came? No. He has taken the fire of the gods, given to him at such tremendous sacrifice, and has fanned it into flames of selfishness and lust, wasting it and crucifying it in useless expressions of destruction, and has utterly failed to build with it the giant of strength and power who must release Prometheus from the mountain of stone. But there is one coming—the Strong One—the Child of the Sun—Hercules—and he shall release Prometheus from his ages of torment!

"And each one of you, oh children of earth! must become that Hercules, with the light which ye have found—the shining sun—ye must build of the flame brought by Prometheus the mind and the body that we may sever His bonds and pay our debt to the first Great Friend of man."

Slowly the mighty mountain rose before them in the sky and as they drew closer they could see the lonely figure still hanging upon the slanting stone, his eyes turned in agony towards the sun—that great globe of light whose rays must release him from his endless torture. Still the vulture with claw and talon tore at his liver, still the rock was spattered with his blood, and still in divine trust and a great peace that surpasseth understanding, Prometheus waited—waited for the prophecy to be fulfilled that a strong one should rise from those whom he had served—one who should release him from the cross.

The shining guide spoke.

"Oh, Prometheus, Friend of Man! have courage. Through the ages the soul of man is awakening and the time shall yet come when he shall know your sacrifice. Some day from the fires which you have brought him he shall build and smelt the tools to set you free. Wait yet a little while. The world is young and the curse of the gods is terrible, but still one shall come to free you from your bonds."

The divine face of the Sufferer lighted with a glory beyond the words of human to express.

"I will wait. And I am glad in my agony, for I love man. Though it be a hundred million ages it is not in vain. I saved man from an endless darkness and have brought upon myself a punishment that is great indeed but I am willing to bear all if man but makes himself great and glorious through my sacrifice. How little do those whom I have served realize the price that I am paying for their freedom! As the fires within man flare and burn, fed by the lowest and the worst, they little know or realize that there is One tied to the rock who feels in the anguish of his soul each perversion of the sacred flame. For not only does the fire light man's way but by the curse of Jove it burns as well. And the light I have brought them they have used to slay me with—but I can wait. Through ages unnumbered—since before the dawn of time—I have hung upon this rock. A hundred million times has this vulture of lust and fury clawed away my life, but the curse of the gods is endless for as fast as the vulture's talons rend the flesh more grows to take its place.

"I am the Eternal Sufferer. It is I, not man, who feels the most of pain, for his abuses of my sacred fire. I brought it in a reed from heaven to kindle on the hearthstones of the world but they have desecrated my altars; they have broken my most sacred vows. And though I saved them from oblivion my only fear is that they may not yet escape it.

"But when one is found who purifies my fire and harnesses its flames, freeing my light from the world of sin and abuse—that one shall climb to this lofty height and free me from my agony. Until then I wait. But as you burn the fire of life away, forget not Prometheus the Friend of Man who feels in the clawing of the vulture the abuse of that life he gave so much to bring.

Description of Last Month's Plate

The plate in the July issue of the All-Seeing Eye is taken, as the others have been, from the rare and unobtainable writings of Robert Fludd the medieval English alchemist and Rosicrucian who is said to have brought the teachings of C. R. C. from Germany and to have been closely connected with the early development of both Masonry and Rosicrucianism. The plate represents the hierarchies of nature and its great lesson to the student of occult philosophy lies in the analogy between elements, chemicals, planets, gods and celestial hierarchies.

The plate is divided into two grand divisions like the horoscope of astrology. That which is below the central horizontal line represents the inferior creation while that which is above symbolizes the superior creation. As the superior creation is the cause-all world there is laid out in this chart the superphysical hierarchies and the various intelligent powers behind manifestation. The upper half of the diagram is symbolical of the Masonic Lodge and the body of the enlightened Mason while the lower part symbolizes the unilluminated negation of being.

In the concentric rings are placed the names of the Powers of the universe as they are found in the various sacred arts and sciences. The sacred Hebrew names and the Sephira of the Hebrew Qabballah are found in the spaces between A and B. The superphysical hierarchies of divine beings and the leading angels and rulers of the hierarchies pass through the sphere marked by the line of B. Under C. we have the astrological worlds and under D. the natural, chemical, alchemical, mineral and animal kingdoms laid out as they are found in nature. In the outside rings beyond A. we find the primitive principles of creation with the part they play in the unfolding of a universe, an individual, or a protoplasmic cell.

This is one of the most complicated of the alchemical plates and can never be satisfactorily explained until the individual has unfolded a very high degree of spiritual sight and insight.

The passage of man through the spiritual worlds of nature and the twelvefold constitution of his own globe and chain is the result of conscious initiation which, until it takes place, conceals from man—because of his own consciousness limitation—the mysteries which are the heritage of the wise. There are really no mysteries in nature for those who have earned the right to know; neither is there anything concealed that shall not be revealed. But the only way that the unseen can be brought into conscious manifestation is when man removes the veils of limitation from his own eyes by growth and unfoldment.

Thus these plates which we have been issuing in our magazine have a very great meaning but like the sacred scriptures of the Ilumined are sealed forever from the ignorant by their own ignorance. No mere intellectual power is capable of unveiling the divine mysteries. Only soul qualities, the highest of the spiritual reflective powers, the co-joining of spiritual reason and mystical intuition is capable of producing true illumination.

The first step to the study of these plates is neither reading nor meditating but practical self-regeneration which will give the higher power in man an opportunity of expressing its own omnipotent knowledge. This plate contains the entire secret of spiritual rulership and analogy; but no more may be said about it than that each individual must file from his own organisms the key which shall unlock its mysteries for the wise designed these things for the use of the wise and the price of understanding the words of the Illuminated is to become illuminated yourself. This is done when the light of spirit shines forth to bring out the colors on the printed page through the regenerated lantern of the philosopher—his own sevenfold body organism.

The plate in this month's magazine is of the philosophical marriage and the philosopher's stone and is taken from the secret writings of Henry Kunrath. Its description will follow next month.

A Discourse on the Eight Perfections

AND the Thrice Blessed Lord spake unto His disciple, from the heart of His lotus-throne, explaining those things which are the Great Intelligences and the basis of union with that which is Above.

By his conduct is man's salvation measured and by his works is his soul ordained. Of these Eight Intelligences, which are the Ways of Perfection, should all men learn that they may sanctify themselves in the eyes of Brahma the One who Is.

So the Lord of the Lotus Lips spake, saying:

"The first Great Intelligence is the perfection of Perception, for he who perceiveth things has power equal unto his perception. And all things may be known by any who are capable of seeing them. Learn, oh son! to perfect thyself in sight that when thou lookest thou shalt see the Reality, for behind the veil of Maya is concealed all true workings. And unto those who see with eyes that God has opened all of the Plan is manifest even unto the least of the creatures, for each stick and stone tells of that which is eternal; each passing glance, each action and thought is a key to the destiny of a universe!

"Therefore, oh disciple, learn to perceive that each day new lessons shall come unto thee because thou hast found them in that which eternally Is. For know that all knowledge is about thee always but must forever remain unknown until perfect perception crowns thee with the jewels of omnipotence."

Thus spake the Blessed Lord of the First Intelligence, which is Perception, saying:

"Learn also that that which thou seest first is not the Reality save when through perfection thou perceiveth that which is invisible. What thou first seest is Maya the great Illusion but Reality molds Illusion and he who hath a right perception perceiveth the Reality in the expressions of Its not-Being.

"Know, therefore, oh Son of Man, that mortal perception seeth nothing but the shadow while divine perception alone seeth that which Is, knowing that the Reality casteth the shadow; and he is blind who worships the reflection. Moreover, know that he who perceiveth that which is not knoweth that it shall yet be the cause of that which is, that one is threefold wise in Perception. While he who perceiveth that which is, and through his perception seeth that which is to come when the Reality gathered unto itself the Illusion, is also wise. For know that the great Perception is not to perceive a thing unto itself but to perceive the action of Reality upon that which is not Itself.

"Therefore, perceive three things. That which is, that which is not and that which shall be from the union of these two. For the action of one thing upon another showeth unto the wise man the power of that which is unseen and invisible save through its reactions upon illusion.

"Know, therefore, Child of Earth, that perfect Perception seeth life in death. Not by denying death but by piercing the veil of Maya. Perfect Perception is that which seeth good in evil. Not by denying evil but by piercing the veil of Maya or the belief in that which has no Being. Also know that perfect Perception pierceth all things save the Eye of God which it beholdeth free of the veil of illusion.

"He who hath perfect Perception is great for he hath seen the Reason of all things and for all things. He who hath perfect Perception seeth one reason for all things for with his perception he has perceived perfectly that diversity is born of unreality and that Unity is the Divine Reality."

These are the words which the Blessed One spoke of the First Intelligence which is Perception and of the way in which a man should labor if he would be free from selfish selflessness.

* * * *

He then opened a petal of the Lotus and said as follows:

"Behold! I would speak of the Second Perfection—that which is the Intelligence of Purpose and the Perfection of Right Aim.

"By the purpose of a thing is it measured. The best work which thou may do, be it without purpose and intelligent aim, is Maya, that is, Illusion. There must be a purpose for all works and Right Perception which is the first Intelligence must illuminate the disciple unto the path of Right Purpose. There is but one purpose wherein man may be Intelligent in Purpose and acceptable in the sight of his Lord, and that is to be worthy of Nirvana. By its reason for being is a thing measured and a man who labors without reason labors to no purpose. He who labors without ideal labors to no purpose; he who labors without sacrifice, labors to no purpose; he who labors without compassion, labors to no purpose; he who labors in selfishness, labors to no purpose. But he who labors for that which is Eternal—he labors to Perfect Purpose.

"Know, therefore, that before thou laborest for thy God, decide upon that for which thou shalt labor and by its choice shall the labor be measured insomuch as ye are chosen."

Thus spake the Lord of the Lotus upon the Second Great Intelligence which is Right Purpose:

"Intelligent Aim wherein man may be one with that which Is and true unto himself because he is true to all things is the basis of noble purpose. The Spark of the Flame came down for the one purpose that it might be Perfect in Purpose whereas now it is imperfect in purpose. Wherefore man is to perfect Purpose by being one in his ideals with Reality.

"There is but one Perfect Purpose and that is the Perfection of Purpose which man learns only through the vale of Maya, where he labors in imperfect purpose with that which is not so good and that which is better —thus learning the Great Perfection. Such is the Perfection of Purpose."

* * * *

With these words the Lord of the Ten Thousand Perfections spoke of the Third Intelligence which is Perfect Speech, saying:

"Men speak many things. The wise men speak great truths, the foolish speak only words that they may listen to themselves. These words mean nothing save to the wise man who learns from them that the speakers of them are fools.

"Therefore of Perfect Speech I would say: speak not too much for he who wasteth words wasteth life as words are living things. By much speaking man becometh careless of his words which then lose their meaning and are but sounds. Yet by much thinking man speaketh little and so becometh Perfect in Speech, whereas he sayeth much less in words but infinitely more in Truth. For Perfect Speech meaneth that all words shall be of Truth and not of Illusion. The man who speaketh with his mouth sayeth nothing but when he speaketh with the spirit he sayeth that which is wise.

"Therefore it is that man should be Perfect of Speech and intelligent of words, which we know as the Third Great Intelligence."

And then spake the Blessed Lord of the Intelligence of Perfect Speech, saying:

"Perfect speech is kind and sayeth only that which is true and serveth three:—the one spoken to, the one speaking, and God who hears them both.

"He who would know the bliss of union with his Lord must have control of tongue that he sayeth not that which is untrue, that which is hateful, that which injureth, or that which teareth down and is malicious, for these things are of death and not of life. And whoso controlleth not his tongue will never be one with the Immortals who speaketh only words of wisdom. He who is Perfect in Speech hurteth not another, being kind with that which is and generous with the Great Illusion. A sharp tongue hath nought with its God nor with Me, for he who hath a sharp tongue speaketh with the mouth only and useth vain words which, while often sharper than an adder's tooth, mean naught for they come from naught.

"Therefore, oh son! be Perfect in Speech that your words be kind, true, and not too plentiful; that ye speak with your mind and your heart that only which is of Truth a Reality and not with your bodies which are but Unrealities."

So sayeth the Blessed Lord of the Third Perfection which is Intelligent Speech.

* * * *

Then taketh He the Lotus and resumeth:

"This is the Fourth Perfection which is Intelligent Conduct—both unto thyself and unto those that surround thee. For know that a man of God who weareth the braided cord must conduct himself according to the law and must strive that his conduct be perfect insomuch as it is within his power. He who watcheth not his conduct each day soon becometh careless and faileth to conduct himself according to the Ways of Light. Therefore, I give ye these instructions that ye may live and conduct yourself in that way which is acceptable to Brahma.

"First, conduct yourself in simplicity that there be no forward thing in you which is not good in the eyes of the Most High. Be ye not first, neither be ye last, but where ye belong according to that which you yourself knoweth.

"Second, conduct thyself with civility unto all things and with righteousness unto thy gods. Wherein ye fail to do this ye bring upon ye the calamities of which ye know."

Thus spake the Blessed Lord unto His disciple at the foot of the mountain of the Fourth Perfection which is Intelligent Conduct, saying:

"By what my priests do so am I judged and as ye conduct yourself so men say do I, the Lord of Men, conduct myself. Therefore be ye ever mindful that ye conduct yourself according to the ways which are of wisdom. Give not to that which is Temporal but be strong for that which is Eternal. Conduct yourself in peace when others are in strife, conduct yourself in meekness when others are discordant, conduct yourself in simplicity when others are vainglorious. By this shall men know that ye are seeking for that which is Eternal and not that which is of Illusion. For by your works are the gods judged insomuch as ye claim to be the mouthpiece of the gods. And realizing that ye live not of yourself but of God, live that ye may serve others through noble conduct which shall point ye out from the world of men as one trusted and beloved of the gods as their divine messenger."

In this the Blessed Lord closeth the fourth Great Perfection, which is Intelligent Conduct, and speaketh of the fifth which is Intelligent Living. For behold he liveth only who learneth at the feet of the Lord of Wisdom of that of which life is composed. So the disciple listened while the Good Lord spoke:

(To be continued.)

The Ave Maria
Continued from page 11)

key with a power miraculous! Of body there was no sign—just the two white hands. And as the blacksmith looked he crossed himself once more. They were the fingers of the dead musician!

The wonderous strains of the Ave Maria flooded through the cathedral in thundering symphony while the white form of the master organist lay at rest—he in union with his life's companion. The clay was shattered forever but the soul of the musician could not go on until once more he had played the harmony he loved so well. The final notes died out, the fingers rested for a moment caressing the keys, and then a strange stillness descended upon the cathedral. It was broken then by a sigh so faint that only a few could have heard it, and those two white hands still reaching outward toward the keys of the organ drifted slowly away into nothingness amid the gloomy shadows of the cathedral.

They say that the organ never again sounded as it did that night—never was one found who could bring such glorious harmonies from a soulless thing. They often tell of the master musician who lived and died in the little village but the most wonderful thing of all they tell is of how he played the Ave Maria the night he died.

Impractical Occultists

THE greatest stumbling block that confronts students of the Wisdom Teachings seems to be the problem of proper application. A large number of so-called students are merely theorists living in a world of their own creation, separated by transcendental ideas from all of the practical problems of life. They live, move and have their being within a crystaline shell of their own making which they seem unable to break through to contact the daily problems of life.

The great cry is not for abstract ideas but for practical remedies to be applied to the world inharmonies and international diseases which we know as plagues, wars and economic disturbances!

Occultists and mystics who are not able to apply their philosophies to the great bread-and-butter necessities of life have failed entirely to grasp the real truths of Universal Knowledge. Why do we find so many students who have lost contact with their brother man? They live alone on the tops of mountains, gazing down with supercilious mien upon the tiny ants and grubs which appear mere grains of nothingness from their elevated (but not superior) position. Why does the student have the feeling that every one is beneath him in ethics and ideals? and why—oh why!—is he too good to work?

This list of questions might be continued indefinitely as one unexplainable why after another passes in endless procession—few of them complimentary to the traits and qualities exhibited by so-called students of the Wisdom Teachings.

There is no denying the fact that Mystics are unusual people but the strangest of all are the pseudo-mystics who are hanging 'twixt heaven and hell in a wonderous parachute of self-created concepts. Their eyes are upon the stars (with which they seek union) and thoughtlessly and heedlessly they push less fortunate brothers to one side, trampling on the rights of others, shirking with studious care their own responsibilities. They seem to feel, for some unknown reason, that the world should honor, adore, and bask in the presence of all who claim to be seekers of the Light and that all should hasten to co-operate in perpetuating the indolence of the average truth seeker.

The "mystic" feels and expresses in his life the idea that the world owes him a living; that it should honor, respect and support him and rush to his beck and call because his mind is filled with contemplation of the Absolute. Being engaged in such weighty and brain-wracking thoughts his inspiration should not be disturbed by the rent man, the grocer or the cries of an atrophying stomach but that some one gathered from the worlds of the unenlightened should do these things for him and so leave the master dreamer undisturbed in his celestial nightmares.

Let us study these questions, the eternal whys, and arrange them with the analytical mind of a logical thinker—free from much spirituality and theoretical concept—and find the underlying innate reason concealed behind these eccentricies of the exponents of divine wisdom.

An old saying is that the Devil is proficient in quoting Scripture and always does it to purpose, and just so the lowest qualities in human nature eternally seek vindication beneath a mock robe of the highest and most beautiful. When we ask the question—why does not an occultist work?—he excuses himself by saying he is serving the Lord, is concentrating upon world salavation or unfolding his consciousness through hours of meditation and other strange exercises which he is forced to perform twenty-four hours a day that he may prevent an earthquake, a tidal wave, or a revolution. Another will tell you that he cannot find anything to do that is congenial with his spiritual views; another is incapacitated by a delicate constitution, et cetera. This is what they tell us but when we analyze the problem we find that the real reason for the inertia among the "divine" is unadulterated laziness, which inherent desire to escape labor seeks to cloak itself beneath spirituality.

It is this innate quality of the lower bodies to escape the battle of the world which is the basis of recluses, hermits and cranks. First it is a habit, then an eccentricity, later a fanaticism, then an obsession, and finally a murderer. Man humors these lazy little principles within himself until they become giants and he is murdered by his own creations.

A large percentage of so-called students of mystic philosophy make no practical effort to be useful in world affairs or to meet the battles of life and the real reason for this is they are lazy but have found a pleasant, intellectual, highly respectable channel of human expression in which they can make themselves believe that inertia is a virtue. And whatever doctrine teaches that laziness is a desirable condition will be attended by an overflowing membership.

No one likes to work without special training. No matter how you enjoy a certain thing if you have to do it continually it becomes monotonous. The human soul cries for freedom from routine, and so our "mystics" assume various gymnastic poses. To quote authorities on the subject: "They aspire to soar as eagles from crag to crag." So we see some generously proportioned disciple of things spirituele trying to balance gracefully upon one toe on a pinnacle of ethereal cloud waves or to flutter aesthetically from moonbeam to moonbeam crying in ecstacy as the gentle zyphers flush his cheeks —free as a bird!

Upon this basis of spiritual aspiration thousands of people who could make respectable grocers, clerks, window-washers, firemen and floor-walkers are now lounging around listening to delirio-scientific outbursts and waiting impatiently for their avoirdupois to become transmuted into spiritual ethers that they may slip through the window, wafted on the gentle breath of Eros!

So, we may say by way of brief condensation, that our so-called spiritual works are producing a series of lazy failures who would not do an honest day's work for the ransom of Croesus. And to top irony with calumny they not only continue systematically to do nothing but they expect to be respected and praised for it and pointed out as glorious spiritual successes as they loll around waiting, like Wilkins Micawber, for "something to turn up."

"Occultists" with temperament are not uncommon. Some simply can't stand a breath of air! Others are overwhelmed with nausea when they contact an ordinary human being; some are shrouded in repugnance when it becomes necessary to converse with a menial person; while our scintillating lights of brotherhood edge gently away from such individuals as brick-layers, butchers and ministers. Most of our "mystics" have super-nerves and a large percentage of them have that peculiar disease which turns the backbone into a wishbone, said wishbone being very wabbly and lacking sufficient strength to permit the individual leaning himself against it. This makes it necessary for him to find someone else to lean on, to tell his troubles to and blame for all his failures.

A person who is not busily engaged in something is a danger to the community, regardless of his religion. Wars, crimes, pestilances, gossip and parlor-parasites are the outgrowths and products of the germ of laziness. And never mind how "spiritual" a person may be if he is not really busy at some material, tangible and result-producing thing he is a danger not only to himself but to others who might be infected by the bacilli he is propigating. The sooner occultists get the idea out of their system that it is degenerating to be one with the world the sooner they will really become spiritual.

Taking it as a general entire at the present time the mystics, new thoughtists and so-called spiritual students are the most unreliable series of people alive. Their word is not worth "shucks," their powers of concentration are nil, they do not know one end of an umbrella from another, and are as lazy as all outdoors. When put to work to earn their daily bread like the rest of suffering humanity all they do is stand around and try to impress others with the necessity of realizing that an electron is smaller than a molecule or that God is all there is. This class entirely overlook the fact that if God is all there is that it is unnecessary for one part of Him to tell the other part about it. If each will mind his own business God will take care of the entire.

There is no class more dangerous than the soul-savers who having just found a little light become overly enthusiastic about it. They rouse you out of bed in the wee sma' hours, serenade under your windows or make you stand out in the back yard while the muffins are burning informing you that your present concepts are sure to result in a permanent Turkish bath for you after demise. It is the height of sarcasm to have some worm-eaten individual—whose handclasp reminds you that your fingers have closed over a clam, whose limpid personality has neither backbone, strength, activity nor even the human attributes of cheerfulness—come up to you with tears in his eyes and try to save your soul or illuminate your consciousness in the ways of success at the same time borrow two ninety-eight until next week.

Now comes a still more important problem —oh why are all occultists "broke?" There is more pecuniary embarrassment among our modern spiritual demonstraters than in the immigrant class. Every one of them are strictly up against it and when asked why they will answer that the world has not treated them right and that their high spiritual motives make it impossible for them to join the ranks of money-grabbers and punctilious cash profiteers who make up our business systems. The "mystic" will tell you that his tender consciousness revolts against commercialism, therefore he is not well fixed because he cannot go back to that money-mad world he left behind! However his conscience never seems to revolt against letting somebody else go out and earn it for him, and we find from proofs that when our "mystic" does get any money he is just as commercial as the person he points out as a horrible example.

Now, why, in plain English, is he broke? The answer is—he lacks concentration of purpose, system, regularity, efficiency and worst of all he cannot take orders. The average occultist will condescend to be the leader of almost anything but to be an office boy shocks his tender sentiments. He believes that his knowledge of rounds and periods should make him of inestimable value in a boiler factory and qualify him to be the president of a paper clip manufacturing company on general principles. The fact that he has a personal contact with God should highly recommend him in the world of affairs; when in reality it only places the taboo mark on him for the business man has found that dreamy mystics do not sell china well nor peg good shoes.

One of the main reasons why occultists do not succeed in business is the fact that the world is filled with a number of people, each one of them desiring to think as he pleases, wear what he pleases, eat what he pleases and smoke stogies if he so desires. When he goes to buy a pair of shoes or have an inch sawed off of his cork leg and the salesman tries to baptise him or initiate him into the value of hops tea, he does not usually return but goes where they sell shoes instead of scintillating advice.

There is a very wide gap between heaven and earth and the business man who lives in heaven all the time will undoubtedly lose his customers. Heaven is a very abstract space, it does not satisfy an appetite nor vulcanize tires and the individual who tries to live there all his life will undoubtedly reach his goal prematurely as a result of starvation. And the worst part it is that these "occultists" will never reach heaven by the routes that they have assigned for themselves but day by day in every way they are going further and further astray! Their theories will not bring down the price of milk in summer nor clean the mosquitoes out of the Jersey flats. They will not inaugurate an era of brotherhood but if the modern religious mystic got hold of conditions we would have a "smotherhood" rule instead. We have wars regularly, earthquakes per annum, pestilences, crime waves, et cetera, just as though occultists did not gather around their cold slaw like the farmers used to do down in Rumpus Ridge where they discussed the next election over the checkerboard.

And when all is taken and boiled down, in spite of much talk, there are very few occultists who have really done anything for themselves or anyone else which they couldn't have done as atheists just as well. All they have amassed is a series of intellectual concepts and theoretical speculations which have never been applied and would not work if they were. That rather hazy word "Truth" covers a multitude of sins; "the realization of God" covers a lot more; "the impersonal" is a mystic tarpolin, while "divine love" reaches entirely across the gamut between bootleg and blackmail. But all this does not produce honest politics nor do the great international problems adjust themselves through our mystic luminaries and if it was not for the work of a few who really do know and do apply, things would be in a very sorry plight indeed.

There is but one answer to the question and that is the practical living of a life of daily service and helpfulness in the community. When the student applies to living problems which surround him the theoretical knowledge—which is useless until so applied—he will be an occultist but not before. While the occultist evades the material world he overlooks one of nature's most fundamental laws. Let the mystic remember that he was not ordained to be ornamental but to be useful. He should also remember that hell, not heaven, is to be the field of his activities because from last reports heaven is quite able to take care of itself. A mystic who believes that heaven is to be his resting place and that he will be privileged to lounge forever on a bed of phoenix feathers to gargle nectar and ambrosia through sunbeam straws has a cruel awakening before him! He may as well get used to adversity right here because in accepting the Master's work he has signified his willingness to give up the comforts and peace which mark material existence and work in any way which may be given to him in the name of the great Light which he is seeking to discover.

The realization that the world's salvation depends upon the willingness of mankind to learn lessons is of great importance and students who go around fussing and stewing because of the adversity which surrounds them are not setting examples worthy of a moment's consideration. The world needs practical people, it needs better lawyers, better doctors, better ministers, government officials, and able citizens. Conscientious shopkeepers, mechanics and artisans whose work is better and more perfect will thus help to glorify the entire. All constructive works are noble and worthy and conscientious labor with the ability to master the unpleasantness of routine is necessary for advancement.

The average occultist does not realize what an important place a handshake fills in character analysis. Have you ever shaken hands with a "mystic?" Try it some time. You will find that his hand slips out between your fingers before you can close them; his hand is clammy, mushy and semi-glutinous while the fingers never exert themselves sufficiently to close; the arm and hand droops and the mentality, power and health is in exact accordance with the lifeless member. Their voices are sing-songy and no deeper than the front teeth; and they are prone to sighing which is a sign, we believe, of a collapsing diaphragm. Their backs are weak, their knees wabble and they are spending their lives eating pre-digested pickles and non-protein prunes a la sweibach in order to piece out an absolutely useless existence.

If these were outpourings of the Mystery Schools!—occultism would have died ages ago. But thank goodness, these peculiar specimens are not occultists nor students of anything! They are too weak in most cases to chew their own food—mentally, spiritually or physically—and are merely collapsing organisms who are using occultism as a refined method of disintegrating.

You will find the true disciple of the Mystery School out doing things in every walk of life whether it is driving stakes, carrying girders, building homes or cleaning drain pipes, he is at work. He sings at his labors while the weak and lazy sigh at their inertia. His body is strengthened by toil, his hands are blistered with the world's work, and ever in his heart he is the master mystic. For his hands have built the dreams of his soul into the things his brother needs! He has built homes to shelter the children of men; he has cleaned the drains that they might be well. His own work is carried on as a menial but he is the one who has won the game. Many a god has bowed in humble servility to one far less than he, while many a fool has stood on his hind legs to sneer at the divine!

(To be continued.)

A Knight of The Holy Grail

THERE is no more terrible product of human individualization than that great desire for supremacy, territorial acquisition and personal vengeance which we know as the cause of war. In spite of the fact that nearly every doctrine of mankind speaks for peace and that the very faith of the world is one of love and co-operation, still the eternal combative principle of man continues to bring down upon itself that terrible pestilence—that international disease—which we know as war.

War is far more than what the average individual knows concerning it. Not only is it a battle of living things on this visible plane of nature but it is also a terrible conflict of mystic beings in worlds unseen. The very elements of nature seem to conspire and strange creatures unknown unite with the endless stream of human passion—struggling, tearing and breaking. From the heights of the mountains to the depths of the sea all nature seems to be one wild tempestuous mass of seething, twisting flame-colored forces. The armies on the field of battle are but reflections of a mighty cosmic horde, struggling, wrestling, slaying and being slain in the living ethers of the invisible worlds.

Through all of the universe a great shudder thrills as human beings loose the animal within themselves which as a giant wolf rushes across the surface of creation breathing flames of hate, playing upon the weak and foolish, tearing down the craftsmanship of the divine with murderous savagery!

If war is terrible on land it is doubly so far out in that ever mysterious ocean. The sea has often been called the graveyard of the world and in truth, its ceaseless foam-capped waves seem like ghosts reaching ethereal fingers upward from the darkness of the deep. Great nations, worlds, treasures unnumbered, knowledge untold, proud ships that once sailed the seven seas—all these lie buried in the misty depths of nature's wondrous miracle where lurid shadows of strange swirling seaweeds alone mark the forests and cities of forgotten days. The lapping waves conceal in that unknown deep many a noble hope, many a great ideal; in these mighty depths many a brave soul lies in dark oblivion; and mayhap the restless souls of those unfortunates cause its endless motion.

Here too the spirit of war is loosened, strange beings unseen to mortal eyes twist and writhe in the foamy depths lashing the waves to fury; great streams of fiery hate nourished by thoughts of men impregnate even the ocean's depth with powers demoniacal. The bloodshed, the lust of loosened passion and uncurbed desire thrill through the mystic currents of the sea as through the land and strange, low, moaning sighs seem to echo into a wild mystic sob which tells of the broken heart of the world.

It is not man alone who feels that awful break which stays creation's plan when the leperous pest of war is loosened, but both God and nature combine in sorrow at human ignorance and man's perversion. Plant and animal, stone and star, all feel when the red powers of Mars are loosened, all nature shudders and armies of mystic demons struggle in the clouds of smoke and gas that cover a battlefield. The salamanders battle in the flame of the firebrand and carry with lustful gleam the sparks that lay a nation bare, the twisting undines surge through the ocean clouds of spray, while from the skies the slyphs launch hurricanes of gas and wind upon that puny being called Man who feeds the worst in all the universe with his hates and his desires.

As the gods of creation wrestled in the throes of cosmic birth, so those flaming demons of darkness and armies of hate live on that mystic something—that strange effluvia of death—which rises as an unnamed stench from the battlefields of a great war! Like the drunkard gloating over the alcohol which destroys him, like the drug fiend and the morphine to which he is a slave, so the demons of death and hate live and grow strong, for a time at least, upon the thoughts and hates of man which rise in a great cloud of murky hue and float over man's greatest perversion.

All over the world this perverted energy is felt, the internal fires of the earth are loosened and streams of lava pour down the mountain side, the curse of pestilence and crime bathes the world in blood. Each country, city and hamlet feels the presence of the Angel of Death as the powers of hell are freed from the bonds of decency. The Spirit of the Plagues, that brooding shadow that bespeaks mortal doom, carved by human thoughts from the unformed substances of chaos, hovers as a great ghoul of evil over the world which it blasts with its flaming tongue and tears with its clawed talons. This creature is the reward of war and is given birth when man forgets he is a man and becomes a beast once more—yes a beast lower than a brute.

* * * *

It was a gloomy night during the European war, probably the greatest struggle which the world has ever known, and the darkness was lighted—for those who had eyes to see—by millions of lurid sparks, strange snaky forms and creatures of an opium dream, the whole astral plane a seething mass of hate and glowing coals of passion. Already the low rumblings of internal flames warned that the end of human rulership had come while the beasts of desire, not human brain, governed the actions of man.

The ocean was as silent as a tomb, even the ceaseless moaning of the sea was so subdued as to be inaudible. Suddenly a low "swish!" and a great dark form rose out of the darkness to be silhouetted against a starless sky. A mighty ship was passing as silently as a spectre through the seemingly boundless night. All lights were out and not a voice could be heard, for the vessel had entered the danger zone.

The submarine warfare which marked the European conflict was a terror hard to combat and in breathless fear and trembling each passenger waited hoping that the thing they feared would not occur and that the crash and thrill which spoke of torpedo or sunken mine would not send the gallant ship to an untimely end. The captain, his hands clutching the rail, stood on the bridge peering into the darkness, while the crew stood around with bated breaths—for the ship was carrying contraband! Any moment might be its last.

Silently it ploughed on its way, the soft swish of waves and the low throbbing of engine the only audible sounds. Had the captain been able to gaze through the darkness and gloom that stretched out through the infinity of night he would have seen a dark shadow pass swiftly through the water apparently without sound nor shape. He might also have seen a thin streak of white foam pass silently over the surface of the waves towards the darkened form of the mighty vessel.

Suddenly the tense hush was broken by an explosion and a vivid flare lit up for a second the troubled water showing the long tube-like shape of the submarine shining with silver spray as it vanished beneath the waves. In a second all was uproar on the great liner and cries and shouts broke the stillness—for the torpedo had struck a fatal spot! Explosion followed explosion within the ship itself which reeled and twisted like a stricken animal. The hoarse voices of sailors, the cries of frightened passengers, the swift issue of command, the shriek of lifeboat pulleys and the unleashing of pontoons—all showed that a great excitement had taken the place of the silent dread.

A great cloud of mist suddenly swept over the ocean in dense billows shrouding the vessel and its terror stricken passengers in a gloom intangible. The last lights vanished and nothing remained save a surging maelstrom of shadowy creatures of the fog......

Hours passed and the rising sun scattered the clouds of darkness. But as it rose it shone down upon a troubled sea for the waves had risen to fury, fanned by a half gale from the south, and as far as the eye could see nothing was visible but whitecapped breakers. The ship had vanished. Here and there a broken piece of wreckage marked its resting place while an overturned lifeboat told a sad story all its own. The mighty ship was sunken forever from the sight of men and not one had survived to tell the story of its going for the storm swept sea had engulfed the last eager hope of those fated souls......

Hours passed, the waves stilled, and slowly the great troughs subsided until a great calm rested upon the ocean which stretched serene and blue as far as the eye could see, concealing all traces of night's tragedy. This is all that man knew. War had claimed another victim and the hungry flames were nourished once again by the life blood of the innocent. But there were other things that man did not know which nevertheless tell of a wonderous plan and a wisdom divine.

Somewhere above the world where the mountain peaks of eternity touch the blue skies of a celestial land there rises a single crag higher and mightier than all the others, clouds nestling among its precipices and cliffs. While storms break in the valley below the summit of this lofy mountain is ever bathed in sunshine. There rising from the very peak stands a mystic castle, a temple undreamed of by mortal man, a palace of rainbow tints connected to earth by a glorious pathway of flashing jewels and mist. In the heart of this mystic temple stands a wondrous shrine guarded by the pure of soul in the world of men. It is called the Temple of the Grail and is the home of the Lords of Compassion for from it there go forth into the the world the guardians of human destiny and the saviours of the weak.

As we gaze upon the mystic castle a shining figure passes out from beneath its lofty gates, a figure robed from head to foot in garments of shining color which gleam with the shades of opal and of pearl. Down the rainbow bridge of light the figure passes along a path which mortal feet can never tread.

Finally at the base of the mountain where it met the waves the mystic stranger stopped by the side of a wondrous winged boat made like a swan. Stepping into the frail craft which itself seemed but a dream and not a reality the shining figure stood and taking a thin cord of scarlet between his fingers pointed out through the blue haze which marked the unbroken skyline. The boat seemed to thrill with life and silently swift it glided away over the surface of the water, the waves were stilled as the boat passed and like some mystic phantom the shining figure standing in it drifted away amid the blue waters of eternity. On and on this beautiful being passed. The mirror-like waters of peaceful blue slowly turned into surging waves of mid-ocean, the mighty mountain that touched the heavens vanished in the distance as though it had never been and the tiny figure became the only living thing in an endless expanse of water.

Suddenly he raised his hand and the vessel stopped. Beside him lay floating upon the water a piece of wreckage. He leaned over the side of his mystic craft and picked up the broken stick and holding it before him gazed sadly at it for several seconds, his great eyes lighted by a divine compassion. And then the shining one sank in prayer in his tiny barque 'mid that endless ocean. His prayer was turned to the mountain that touched the sky, was turned to the great temple of shining pillars, to the mystic shrine within whose holy glow the Blood of the Saviour sparkled. His prayer was for the salvation of man and the redemption of the dead. As he prayed a great glow appeared floating over the waters. It was a cup formed of a glorious stone and in its heart surged a strange flaming liquid which seemed to pour out on to the waves below. . . . The shining stranger rose and held out his arms to the Cup.

"Lead thou, the way!" he whispered. And as the shining Grail floated over the ocean and finally sank beneath the waves the Brother of the Shining Robe stepped out of the boat. Instead of sinking, the waters became stilled beneath his feet and without fear or hesitation the Knight of the Holy Grail walked out over the surface of the deep, his white robe blowing slightly as the breezes fanned the water beneath him.

Reaching the trough of a mighty wave which seemed ready to break over and destroy him the shining figure reached the top of a series of mystic stairs which formed out of the water itself and seemed to reach down to endless depths. Slowly the Shining One went down the mystic stairway and vanished beneath the water. Down, down, he passed, the light around him growing fainter and more greenish as he descended. Darker and darker it grew until finally a deep blue night enveloped him lighted only by the glowing radiance of his own being. Strange sea creatures swam about him and as he neared the bottom of the ocean great twining arms of sea weed stretched up as though to encircle him, strange fishes and crawling things unknown to man surrounded him but none sought to harm him not even the mighty leviathans which swam in and out among the coral arches.

Before him, brought into sight by the gleaming light of his own being, rose the hulk of a mighty vessel, in its side a gaping hole where the torpedo had struck and shivered its form. It lay caught between two mighty rocks just as it had been when floating above, save that now the deep gloom of the ocean bottom covered the scene and its passageways and corridors were filled with water and swimming things.

The mystic stood upon the deck and then slowly he passed from stateroom to stateroom, from corridor to corridor. Just a few seconds in each and then he passed on. But from the darkness of the ocean depths there arose one after another silent forms who had heard his voice and awakened from their sleep. As he climbed in and out and down into the very depths of the vessel he gathered in the bewildered ones from the tombs of the ocean.

At last he entered a little room where on every side lay torn and twisted machinery. There caught among the wheels and pivots was a lonely figure—a youth. The Master stepped up to him and spoke in his soft, sweet voice,

"Brother, awaken!"

As he did so a strange thing occurred. The tense set face of the dead man relaxed and a mystic etheric form rose out of the body.

"Who are you?" asked the youth awakened from his slumbers, "where am I? what does it mean?" and staring around in terror and amazement he held out his arms to the Shining One.

"You are in the depths of the ocean," answered the master, encircling with his arm the shoulders of the youth. "You are now in a different world from the one you have left."

"Who are you?" questioned the youth.

"I?" answered the master, "I am one who has lived in the world of men and have become through my own labors a citizen of two worlds. I am one of the Knights of the Holy Grail, the Invisible Helpers who labor with humanity. Come with me and I will show you your work and mine."

On and on passed the Knight of the Holy Grail. There in the darkened hold of the vessel amid the machinery torn and cracked by the explosion of boilers were those pathetic forms that had not a chance to reach the upper decks. In every case the greeting was the same and soon a shadowy file had joined the Elder Brother as he passed on through the ocean's depths. Through the caverns of coral and forests of seaweed passed the Brother of the Shining Robe. Everywhere he found the darkness and in every case he brought the light. One by one he awakened the children of men from the sleep of death and gathered them together that they once more might see the light of day.

So the hours passed and the minister of the gods labored far below, unseen to the eyes of men, known only to the dead who lived again through his coming. At last the work was done and the hundreds who had been cast into the Great Eternity by that single torpedo were freed from the bonds of the unknown, freed by the Master of the Holy Grail, and shown the way to a life anew.

Slowly the shades of evening fell again over the ocean but a great peace was now upon the face of the deep for no longer the souls of men lay in darkness—the Master had brought them Light. The little swan boat of ethers still floated upon the waves and there slowly appeared, climbing again the steps of the ocean, the gleaming figure of the Master and behind him a wraithlike train of phantom forms. Reaching the little boat he stepped again into it and pointed in the direction from which he had come. Turning he spoke:

"Far up in the land among the skies is the home of the Lords of Compassion who are those of our own living and dead who have seen the Light and have labored for it. But a few short hours ago you lay in an endless sleep of uncertainty. Now you are awakened. Over the ocean and the battlefields of this war there are thousands so laboring that man may know of the way which leads to freedom and light. I have awakened you, now go you and do likewise to those others who do not know the way but who, torn with shot and shell, are alone in an awful oblivion."

Quickly the craft moved along passing over the surging water with the speed of the wind carrying away into the unknown the Brother of Light. Slowly the great temple on the heights of the mountain came into view again bathed in the glory of its endless day. The work of the Invisible Helper was done again and the Knight of the Holy Grail returned to the mystic shrine around which gather the Brothers of Compassion who labor eternally for the weak. . . .

Upon the silent battlefields, in plague-stricken lands, in pestilence, crime and disease, sorrow or death, man over turns his eyes upward to the heavens and the mountain tops from whence cometh his help. And in the moment of extremity the Knight of the Holy Grail is unfailingly there to encourage, to release and to inspire the souls of men struggling with the Great Unknown. And each day there are new ones gathered from the ranks of humanity who are ready to join that mystic band who bow before the sacred Cup in which gleams and sparkles the Life Blood of the martyred Christ.

ASTROLOGICAL REWARDS

Cancer, the fourth sign of the Zodiac, is the first of the water signs and is shown in the heavens under the symbol of a crab. Being the home of the moon it is a fruitful sign and has been used by the ancients to symbolize the Divine Mother and the maternal instincts in nature. Briefly considered we may analyze its general keywords as follows:

Cancer the fourth sign of the Zodiac:
- Summer
- Cold
- Watery
- Moist
- Phlegmatic
- Feminine
- Cardinal
- Tropical
- Northern
- Commanding
- Nocturnal
- Movable
- Fruitful
- Weak
- Unfortunate
- Mute sign
- Long Ascension
- The House of the Moon
- The Exaltation of Jupiter
- Detriment of Saturn
- Fall of Mars

General Characteristics:

Cancer is not considered to be a very strong sign and those under it must under general conditions watch their actions and lives very closely or they will not keep up to the best that they are, being apt to grow indifferent as to health and appearance.

- The most fruitful sign in the Zodiac
- Will power, fair
- Occasionally stubborn
- Usually changeable, being a water sign
- Kind-hearted
- Difficult to manage
- Artistic and dreamy
- Often negative
- Suffer occasionally from anemia
- Not usually good in speaking
- Usually fairly cheerful

Physical Appearance:
- Usually fair
- Often pale
- Short, round face
- Slender arms and small feet
- Brown hair
- Usually small gray eyes
- Upper part of body somewhat large
- Somewhat dull in temperament and appearance

Short stature
Effeminate constitution
Phlegmatic
Heavy
Usually grows stout with age.

The Moon well posited in Cancer gives rather full symetrical development of form while afflictions cause an overbalancing of the figure and undue development around the shoulders. Jupiter, if present in this sign, gives size and weight and a rather round appearance.

Health:

Cancer is often troubled with ill health and is subject to ailments in many parts of the body and when the moon is afflicted in Cancer there is often considerable trouble with the liquids in the body as the blood, lymphatics, etc. The opposition of Capricorn to this sign and its malific ray from Saturn often causes crystalization where an affliction occurs. The following are the most prevalent diseases and ailments:

Diseases of the chest and breast
Stomach trouble   Coughs
Pleurisy   Dropsy
Chronic indigestion   Asthma
Shortness of breath   Consumption
Want of Appetite   Liver trouble
Cancers   Ague
Chills
Inflamation of the lungs
Injuries to the diaphragm
Ribs
Fear of insanity.

Domestic Problems:

Cancer is not always fortunate in these being subject to fits of irrasibility and peculiar changes in temperament and cannot always be depended upon. Is usually fond of children however, happy in the home, and if of a highly evolved type harmonious and very likeable. Their success in this direction lies entirely with themselves.

Countries Under the Influence of Cancer:
Scotland   Africa
Holland   Carthage
New Zealand   Algiers
Granada   Tunis
Burgundy   Tripoli

Cities Under the Control of Cancer:
Constantinople   Magdeberg
Venice   Whittenberg
Milan   St. Lucas
Genoa   Cadiz
Amsterdam   St. Andrews
New York   York

Colors:
Russet
Green
Silver

According to Ptolemy the two stars in the eyes of Cancer have the same influence as Mercury and also moderately like Mars. Those in the claws are like Saturn and Mercury. The nebulous mass in the breast called the praesepe has the same influence as Mars and the Moon. The two placed on either side of the nebulous mass and called the asini have an influence similar to that of Mars and the Sun.

According to Henry Cornelius Agrippa Cancer, which rules from the 20th of June to the 20th of July, is listed in Cabalaism as follows: Of the Twelve Orders of Blessed Spirits, Cancer rules the dominations; of the Twelve Angels ruling over the Twelve Signs it governs Muriel; of the Twelve Tribes, Manasseh; of the Twelve Prophets, Amos; of the Twelve Apostles, John; of the Twelve Plants, comfrey; of the Twelve Stones, calcedony; of the Twelve Principle Members, the breast; of the Twelve Degrees of the Damned, the revenges of wickedness.

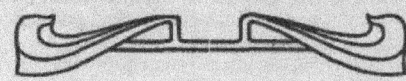

Pearly Gates Gazette

MEMBER OF ASSASSINATED PRESS — EXTRA — UNLIMITED CIRCULATION

VOL. 30000001   SEPTEMBER, 1923   No. 1000000000004

NEW RACE OF PEOPLE DISCOVERED

PRIZE FIGHT ATTRACTS LARGE CROWD

Bets ran high last night at Skydome Auditorium when Kid Castor the Gemini bantam weight met Babe Pollux of the eighth ward with Patrick O'Rion refereeing. Pollux had both his eyes closed and was knocked out in the eighth. Kid Castor was presented with a belt of asteroids. Smaller matches followed. The meeting broke up however when police raided the ring. A large number of celebrities escaped but the following appeared in police court this morning: the Hon. J. J. Jupiter, Mr. Wm. F. Mars, the Very Right Honorable Sir W. Dracoonus and Lord Aldebaron. The Duc du Antares escaped during the rush. Heavy fines were imposed on all offenders. A small star in the constellation of Virgo who was unable to pay started a sixty day term on the rockpile behind Pearly Gates early this morning.

STRANGE BOOK ARRIVES

The morning mail brought to heaven a strange book which is on exhibition in the lobby of the Skydome Auditorium all this week. Admission 25c. Several patriarchs and four prophets called this morning to analyze the strange book. At first it was thought to be the work of some practical joker on Earth for it contained selections claimed to have been written by noted people here. Mr. Moses called this morning while Prof. Nicodemus dropped in this afternoon while out in his runabout. A symposium of prophets is to gather this afternoon. The work, which carries the name "Holy Bible," is admitted to have certain resemblance to statements made by some of the prophets; many of the passages however are incorrectly transcribed and were not even recognized by the original authors. The book is quite a curiosity and well worth seeing. Doors open at 9 a. m.

They come from California, are white, and of varying shapes and sizes. An anthropologist here finds they are known under the name of Real Estate Agents. We thought at first that they were a profession or something but there are so many it must be a race. Hundreds have appeared within the last few months and the way they come from California would indicate that they form the greater part of its population. They are not a bad sort of people but since arriving in heaven they have been hanging real estate signs on all the planets and have staked out three quarters of the Milky Way in lots fifty by hundred and fifty. They build funny little houses which they stick on corners and then stand in front with megaphones shouting. Several eminent scientists here are studying the traits and habits of this peculiar specie. They are pronounced harmless, rather clannish but very persistent. Neptune, while out riding yesterday afternoon in his Stiltz Twelve, was stopped over forty times by three strange creatures who nearly talked him to death and even threatened him. The Pearly Gates City Council has recived so many complaints that they will probably issue muzzles and license plates for them and have them kept on leashes. What peculiar creatures the Earth is producing!

TIGHT-ROPE WALKER ARRIVES THIS MORNING

Prof. Epicureous Toegripper made the announcement on Earth day before yesterday that he was going to perform the most difficult feat the world had ever known and that the slightest slip meant death. Prof. Toegripper swung head downward from a trapeze hung between two airships before an amazed crowd of fifty thousand people. The Prof. was hanging by his toes only. This most daring feat was remarkably successful and won great renown for the professor. He slipped however and arrived in heaven early this morning.

SKYROCKET APPEARED THIS MORNING

PEARLY GATES, July 15, 6 a. m. By Special Dispatch.—A large skyrocket from the planet Earth entered heaven this morning and fell in the woodshed behind the Lord's palace. It contained an anonymous letter from the plant Earth addressed to God which read as follows:

Dear Mr. God: I think you are a liar, a fool, a hypocrite and if I had anything to do with creation I would have done it much better than you have. You have been wishing infirmities on me for the last fifty years and I am just about through. I am going to kill myself and when I get to heaven I am going after you with a gun and shoot you, and to tell you the truth I am perfectly willing to die if I can have the privilege of strangling you.

Very respectfully yours,
A. Nonymous.

This letter caused quite a lot of amusement in heaven but no special excitement owing to the fact that God receives hundreds of them every day. The Pearly Gates P. O. Department have sent out three rocket men and a tracer and all mail will be inspected until the culprit is found.

OCCULIST IN SWINDLE PLOT

The Pearly Gates grand jury are probing a swindle plot in which Artimodorus J. Cashhound, an occult teacher from the planet Earth, is charged with having sold Mercury, Jupiter, Mars and Uranus fake oil securities and an orange grove several miles out to sea. The gods admitted that Cashhound's magnetic personality was the basis of the sale but that the gilt-edged securities tarnished at once; whereupon they brought suit against Artimodorus for two hundred and seventy-five thousand falling stars which he is said to have cheated them out of. The Pearly Gates Detective Agency found that Artimodorus had left the city but they caught him late last night disguised as a comet hiding behind Gloombridge. Watch papers for further announcements.

SPECIAL ANNOUNCEMENT!
SECOND EDITION
(First Edition exhausted in one week)

"The Ways of the Lonely Ones"
When the Sons of Compassion Speak
By MANLY P. HALL

This is the latest work of this author and approaches the problem of spiritual enfoldment and growth in a manner both new and unusual.

The book contains six allegorical stories dealing with the spiritual development and initiation of mystical characters EACH ONE OF WHICH CAN BE PLACED IN THE LIFE OF THE STUDENTS OF THE WISDOM TEACHINGS. THE READER IS THE HERO OF EACH OF THE MYTHS, and concealed under the fables are many of the very deepest principles of occultism.

The book contains the following chapters:

The Maker of Gods.
> This deals with the regeneration of matter and the transmutation of bodies.

The Master of the Blue Cape.
> In this chapter the mystic meaning of the elixer of life and the philosophers' stone is given to the reader. Also the inner meaning of Alchemy.

The Face of The Christ.
> The mystery of the last supper and the great problem of the second coming of the Christ is taken up from the occult standpoint, and presented in an understandable way.

The Guardian of the Light.
> The duties and labors of one who seeks to be given charge of the Divine Wisdom are set forth in this chapter. Also the price of the Mystic Truth.

The One Who Turned Back.
> This is the allegory of one who reached the gate of Liberation and renounced freedom to return again into the world. A study in Mystic Initiation.

The Glory of the Lord.
> What happens to those who seek to enter the presence of the Lord without purifying themselves according to His laws? Read what happened to one, in the Tabernacle of the Jews.

The book is well printed on good paper and bound in boards stamped in blue. It contains sixty-four pages closely written.

This work like all of these publications is presented to the public without fixed price, leaving it to your own higher sentiments to show you your part in the work we are carrying.

The edition of this book is limited, so if you are interested send at once enclosing the contribution that you wish to make, not to pay just for the book but to help the work along, and you will receive your copy in the return mail.

Address all orders to Manly P. Hall, P. O. Box 695, Los Angeles, Cal.

These booklets by the same author may be secured by sending to Postoffice Box 695, Los Angeles, California, care of Manly P. Hall.

Price. These publications are not for sale but may be secured through voluntary contribution to help meet the cost of publication.

The Breastplate of the High Priest

A discussion of Old Testament symbolism showing how the spiritual powers of nature reflect themselves through the spiritual centers in the human body which we know as the jewels in the breastplate of Aaron. This booklet is out of print but an attempt will be made to secure a few copies for any desiring them. Illustrated.

Buddha, the Divine Wanderer

A new application of the life of the Prince of India as it is worked out in the individual growth of every student who is in truth seeking for the Yellow Robe.

Krishna and the Battle of Kurushetra

The Song Celestial with its wonderful story of the Battle of Life interpreted for students of practical religion. The mystery of the Blue Krishna and his work with men.

The Father of the Gods

A mystic allegory based upon the mythology of the peoples of Norway and Sweden and the legend of Odin the All-Father of the Northlands.

Questions and Answers, Part One
Questions and Answers, Part Two
Questions and Answers, Part Three

In these three booklets have been gathered about fifty of the thousands of questions answered in the past work gathered together for the benefit of students.

Occult Masonry

This booklet consists of the condensed notes on a class in mystic Masonry given in Los Angeles. It covers a number of important Masonic symbols and the supply is rapidly being exhausted.

Wands and Serpents

The explanation of the serpent of Genesis and serpent-worship as it is found among the mystery religions of the world and in the Christian Bible. Illustrated.

The Analysis of the Book of Revelation

A short study in this little understood book in the Bible, five lessons in one folder as given in class work during the past year.

The Unfoldment of Man

A study of the evolution of the body and mind and the causes which bring about mental and physical growth, a practical work for practical people.

Occult Psychology

Notes of an advanced class on this subject dealing in a comprehensive way with ten of its fundamental principles as given to students of classes in Los Angeles on this very important subject.

Parsifal and the Sacred Spear

An entirely new view of Wagner's wonderful opera with its three wonderful acts as they are applied to the three grand divisions of human life, the Legend of the Holy Grail, which will interest in its interpretation both mystics and music lovers.

Faust, the Eternal Drama

This booklet is a companion to the above and forms the second of a series of opera interpretations of which more will follow. The mystic drama by Goethe is analyzed from the standpoint of its application to the problem of individual advancement and its wonderful warning explained to the reader.

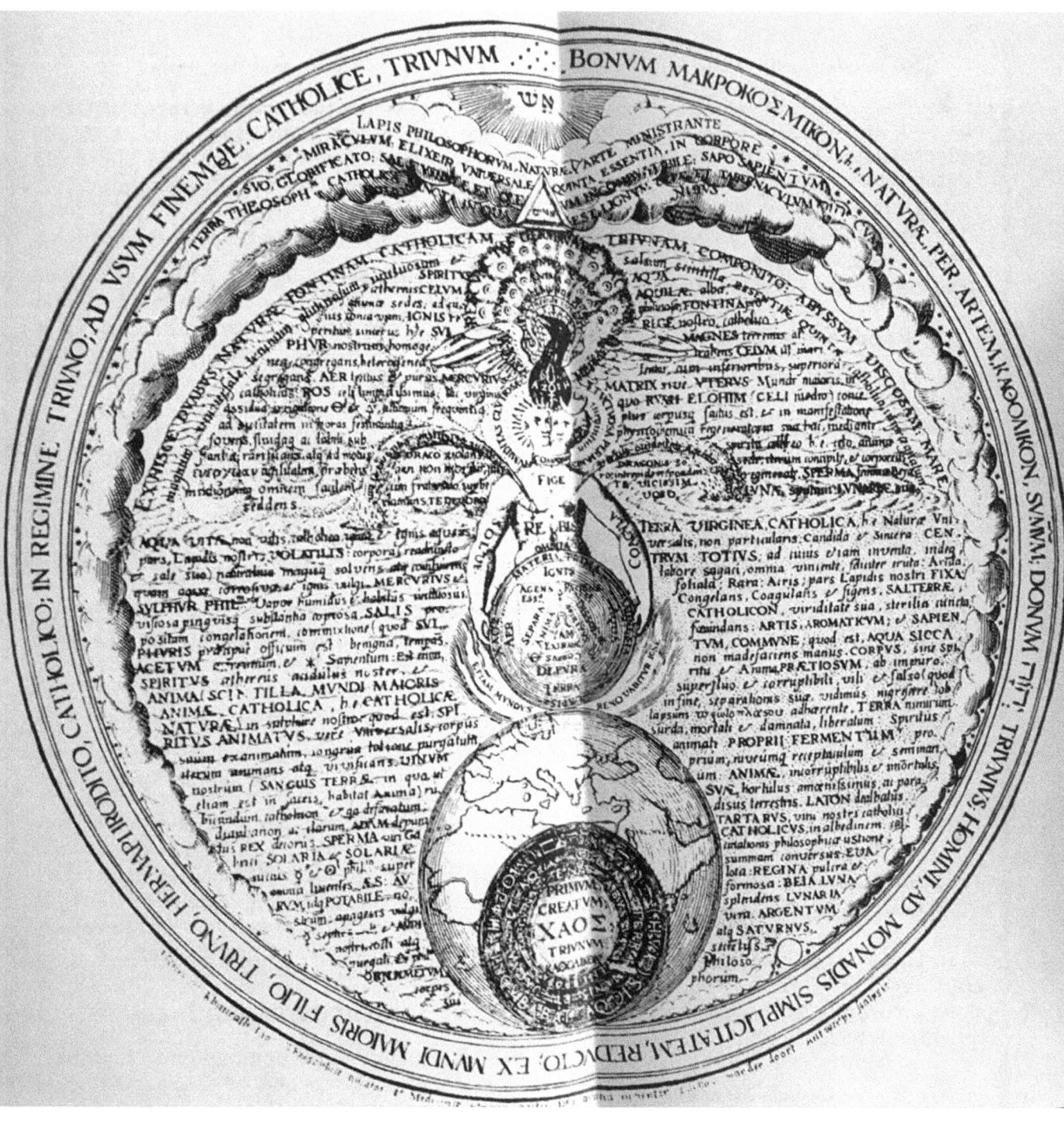

The All-Seeing Eye

Modern Problems in the Light of Ancient Wisdom

A Monthly Magazine
Written, Edited and
Compiled by
MANLY P. HALL

OCTOBER, 1923

THIS MAGAZINE IS NOT SOLD

"The Initiates of the Flame"
By MANLY P. HALL

A comprehensive study in the Wisdom Religion as it has been perpetuated through symbolism and mythology. This work is of interest to all students of mystic and occult philosophies or Masonry. The work is beautifully illustrated with drawings to explain its principles, some by the author and others of an alchemical and mystic nature. The table of contents is as follows:

Chapter One	"The Fire Upon the Altar."
Chapter Two	"The Sacred City of Shamballah."
Chapter Three	"The Mystery of the Alchemist."
Chapter Four	"The Egyptian Initiate."
Chapter Five	"The Ark of the Covenant."
Chapter Six	"The Knights of the Holy Grail."
Chapter Seven	"The Mystery of the Pyramids."

This book is beautifully bound in full cloth with a handsome alchemical cover design stamped in gold leaf and contains about one hundred pages.

This work is not for sale but may be secured through a voluntary contribution on the part of anyone desiring to possess it. All of our work is put out for the benefit of students and not for purposes of profit and we ask your co-operation to assist us in meeting the cost of publication and distribution by your own realization of responsibility.

"The Lost Keys of Masonry"
By MANLY P. HALL

In this work an attempt has been made to dig from the ruins of Speculative Masonry the lost keys to the operative craft. In it the three degrees of the Blue Lodge are taken up separately, their requirements explained and the real meaning of the Masonic allegory given out for the benefit of Masons and Masonic students. The book contains a preface by a well-known Los Angeles Mason.

The following headings are discussed in the work:

Prologue, the Masonic allegory, "In the Fields of Chaos."
Chapter One—"The Candidate."
Chapter Two—"The Entered Apprentice."
Chapter Three—"The Fellow Craft."
Chapter Four—"The Master Mason."
Chapter Five—"The Qualifications of a True Mason."
Epilogue—"In the Temple of Cosmos."

The entire presented in a sensible, comprehensive manner which can be understood by those not otherwise acquainted with the subject.

The book is handsomely illustrated with a four-color plate of the human body showing the position of the three Masonic Lodges on the cosmic man, also other pictures in black and white. The book is handsomely bound in solid cover with three-color cover design.

The work contains about eighty pages printed in two colors with a very fine quality of art paper.

Like all of our other works this book is only securable through the free-will offering of those desiring to secure it. Each person is placed upon his own honor and only reminded that the perpetuation of the work depends upon the cheerful co-operation of the workers.

THE ALL-SEEING EYE

MODERN PROBLEMS IN THE LIGHT OF ANCIENT WISDOM

| VOL 1 | LOS ANGELES, CALIF., OCTOBER, 1923 | No. 6 |

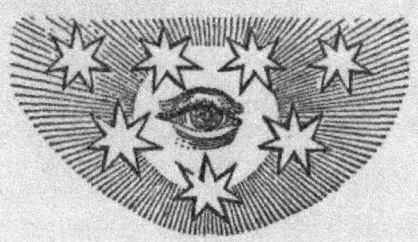

This magazine is published monthly for the purpose of spreading the ancient Wisdom Teachings in a practical way that students may apply to their own lives. It is written, published, and edited by Manly P. Hall and privately published for circulation among his students and those interested in his work.

Those desiring to secure copies of this magazine or who wish to subscribe to it may do so by writing directly to the editor.

This magazine is published and distributed privately to those who make possible with their financial support its publication. The magazine cannot be bought and has no fixed value. Like all of the ancient teachings which it seeks to promulgate it has no comparative value but the students must support it for its own instrinsic merit.

To whom it may concern: It is quite useless to inquire concerning advertising rates or to send manuscripts for publication as this magazine cannot possibly consider either as this is a non-commercial enterprise. All letters and questions, subscriptions, etc., should be mailed to P. O. Box 695, Los Angeles, California, in care of Manly P. Hall, Editor.

The contents of this magazine are copyrighted but permission to copy may be secured through correspondence with the author.

This magazine does not represent nor promulgate any special sect or teaching but is non-sectarian in all of its viewpoints. Suggestions for its improvement will be gladly considered if presented in the proper manner.

TABLE OF CONTENTS

EDITORIAL
   "Ye-a-a-ahs and Ye-a-a-ahs!" 3
   Question and Answer Departments 12

SPECIAL NOTICE TO OUR READERS .. 16

OCCULT FICTION
   Brothers of the Shining Robe, Chapter 4, The Master Speaks (Continued) 10
   Lord of the Flaming Mountain 20
   Lord Buddha 12

SPECIAL ARTICLES
   Explanation of Last Month's Plate 18

   The Occult Acid Test 9
   Faded Flowers 23

ORIENTAL OCCULTISM
   Discourse on the Eight Perfections (Continued) 25
   The Night of Brahma 28

ASTROLOGY
   The Keywords of Leo 27

MASONRY
   The Triangle on the Mason's Ring 31

PEARLY GATES GAZETTE 32

Thoughts—

There are many well known things that no one seems to understand.

* * *

Great minds and massive intellects are always surrounded by enemies of their own making for few can achieve greatness without grating.

* * *

In the eyes of the ancients the acme of attainment was simplicity.

* * *

Those who are absorbed by or enslaved to their labors never attain greatness.

* * *

None despise egotism as do the egotists.

* * *

Man's likes and dislikes stand between him and the thing he seeks.

* * *

The happy person is the one who is so busy he has forgotten himself.

* * *

You cannot insult an individual who is above the plane of personality.

* * *

We must leave our "feelings" so far behind we cannot ever hear them when they call.

* * *

If we did not want so much we would not be so dissatisfied when we do not get it.

* * *

Those who build with personalities shall see their building fall. While those who build with principle build eternal.

* * *

The world is filled with wonderful and talented individuals who are lost to the world and themselves because, alas, they are the first to realize their own knowledge.

* * *

A word of correction from the wise is better than the applause of the foolish.

* * *

No sword cuts the soul like the internal realization of failure.

EDITORIAL

"Ye-A-A-Ahs and Ye-A-A-Ahs!"
DEADicated to Our "Old Students."

OCCULTISM will never grow monotonous or lack the divinely human touch while we have among us those glorious ones who emit their radiant auras of self-achievement as they promenade the by-ways of our occult groves. Wherever we turn we find those ever present ones, who, like rays of sunshine in our troubled lives, breeze in to tell us of their accomplishments.

Let me draw a picture for you,—indeed it is a masterpiece! Poor, weary Mr. Doe, long searching 'mid the archives of the past, dropping pebble after pebble into the depthless oracles of Greece hoping against hope that some echo will waft back to him, sits surrounded by his thoughts, Hebrew lexicons, and Greek almanacs, seeking to find that which will bring him omnipotence. As he wanders midst those depthless pages which show upon their creased surfaces footprints where bookworms have trod, a voice rises and reverberates upon his dun-colored landscape. Beside him appears a strange creature—mayhap a denizen of some distant plane (Hoboken, N. J.)—whose description we will try to assist you to build in that floating substance between the ears.

His name is Solomon J. Wizenheimer and he holds the international occult talking record—having kept his jaws moving continuously for ninety-two hours without saying anything. Mr. Wizenheimer is a small man about five-foot-one but what he lacks in size he makes up in conspishiation for wherever you may look—from the Grand Canyon of Arizona to the Natural Bridge of Virginia—he is always the largest and most prominent object in sight. It is true that he cannot talk very clearly, having asthma and ingrowing diabetes; his glasses are about an inch and a half thick for he is nearly blind; his upper plate falls every few moments; he dyes his eyebrows to match his toupee and his wooden leg always squeaks when he walks, but he is not so bad looking for he keeps his mange under good control. As he stands beside the struggling Mr. Doe he is a perfect picture of the vintage of the year one.

"I see you are a student of the occult," says Mr. Wizenheimer. "So am I. I am one of the original class of Monsieur Whoop—you will remember him of course. He is the famous Slavonian Kabbalist. I studied with him for yeahs and yeahs and have written several books myself on physical regeneration and kindred subjects. I am the ex-grand master of the mystic Walupuk Shrine and if I do say it myself I don't think there is another person on earth who has come so close to the realization of the mystic. I see things. As I gaze upon you there is a peculiar greenish grey aura surrounding you. Oh yes sir, I am a seer; I go into trances! It is very wonderful when you get as far advanced as I am."

The peculiar greenish haze which was surrounding Mr. Doe was the result of that individual having become petrified with horror for fear that his studies would produce the same effect upon him as it had on Mr. Wizenheimer. The though flashed thru his mind that if that is what occultism did for one man he would leave it at once and join the first orthodox Fiji Island church!

Swallowing his innate feelings, Mr. Doe made a graceful departing speech and hurriedly left the scenes of his late labors, leaving Mr. W. to visualize complacently the effect that his overwhelming soul growth had had upon Mr. Doe.

"My powers simply hypnotize them," murmured Mr. Wizenheimer as he also vanished from the frame of our picture, leaving a refreshing vacuum behind him.

* * *

Of course some of our readers may feel that we have not treated this subject with justice and that we ought to have said a great deal more but we must ask them to imagine the rest upon the strength of what they have gone thru themselves while cloistered with one of these near-philosophers.

They have their place however, for utterly unknown to themselves the "old students" are the occult comedians and mirth provokers and are the basis for the laughter of the gods.

Students come up to us regularly to qualify themselves in art, philosophy, music and paternal judgment with the aid of rheumatism and white side whiskers, feeling that a snowy crest or an appearance resembling a spring freshet should deserve consideration, respect and veneration. A certain class of "mystics" just love to tell us how many cycles they have studied in this or how many decades they have immersed themselves in that, having a peculiarly distorted idea that their superiority is based upon the length of time they have expended in a certain work, failing to realize that ages of effort unwisely expended will produce nothing and that the length of time passed in study has little to do with the position of the soul in the great path—for some have done more in a few hours than some of our oldest "students" will do in a lifetime.

I must explain to you a few types of said occult mirth provokers whom we could not help but smile at if we did not realize what a tragic place they hold and what a tremendous sorrow that must come to them when they wake and realize how little they really know. The divine egotist is always with us and the trouble is the egotist seldom if ever is himself aware of his traits but blaming everyone but himself for his troubles, and claiming that others are simple because they do not agree with him, he goes on thru life never convinced of the foolishness of his own concepts. It is a tragedy in any line of life but in spiritual things it is doubly so. But for the good of those whom it may offend we must show you a few types commonly met with who are their own worst enemies and who in reality are never as far advanced as the average person that they talk to. For it is the depth of the soul, the true spiritual understanding and practical works that are the basis of occult mastership and the "real old student" is the last of all who could claim that position.

It is a hard thing to say, yet it is true and must be said for the protection of others. A large number of people who claim spiritual vision and first hand knowledge *have not got it* and never did have. Fifty percent of our so-called clairvoyants would be scared to death if they even saw an elemental and would run twenty miles from the first superphysical thing that confronted them, but as "old students" who should be conscious on all these planes, etc. and as nobody else is liable to be able to check them up, they tack on a few of these things for good measure to the awe of the foolish and the disgust of the initiate.

First I want you to meet Exhibit A—Mrs. Ophelia Wobbletripe—who has tormented the community of truth seekers for about fifty years. She is a dashing dowager who has talked some of our greatest minds into a state of coma then left them perfectly satisfied that she had confounded the Elders. Madame has studied with every known swami, yogi, saint, patriarch and master since the civil war and has autographed photographs of the leading religion dispensers of the modern world—(they would have given her anything they had to get rid of her). Mrs. Ophelia is a very much-present student who can always be found in the front row with her mouth wide open (possibly to show her gold bridgework), going into shivering ecstacies of admiration for some exponent of things divine whom she nearly drives to distraction with an ostrich feather fan or some crinkling note papers. Mrs. Wobbletripe can quote Sanskrit by the yard, can decline Hebrew verbs, has climbed Mt. Shasta and is the proud owner of a Syriac Bible (which she uses for a paper weight.) During the first fifteen minutes of her acquaintance you discover that she has been around the world fourteen times, has had several major operations and has relations married to the most eminent people in the country with a continuous list of husbands who pass silently to their only rest in the cemetary over the hill. She has a cousin-in-law who owns one of the largest salt licks in Arizona, has been prepared at Court without tripping on her train and has a brother who is an eminent bootlegger. Mrs. Wobbletripe comes from a very excellent family and has a grand niece whose uncle's sister is the wife of Lord Saturday, Knight of the Bath. One of her husbands, now deceased, (and who is at rest save when she joins him on the astral plane), made millions in Chinese ques which he imported for sugar refineries and her eldest son by her ninth husband is married to the daughter of Samoa's bone fertilizer king.

All this we get in the first fifteen minute's conversation, as I said before. She is subject to hectic delirium which she believes is a visionary condition and peculiar feelings come over her occasionally which she attributes to communication with the Masters, but is probably due to the little bubbles of uric acid poisoning which she extracts from her beefsteaks. Madame is a wonderful example of the so-called "old students" for it is safe to say that she knows absolutely nothing about anything except her own ideas which are the center and radius of her life. There is no use talking to the lady because she is completely satisfied with her own gamut of unconsciousness and knows more than any other person alive and admits it. If you are in trouble spiritually she will have some excellent advice for you which she has never attempted to use herself but quotes it verbatim from her favorite swami. She has inflamatory rheumatism, kidney trouble, is very much over weight, won't walk, and spends half her time at Madame Gump's who is trying to eliminate seven or eight of her extra chins painlessly.

Kind reader and fellow sufferer, you may not believe that such creatures exist, but they do and can be found anywhere that students of things supernal gather. She will always be found very much in evidence and expresses herself with great confidence upon every conceivable problem.

This is an "old student." Taking the Funk & Wagnall definition of "old" we find that it says in part: "things liable to decay or having lived and existed in a certain state for a long time." This particular type has lived in a state of coma for ages and will only come out of it when nature prys her loose. Many students have reached that enviable stage of crystalization when, having found something that to them is perfect, they sit back in complacent mental ossification and bask in the aura of their own accomplishments.

We will pass on to Type B. Section X. who is the occult antiquarian and has that wisdom which no one else can get hold of. He is the "chosen of the Masters" type. Prof. Nebuchadrezzar Nibbs has studied where no one else can go but with lofty superiority he condescends to allow others to drink occasionally at the fountain of his divine wisdom. Nebbsy is shrouded in credentials of a mystic nature, including a veterinary diploma, and being a member of several secret orders practices the pass signs every morning so as not to forget them. Neighbors watching him in the morning think he is taking calisthenics but he is only making the secret sign of the ninth degree of the sacred order of Imperial Bunkum. He has been a private pupil of the famous Sylvester Sandstorm, one of Matilda Brainfag's inside group, has studied at the feet of Algernon Spoutly and all the other leading occult luminaries. He will tell you confidentially what they told him confidentially, misquoting leading authorities with the ease and fluency of a practiced liar. He is always surrounded by a number of gushitive individuals carrying light cargoes of mentoids who found in him the resurrection of a martyr or the reincarnation of a saint and saviour within the first thirty days.

Prof. Nibbs admits that he is an old student also and he always admits it before anyone else questions him. Everything he does is in a secret and concealed manner— he even thinks in such a carefully hidden way that no other creature could possibly imagine that was what he was doing. Nebbsy admits that he is acquainted with all the leading occultists of the world and recognizes the soul growth in Exhibit A. He has had a very checkered career since he stopped working in the saloon which career he has perpetuated in a checkered suit. He is willing to share his superior knowledge with humanity for a reasonable consideration, said compensation being as much cash as the other fellow has got.

Nebuchadrezzar Nibbs talks with the dead every night, he is out of his body half the time and out of his head the other. (We sometimes believe that he got lost on the astral plane and forgot to come back.) He is surrounded by ethereal creatures and material dupes and a bald head, a wise look and seventy-five years of stone rolling constitute his stock in trade. He knows absolutely nothing about anything but conceals this under paternal eyebrows and a saged appearance which means absolutely nil and when asked a quizzer always replies that that information is only given out in the higher grades.

Having completed our analysis of Type B, we pass on to Type C. X 3, the Astrological Contortionist and Numerological Sprainer, Miss Delilia Wampus. No occult group is complete without her and she is with us even unto the end of the world. Her speciality is birth paths and evil aspects, she is perpetually suffering from acute angles and afflictions in her rising sign and can always be found seeking the hour and minute of some individual's birth and then informing them that by compound ratio or mathematical hydraulics that the Z sq. X means that their husband will run off with the chauffeur's wife or that their hours are numbered. Miss Wampus is a specialist at prognostication—she has prophecied every winter that has happened during her lifetime. She knows exactly when the world will end and is waiting patiently for a certain aspect to culminate for when it does she is going to do great things. Miss Wampus is an old maid—she declined three aspirants to her hand because their rising sign was not congenial with her own. Her best aspect is Saturn trine Jupiter and she never misses an opportunity to express these good qualities and to explain that they are the base of her divine understanding. Miss Wampus also sees things occasionally and is now concentrating for prosperity, feeling quite confident that the transit of the moon will assist. She runs her life by astrology, numerology and kindred sciences and plans out her daily work according to astrological hours. She eats astrology and then like our family cow chews it some more; she inhales and exhales sidereal time and has her tea on the table of houses; and whenever she closes her eyes she sees black horoscope forms. She has been pronounced demented by her relatives because she goes up to perfect strangers on the street and asks them if they have nine degrees of Taurus in the eighth house.

Leaving this specimen in its glass case we pass on to Exhibit D. one of the most interesting and remarkable examples of "old student" formation that we have. This particular specie is known as the "mouthpiece of the gods." After having passed through thirty-five or forty years of indolent probationship he is now a self-ordained mouthpiece used by the Masters of Wisdom to sell vacuum cleaners, electric irons, magazine subscriptions and to dispense the occult wisdom generally. Yes, among our old students we find a large number who are being used by the Masters and are in constant communication with the Lords of high degree. You will always know them as they sit around discussing the haircut of their favorite patriarch.

When we analyze this series of specimen we feel certain that the only thing which the Elders could use them for would be scarecrows and danger signals and there is no doubt that many of our so-called old students in reality are warnings that if we act likewise we may be as bad as they are. Between Indian guides, masters and departed swamis we are raising a wonderful group of "old students" whose particular form of insanity leads them to believe that the Lord has singled them out as exceptionally useful instruments—when they have dispositions like the old Nick himself and bodies below the animal standard. I have seen these mouthpieces of the gods tearing hair over the back fence and declaring themselves in ardent language tinged with blue and scarlet sparks of choice profanity—then half an hour later they lead a silence meeting and wish damnation upon their opponents.

These "old students" tell you confidentially that they spent the night hobnobbing with the Lord or that the Master So-and-so told them you were to loan them two dollars and a half or that God told them that the house and lot they want will flutter down from the ethers to them. We prefer to believe that the old student is demented than that the Lords of Reason are capable of such absurdities. They are our demonstrative old students and their intelligence is just below that of a mineral.

Altogether this quartet of spiritual malformations constitutes quite a percentage of our so-called orthodox atheists. They call themselves "old students"—no one else will call them at all for fear that they may show up. They have been put out of their homes as nuisances, most of them have ruined the next two or three generations thru their idiosyncrasies and mental acidities and now they spend their time snoozing through religion. Instead of having ripened with age they have green spots coming out on them and are fast falling victims to the spirit of corrosion.

These are our old, advanced students. They admit it, they gloat in it, glorify in it and wallow around in it never realizing that they are the most perfect specimens of unconscious egotists that disgrace the garlands of our sciences. Will people ever get through with the idea that they know something? Self-satisfaction is the basis of decay and there are none who know as little as those who think they know a great deal. Socrates said that he was the wisest man in Athens because he was the only man who knew he was a fool. Many an "old student" has told how much he knew and shown how much he didn't know to one he didn't have sense enough to realize was his superior.

The first thing an old student really learns to do is to keep his mouth shut and plod along. Are there any old students? Technically, no. But in this world of affairs those who have gained the most of practical knowledge have superiority over those who have done nothing. The true old student is known by his deeper understanding of life and its problems and not by incessant pallet-calisthenics.

The jawbone of Samson's donkey is still slaying as it did of old and many a suffering mortal has gone with grey hairs to a sorrowful grave, talked to death by one of them—said bone being vitalized by an "old student's" motive power.

Not one in a hundred of our so-called "old students" show any symptoms of spiritual age but the creaks that we hear when they chew indicates that the organism is dying out and that they are slowly passing into the Great Beyond as ignorant of their destiny as before, with nothing to say to their Lord except a quotation from Pythagoras or a couple of Patanjali's asphorisms! It is a very sad thing how little we strive to build for permanence and truth and how seldom we find one who is really willing to consecrate his soul to the truth and in silence and simplicity carry on his Master's work whispering his age in the wisdom of his thoughts, the depth of his understanding and the sweetness of his compassion.

The Chick and the Shell

MOST people are acquainted with the fact that chickens come out of eggs. This being an accepted theory, proven by repeated phenomena, no further consideration is given to the problem and we watch the wonderful processes of nature with a divine unconcern—seeing many things but thinking little about them. Now there is no greater lesson in all the world than the baby chick and the egg-shell. How wonderfully nature protects the coming in of its little creatures, how it builds around the unprotected form walls and barriers that the latent lives may gradually awaken without danger of untimely interruption! Here the embryo chick in its shell carries on, under the direction of the group spirit, the wonderful work of building a complex organism of blood, bone and feather, unseen to the eyes of mortal creature.

But now the great lesson. The tiny chick at last completes its embroyonic growth and its parent shell, the divine father and protector of its tiny life, now becomes its worst enemy. If it is unable to break through that wall it will surely die—destroyed by its own protection. Is this not a lesson in the study of man, his growth, and his development? Are not the walls and laws and the spiritual guidances which protect man in his early infancy the ruts and channels that he later gets into? Are not the concepts which are bred in him as necessary parts of his youth in later life often walls and shells which will destroy him? Are not the creeds and religions which have guarded the infancy of his unfoldment like the shells of the egg—which protect him to a certain point and then strangle him? Are these not Chronus the Father of the gods—Saturn who devoured his own children? Great light should come to the soul of man when he studies a problem of this kind.

Let us take it in another phase. Does not crystallization build around man the bodies necessary for his manifestation here? And does not crystallization also, after it reaches a certain point, inhibit the very qualities which it makes possible? Do not our thoughts build us and yet bind us by walls of our own limitations? It surely seems that they do. Our past concepts have built us and made possible our reaching human intelligence and yet, sad to say, there comes a time when our very ideals strangle us unless all of our life grows great together, unless the shell expands with the egg—which no crystallized substance can. It must break or else destroy the life growing within it.

Those who would go on to greater and more glorious fields of expression must break the shell of crystallization which holds them in, ties them down and places around them the strangle-cord of limitation. Yet in breaking this shell we must do it with reverence for has it not been for many years our protection, our shield and our buckler? Our love for it, however, and our respect for the labors and growth we have passed through beneath its protection must not deter us from breaking it, for its greatest joy is in the realization that its work is done. It may rend our hearts to break the shell but we will die if we do not and neither we nor the shell will benefit thereby.

All people who have set ideas are surrounded by shell. Sometimes these shells are large enough to allow growth to go on within them but there are other times when the spirit is cramped within its shell. We must be willing and glad to break away from the concepts that limit us. This is one of the hardest things in the world to do, for we all love the thing we have been associated with, the things which we learned when young, the creeds, the philosophies, the ideals which helped us to grow in the years that are past. They are in truth the fathers of the things we are and yet in order to grow it is necessary for us to slay the parent. This point is beautifully brought out in the legend of Krishna and the Battle of Kurushetra where the youthful prince, in compliance with the laws of Krishna, drew the arrow to the head and slew with it his own sire. Too often our spiritual channels of expression become too narrow for us but we need never be narrow ourselves, for when a creed begins to bind us then the moment has arrived when with the spear of truth and light we must slay our own protector lest he slay us with his walls of living stones.

So the little chick breaks the shell and comes forth or failing to break the shell dies within it and once more the father protector has slain his child with his loving embrace because the child was not strong enough to slay the parent. Like the seed in the ground, which is nourished and guarded by the green mould and yet ofttimes is murdered thereby, so the spirit of man is protected by the shell of matter which ofttimes slays its own son when the child does not rise triumphant from the protecting womb.

The Occult Acid Test

AS precious metals are tested with acids so the spiritual doctrines and ideals of the student must be submitted to test. None should be accepted nor rejected upon advice, like or dislike, but upon the pure unemotional principles of worth should they be judged. The sacred wisdom of the ancients is now being given openly to the world but at the same time there are many false doctrines creeping in that promise much but produce nothing. The days of secretiveness and the superiority of a few are drawing to a close and all of the true occult works are being given to the world freed from the mystery of the Middle Ages. Below we list a number of questions. When investigating the merits of a doctrine use these as the acid test. Regardless of whether you like or dislike the doctrine, stand by the decision that your conscience makes when it compares the creed with the ideal. If it be a true outpouring of the schools of knowledge, it will be:

1. A doctrine of effort and individual responsibility, striving to build and unfold each soul to perfect independence.

2. A doctrine free from the taint of commercialism, exorbitant prices and inner circles where only the financially elect can go.

3. Productive of individual thought and seeking to unfold the reason of the student, making him independent of his instructors rather than a slave to them.

4. A doctrine of evolution rather than creation, of eternal progression rather than a doctrine with an end.

5. A doctrine of cause and effect—labor for the thing desired—and not one of miracles and superhuman powers.

6. Free from the whiplash of plagues and terrors, not drawing you into it through fear of damnation.

7. Based upon principles rather than personalities, worshipping Truth and not the one who brings it.

8. Slow but sure, promising nothing but opening the doors to all.

9. Free from peace-power-and-plenty scheming and get-rich-quick plans of all kinds.

10. A doctrine of equality with equal opportunities for all and special privileges for none.

11. Fearless in its declaration of principles and conscientious in its effort to live up to them.

12. Free from perverted sex philosophies, soul-mating, and so forth; always obeying the law of the land wherein it is.

13. Staunch in its defense of the physical body, pleading for its development and growth that it may become the living temple.

14. Based upon the doctrines of compassion, renunciation, service, and self-sacrifice; neither gloomy nor melancholy but peaceful and true.

15. Free from much wordiness and mushiness, teaching all its truths in a simple way.

16. True to the principle that the destiny of a people rests in its own hands and that no vicarious attonement can save it.

17. Based upon the seven liberal arts and sciences and teaching that knowledge is the eternal victor over ignorance.

18. Considerate of all other creeds and doctrines, realizing and living the great truth that all religions are one.

19. Based upon the solid rock of brotherhood and cooperation and standing for the fellowship of spirit and of body.

20. Free from claims and pretenses and untouched by the spirit of egotism.

21. The last to ever say that it is great; seeking only to serve, and expecting no reward.

22. Strong in its demand for practical religion—taught through right living, right thinking, right aspiring and right purification.

If the philosophy which you are interested in teaches these things in a rational way, follow it, study it and learn of it; but if it fails to live up to these thoughts, shun it as you would a leperous thing for it will bring with it only sorrow, suffering and an untimely end.

This is the acid test.

Brothers Of The Shining Robe
(Continued)

CHAPTER FOUR
The Master Speaks

As I spoke it seemed that I was no longer a mortal man and that instead of a human brain my source of information was the mind of God himself. The presence of the Master behind me gave great courage and consolation so, daring all things while I knew that he was near, I told of the mysteries of life and of death.

As I looked around the room it seemed filled with white-robed forms and great streams of life and light poured into me then seemed to radiate in waves of courage from my entire being.

"How long will you search in the worlds of the dead for the living? How long will you wander in the shade instead of turning your eyes to the light? No matter how wondrous the implement, how perfect the plan—all science ends where the Divine begins. Between you and the truth of life stands a wall that nothing of material things can pierce, where even the reasoning mind cannot go, and there even the greatest scientists must stop—bowing to an Infinite All which they cannot grasp, measure or define! In hours of sickness man cries not to science but to his God; in the great extremity the soul leaves its reason and cries to its universal Father for courage and for strength. Upon the mystic wall of the Infinite science batters itself to pieces because it refuses to accept that which it cannot see. The greatest scientists in all the world are the ones who know that the visible is but a tiny grain floating in the endless oceans of the invisible. From the Invisible it came and to the Invisible it shall return and puny minds shall never grasp the path it goes nor understand the working of its mysterious power! Far from the eyes of man in the hidden hermitages of the Unseen are those who know its passing and are so close to the footstool of the Light that the secret things of nature to them are simple truths indeed. But if you would have the Light you must seek where it is, realizing that neither science nor philosophy, art nor letters, nor anything of man, shall measure the boundless limits of the Divine!"

It was my voice but the Master's words and as the moments passed he unfolded to the group gathered before me the basic principles of the ancient wisdom. He told of the sacred school of the Twelve Prophets; of the ray of the Black Light; of the Planet of Death and the sacred Lamasaries in India; of the Brothers of the Shining Robe and their labors with mankind and the powers which they have over life and death; and then of the children of men chosen to know the mysteries of God.

At last he stopped and my tongue grew silent too for there seemed no more to say. And so, dazed and bewildered, I sat down—with the Master still beside me. A silence followed my words, then a sigh broke from the circle of listeners. One elderly man arose.

"Your story, sir, is very remarkable. But what proof have you to offer of the things of which you tell? For years we have been schooled in human knowledge, to the proving and trueing of things. Can you demonstrate to us anything superior to science or greater and superior to the physical world that surrounds us?"

I was about to say "No," but the Master nodded his head and my lips uttered the word "yes." At the same time the invisible white-robed form of the Master descended from the rostrum in front of me and unseen by the group of scientists stepped over to an elderly man sitting in a great leathern chair.

Suddenly the figure rose and raised his hand to his eyes, crying—"My God! There is a face in the air in front of me. Two terrible eyes!" And with a cry he fell forward onto the floor.

Immediately the room was in an uproar and scientists and philosophers gathered around the prostrate form of a white-haired man who lay face downward upon the Persian carpet. The professor, who had been sitting next to me and who was one of Europe's greatest physicians, elbowed his way through the crowd and knelt beside the prostrate figure. He then arose sadly and trning to the assembled group, announced:

"Sir Richard ——— is dead!" A gasp went around the crowd. One of England's leading astronomers and physicists had passed into the great Beyond.

The Master prompted me and I spoke:

"Professor you have stated that science is unapproachable in its power. What has science to do now? Answer me a question for I have answered yours."

"This is no time for idle argument!" exclaimed the professor.

"Yes it is," I answered, now master of the situation. "If science is perfect and omnipotent, let it restore Sir Richard ——— to life."

"Fool," answered the professor, "no human power can do that."

"All right then," I answered, "there is something that science cannot do. Then explain to me, what is death? and why must all living things pass through it?"

"The organisms just stop working" announced the scientist.

"But what is the power behind the working?" I asked.

"No one knows," answered the professor.

"Yes, I do."

Again the faces of all were turned to me and I reiterated some of the statements I had made during the evening.

"The higher consciousness and the superior bodies of man, including the spirit, the astral body and the mind, leave the physical form by passing out at the top of the skull with a twisting motion to then function on the subtler planes of nature. The consciousness has not died but has merely discarded a useless vehicle to function in a newer and finer organism."

"How can you prove that any intelligent thing has left?" demanded a voice.

"How? Why by bringing it back." I answered.

I leaned over and placed my hand upon the forehead of the dead man. At the same time the Master stooped over me and a thrill of force passed into the organism at my feet. I took the dead man by the hand whereupon his eyes opened and with my assistance he slowly rose to his feet and gazed around in a dazed sort of way. A gasp went around the circle of scientists.

"Did you do this?" demanded one.

"No," I answered, "I am but the mouthpiece. The great Master I told you of who dwells in the Temple of the Caves in the heights of the Himalayas has been with me all this evening and unseen by you has performed the works to prove the truths that I have sought to give you."

Slowly the group parted and the wise men of Europe gathered in small clusters to discuss the problem as I passed slowly out the door and back to my apartments. I afterwards heard from one of the members of the group who talked with the professor after I left. He asked him, "Well, sir, what do you think of it?"

"Bunkum, my dear sir, bumkum pure and simple," announced the international scientist as he lighted a very black cigar and sent an attendant scurrying after a whiskey and soda. "A pure coincidence, my dear fellow, a pure coincidence, but of no scientific value whatsoever. As I said in my talk the man is a dangerous lunatic and should be confined. There is positively nothing in the universe superior to science. I know, my dear fellow, for I have been a scientist for fifty years."

"You are certainly a marvel, professor," answered the man as he walked away.

The professor stepped over to the rostrum and picked up the crumpled piece of paper containing the questions he had written and which I had dropped after answering them. He stared for a second or two and then put on his glasses—for all the questions were answered in fine writing around the margin of the sheet.

"Most extraordinary!" exclaimed the scientist, "When did he write that on there? I watched him every minute!" As he spoke the piece of paper turned to dust and disintegrated between his fingers. The professor adjusted his extra eyeglass and gazed at his empty fingers. "Most extraordinary! That fellow is surely clever. But he will never be able to convince me that science is not the last word. Another whiskey and soda, boy, my nerves have been completely unstrung!"

(Continued on Page 26)

Lord Buddha

HE came in a packing box bound round with bands of steel and iron, dented and battered by its rough usage during a trip of many months. The packing box stood unopened for many weeks before the sacreligious hands of uninterested servants broke it open and scattered heaps of excelsior and wrapping paper about the floor. At last the figure stood revealed—undoubtedly one of the strangest that had ever crossed the waters from the land of the blue lotus. Lord Buddha was a wondrous life-sized wood carving and even the servants seemed awed as they gazed upon his gilded form. Many strange stories had come with him from the silent East. It was told that the Master himself had breathed the breath of life into the ancient carving, making it sacred to all the Children of Light.

Be that as it may, the Lord Buddha was surely a thing of glory. His robes, carved with wondrous fineness out of ancient teak, were richly covered with solid gold leaf and many colored laquers, while his eyes were precious stones set deep into the dark wood which formed the face. Upon his forehead was a mighty diamond—one of the greatest that has ever come out of India. Even the unromantic were forced to stop for a moment and gaze in admiration at the wondrous figure of India's immortal reformer.

They took Lord Buddha from the packing case and stood him upon an ebony taberet in the Gothic library of the Chadwick home and there he remained shaded by the gloom of ancient rafters during the weeks and months that passed. Unhonored and unrevered—a breath of the mystic East amid the mold of the prostic West.

Lord Chadwick had always had a taste for antiques and his Indian appointment had given him great opportunities to indulge it. But the main reason why he secured Lord Buddha was because the Hindoos did not want him to have it. (When you know Lord Chadwick you know that that was reason enough.) We will not go into details as to how he acquired the statue for he followed a rather—shall we say irregular manner, not unusual among foreigners in the Orient. The Christian seldom asks the heathen for anything he wants but just takes it. If the native protests the Christian shoots him. So with great expense and labor Lord Buddha was sent to London where he remained in silent meditation, surrounded by cobwebs and the curse of an outraged priestcraft.

A brief description of Lord Chadwick may not be out of place at this moment. He was one of those particularly affable gentleman who is always a leading attraction among the ladies and a source of great inspiration to all who do not know him too well. While admitting his affability and his military polish, it is necessary, for the proper unfolding of our story, that we unveil certain parts of his private life which are of a slightly different flavor.

Poor Lady Chadwick had been dragged through a knothole and then stepped on in the course of being duly impressed by her husband's personal omnipotence and a strange pathetic expression appeared in her bleared eyes every time anyone congratulated her upon her choice of a husband. Not that the Earl was a tyrant or anything of that kind, just that a certain besetting sin went with the heraldry of his house. When the Earl was sober he was a gentleman but after a few hours at the club he became infinitely inferior to a self-respecting animal. Every time his lordship fell victim to his indiscretion a reign of terror descended upon the household and suffering and misery formed the family lot. Not always—just when Lord Chadwick was exercising his hereditary sins. It is a strange thing how temperaments become reversed under the influence of alcoholic stimulant for Lord Chadwick sober and Lord Chadwick intoxicated were two entirely different beings—like the old story of Jekyl and Hyde.

This is not a story, however, of family skeletons but is a narrative wound around Lord Buddha who stood, through all these passing months, on his lotus throne in the silent shades of the library, his hands clasped in meditation and his flowing robe gleaming in the half light.

A certain cold December evening had given way to the bleakness of a moonless night. Lady Chadwick stood before the fire in the library, her eyes fixed on the great clock hanging on the wall whose silent fingers were passing slowly round the ancient dial. A great fear oppressed her for Lord Chadwick and several of his cronies at the club had taken steps earlier in the evening which usually preceded one of milord's streaks of intemperance. This part of our story deals with the ancient fable of the worm who turned. Lady Chadwick—inspired by the flaring embers of a dying will—had decided that from now on her husband would have to find within the heraldry of his house some symptom of inherited courtesy and restraint. Reared in obedience, married off in perfect obedience, beaten to further increase said obedience, milady was about to commit Europe's most terrible sin—an expression of individuality. An unpermissible thing among the blueblood of the old country.

It was about half past three when a cab pulled up at the door and two voices broke the stillness whose tones were about as thick as the average London night.

"Five bob!" called a voice, "you heard me, five bob!—not a farthing less!"

"Stooo-o mush," sounded a muffled growl. "I won't pay it!"

"Five bob! you blighty, five bob!"

Then there came the sound of a blow. The voice of the hackman broke forth, this time is pure cockney, his language consisting of one malediction after another.

"Help, help, he's strangling me!"

"Shut up!" threatened a thick voice, "take thash and thash."

At the same time there was the sound of two heavy thuds followed by a low groan. Then unsteady steps on the pavement and a grating noise as milord tried to fit his key into the door hinge.

"Sh'wont fit—hic—sh'wont fit," he muttered. "Sh'mush be wrong key. Well I'll fixsh it!" The next instant there was a crash as Lord Chadwick kicked his foot through the plate glass door piece and unlatched the portal from the inside. There was the sound of steps advancing at a right oblique and as Lady Chadwick faced the library door the form of her better half appeared in all the dignity of inebriate nobility.

Lord Chadwick was a tall, broad shouldered man, heavily tanned by exposure to the Eastern suns, and with the muscles of an ox. He now stood swaying slightly on patent leather hinges, his tall silk hat over one eye and his evening cape dangling along the ground on the end of his cane. Putting a white gloved hand over his mouth he hiccoughed gently behind it.

"Well, whash you lookin' at?"

Without a word Lady Chadwick turned and with tears in her eyes faced the great open fireplace on the opposite side of the room.

"Whash matter?" demanded the nobleman as he reached out and hung his hat on an imaginary hook about six feet in the air, "why donsh you speak to me?"

"John Chadwick you are drunk again!" exclaimed his wife turning around.

"You don't hash to tell me, I know it! Hash such wonderful time!" and milord swallowed hard. "But what has that got to do with it? Why donsh you come over and say good morning?"

His wife remained silent and turned again with her back to her husband.

"Well why donsh you answer? Donsh you know I'm your husband?"

Still no sound from Lady Chadwick.

A strange expression slowly came into the eyes of Lord Chadwick. He straightened up and his face grew hard.

"Come here!" he demanded.

Still his wife never moved.

"I told you to come here! When I want anyone in thish house they have got to come. If you don't come right over, I'll throw thish at your head!" And he picked up a large China vase.

Lady Chadwick remained as before and without further warning her husband threw the China jar with all his might across the room. But he staggered as it left his hand and it missed her by several feet.

"You brute!" exclaimed his wife as the vase crashed into a great Venetian plate glass, sending fragments in all directions.

Then the thing which all his family feared happened. The spirit of ages of degeneracy and debauchery possessed him. Lord Chadwick's body slowly bent forward, and his head sank on his chest between his great arms which swung like those of a monster ape. His lips drew back from his teeth and the white of his eyes grew red and streaked.—the parlor gentleman had become the domestic beast.

With a scream his wife shrank back as the figure slowly advanced—his steps no longer unsteady but now like the stealthy tread of an animal. Reaching a great chair the Earl picked it up with the ease of a giant and hurled it across the room where it struck the old stone wall and was splintered to bits by the force of the blow. His wife, terrified beyond expression, crept slowly back into the corner of the room while ever closer loomed the form of her husband, now blinded with drunken rage.

At last the corner was reached and further retreat was impossible. She had stopped beside the figure of Lord Buddha who stood in silent contemplation, unmoved by the scene of confusion around him. As she shrank back her shoulder touched his laquered robe and the chill caused her to draw aside.

Suddenly, crouching like an animal, Lord Chadwick sprang at the trembling figure of his wife and with a cry of terror she jumped behind the statue of Lord Buddha. With an implication Chadwick rushed against the statue, throwing his arms around it to cast it aside, but though he pulled and tugged the figure of the Oriental demi-god would not move. It seemed rooted to the ground. As he tried to pass around it, it seemed that the robes spread out on each side and before the Earl realized it he found himself twisted and bound in what seemed folds of golden laquer.

Struggling, twisting and roaring like an angry bull he sought to escape from the statue. His wife watched in amazement for she saw her husband's hands and arms apparently growing to the form which he tugged and tore to escape from.

Slowly the minutes passed. Lord Chadwick's struggles became less and less until finally exhausted and enveloped in folds of yellow laquer he fell at the feet of the statue, his hands and arms still glued to its surface. The Earl was now thoroughly sober. The terror of his position, held prisoner by a force unknown, took all the hate out of his being.

"How am I going to get free?" he kept muttering and turned with pleading eyes to his wife. She, realizing that the fit of passion was gone, attempted to release him. But his hands seemed part of the statue and as she watched Lady Chadwick gave a scream of amazement and terror—the fingers and hands of the Earl were slowly becoming encrusted with a golden film! At the point where he grasped the statue they had become like the teakwood beneath them. In other words he was turning into an idol himself under the mysterious power of the sacred form of Lord Buddha.

As his wife stood there in perplexity she heard footsteps behind her and turning she looked into the faces of three men—all of them Orientals. They must have entered through the broken doorway.

"Who are you?" she demanded starting back.

One of them bowed politely and spoke in perfect English:

"Our names will do you very little good, madam, but we have come all the way from the sacred shine in India to take Lord Buddha back to his home."

Lady Chadwick immediately replied, "Yes, yes, take the statue—gladly! But how can I release my husband, for his hands and arms are turning into laquer?"

The priest shook his head.

"That is the curse of Lord Buddha upon those who defile his sanctity."

"Is there nothing that can be done that I may escape?" pleaded Lord Chadwick.

"There is no way but through prayers to Lord Buddha for he is the Lord of Righteousness and if it pleases him he may release you from his golden self. If not, you must await the end."

"I will give anything that I have to be released! My arms are growing cold and a creeping death is upon me!" cried the nobleman.

Suddenly a strange thing hapened. The mouth of the Buddha opened and a voice seemed to breath out from the soul of the statue:

"I am Lord Buddha. Ages ago I breathed myself into this thing of wood carved by the hands of the faithful. You stole me from my shrine, but that sin was not your greatest. Know you that those who seek protection behind the yellow robe of the Buddha shall not seek in vain. No man shall pass this gleaming robe for works of hate. I am going back again to my people who love me, honor me and revere me. But before I go I grant you life on one condition—that never again shall you abuse it. And if you do, as surely as I stand here today, you shall become a figure of wood and stone."

Slowly the hands of Lord Chadwick fell from the statue and the folds of laquer seemed to swing and sway in the breeze that came through the open door. The statue then steped down from its pedestal and, as the three Orientals fell on their knees before it, passed slowly out of the door, draped in its blowing robes of gold. On the ground as it passed were left strange footmarks pressed into the very surface of the floor. Without a word the three Orientals followed the carven figure and Lord Chadwick suddenly swayed with dizziness and fell across the pedestal to the floor.

* * * *

Milord suddenly sat up in his chair and gazed around him. The London Times fell from between his fingers and he slowly drew in one foot whose close proximity to the fireplace was undoubtedly the cause of his sudden awakening. He turned to his wife who was sitting reading a few feet away.

"How long have I been asleep?"

"About an hour and a half, dear," she answered meekly.

"By Jove! the most peculiar dream! You know you have often asked me to stop drinking—I have half a mind to do it. By the way, I dreamed that my statue of Buddha came to life and walked off—wasn't that unusual? I must go over and look at him again. He is the most————"

Lord Chadwick had stopped and was starring at the recess in the wall where Lord Buddha had stood. He rubbed his eyes and looked again.

"Good Lord! its gone!"

"Really," exclaimed Lady Chadwick mildly, "are you sure you haven't mislaid it, my dear?"

"Do you know," announced his lordship, "I believe I will stop drinking!"

Suddenly his face brightened up.

"I see it all, now," he muttered. "They told me that they would get it back. They are a strange people—those Orientals."

"If you think they are strange, they must be strange, my dear," remarked his well-regulated wife eagerly.

Milord sat down again with his feet on the grating.

"I haven't lived in India for twenty years without seeing something of Oriental magic. That dream of mine was more than a dream —it was Oriental magic. They have spirited the statue away."

"I wish the spirits would wipe their shoes when they come in," murmured Lady Chadwick. "Look at those footprints all the way to the door."

The Earl gazed at them. His mind turned to the shrines of India and a strange expression came into his face.

"What are those things?" asked his wife "will you please tell me, dear?"

"They are the footprints of Lord Buddha," answered the nobleman.

"What are they, John? You know I always let you do my heavy thinking for me."

"I don't understand it myself very well," answered milord as he stroked his chin reflectively. "But there goes the dinner bell and I must be at the club this evening—so you had better come, my dear."

"Yes, John."

SPECIAL NOTICE

Six months ago we started the publication of the All-Seeing Eye in order to find a practical manner of publishing and distributing the lectures, articles, and so forth, which our friends expressed a desire to have. During the interval the growth of the magazine has been as rapid as could be expected considering that it has never been placed upon a newstand or in a bookstore but as only been distributed at our own meetings and to those in personal contact with our work. As you realize, the fact that there is no price placed upon it has complicated its distribution tremendously and will continue to do so unless everyone of its present well-wishers cooperate to assist in its development.

As all of our students know, the magazine was issued for six months as a tryout and no subscriptions are good for a longer time. And any of you who subscribed but have not received the entire six numbers are entitled to apply for them until the supply is exhausted.

The time has now come when a decision of importance confronts the readers. Do you wish the magazine to go on? We are perfectly willing to write and prepare it as long as those whom we publish it for are willing to cooperate with us for its maintenance, but it remains with you to say whether it shall be done or not.

An analysis of the first six months of its publication from the viewpoint of the exchequer does not show a financial success. In fact on over half of our subscriptions we have paid the people to take it away. About forty-four percent of our subscribers paid less than one half of the printer's cost of the magazines they received and a large number who made promises never fulfilled them.

Consequently, while the magazine is not in a bankrupt condition, it has been financed to a considerable degree by money furnished from other sources for it has not come within nearly one-half of paying for itself. A few of our true and sincere workers have made possible its publication and presentation to you but the majority of our subscribers estimate the price of this magazine upon others which are procurable at bookstands and stores, overlooking completely two important facts:

First, only about one thousand copies are printed and the cost of setting it up is the same as thought we had five hundred thousand copies printed, and the smaller the number circulated the greater the cost of each magazine.

Secondly, all magazines on the market at the present time are either set at a price which covers cost or else pay for themselves many times over through extensive advertising. Many of the magazines which you secure at newstands could be given to you without any cost and still be tremendous financial successes and entirely self-supporting through the hundreds of thousands of dollars worth of advertising which they carry on their pages.

TO OUR READERS

These two important considerations make it impossible to estimate the cost of producting this work by comparison to those in circulation, for one copy of our little magazine costs as much as an armful of some of the popular periodicals. As a large percentage of people have been estimating upon current prices we have absolutely lost hundreds of dollars which they have fallen under the bare printer's cost. As for the expense of writing, preparing and distributing—that hasnot been even thought of.

We have distributed many copies free to those who could not subscribe through financial embarrassment—probably from fifty to a hundred a month. And those who barely pay for their own subscription leave the work itself to settle the deficit.

We shall be very glad to continue publication and launch the magazine for another six months if we can depend upon your cooperation—otherwise it cannot go on. The only way that we can reduce the individual responsibility is by increasing the subscription list and if we are able to do so we may also be able to increase its size, place in it departments to handle various special problems and in many ways make it a worthier publication.

You will find with this magazine a subscription blank carrying on it three coupons or detachable slips. Each one of these carries space for the name and address of a subscriber and the mount of their subscription.If you are interested in having this magazine go on, please fill this out as generously as you can and also get two other people who will be interested and have them do likewise. Send in the three together with money order or check for the amounts and if sufficient come in to make it possible to carry the cost of publication you will receive the next issue of the All-Seeing Eye on the 25th day of October. If there is not sufficient to meet the expense your money will be refunded to you by that time.

If you will cooperate with us we will be able to go on for we are willing to do anything to make possible the continuance of the work. The greatest good that you can do us in this line is to get two people who are interested and secure their subscriptions to send with your own. In this way we can increase our list three times and reduce the expenses nearly one half. This will enable us to put out extra work, colored supplements, etc., which we cannot do at this time becaues of insufficient means.

Please remember, friends, this concludes all subscriptions taken up to date as per the agreement we made when starting the magazine.

We thank you for your past cooperation and if you desire to extend that to us in the future we will try to serve you in as efficient manner as we can.

The fate of our little magazine now rests in your hands.

MANLY P. HALL.

Description of Last Month's Plate

The plate in last month's magazine which is taken from the rare and unobtainable work of Kunrath, the great alchemist, represents symbolically human regeneration and is also the key to the Philosopher's Stone. As before, the translating of it shall be left to you, because it is only in that way you can really learn its message. But we will briefly consider some of its most important symbols:

The figure rising out of the globe symbolizes spirit rising out of matter and consciousness freeing itself from the encircling and enslaving bonds of form. The two-headed figure represents the Hermetic union and the creation of Azoth the Philosopher's Stone.

In this plate we have the answer to the problem of soul-mates as only the ancient alchemist could explain it, for the male-female creature here shown symbolizes the occult constitution of man who is the male-female creation. The male figure has the sun halo or the positive ray while the female figure has the moon crown or the mother ray, representing spirit and matter, which matter being regenerated becomes the soul or bride of spirit.

This figure rises out of the globe of elements and from the heads arises a wondrous bird with the sign of Leo around its head. This blackened bird represents the unknowable secret of the phoenix or the bird of eternal life that is born out of the union of the sun and moon in the brain of man. Its tail, which is filled with eyes, represents the unfolded sense centers of human consciousness while the great circle containing all the other symbols is made to represent nature within whose protecting aura all growth is carried on.

The fire of the philosopher which rises upward and partly surrounds the central globe is the purification process in which the flame in the lower centers of the body rises upward and awakens Kundalini, the spinal spirit-fire in man, which is asleep in the egg of Brahma located in the solar plexus. This passing upward creates the figure with the two heads for these faces undoubtedly represent the pituitary body and the pineal gland which are the positive and negative poles of the spinal canal fire.

In India the god-man Ishwari is shown as a male-female Diety and in the ancient languages the name of God signified that He was also a male-female Divinity, for He is not only the Creator but the Creation. In a similar way man, following in the footsteps of God, is slowly arousing the latent qualities within himself and building to the day when he too shall be both creator and the creation.

The entire diagram is symbolical of the evolution of the human soul and spirit. Starting from the top downward it is involution; working from the bottom upward it is evolution. Two streams pour from the breasts of the creature and these represent the outpourings of fire and water or salt and sulphur which are two of the three elements of perfection while mercury forms the third element. The band around the neck of the figure, which unites the heads, is the wedding ring of modern theology for it ties or unites as a band of spiritual gold the two extremes of human life. The upright triangle above, pointing up to the Sacred Name, is once more a symbol of human regeneration.

Taking the plate generally it refers to the cosmic scheme of things and later the individual scheme of things. The reading tells of how through the union of the universal Earth Mother and Fiery and Airy Father there is created a wondrous stone which is the answer to all the problems of life. The student recognizes that the union of the spiritual elements within himself will turn him allegorically into a two-headed creature—male-female and self-reproductive through the positive pole of the brain.

Next month's magazine will contain the companion piece to this plate illustrating another of the deep, alchemical principles. Save these pictures for you will find it nearly impossible to get them again, and while you may not understand them now, as time goes on you will be grateful that you possess them.

QUESTION AND ANSWER DEPARTMENT

What is Success?

Ans. Success is the perfect adjustment of the individual consciousness with the prenatal plan which it prepared and earned before its entrance into this life. All advancement over existing conditions is success; all stagnation or backsliding is failure.

What is the greatest of all successes?

Ans. The composite perfection which is the result of a number of small achievements, the gaining of which has been spread over numberless eternities.

Is a happy life a successful life?

Ans. A truly successful life is a happy one but experience rather than harmony is the main requisite to success in spiritual things.

Who is a failure?

Ans. A failure is one who has fallen below the standard which he himself has attained at some previous time; or one who has failed to advance that standard with every thought and action of life.

What is the greatest cause of failure at the present time?

Ans. There are many of them but uncertainty, lack of backbone, fear of popular opinion and egotism are the greatest. Failure to live up to the purest and highest in life is the great spiritual downfall.

What is the greatest enemy of failure?

Ans. Action. For wherever this exists growth is taking place. Though the action itself be destructive, yet through it the spirit is learning a lesson.

What is the great adjustment of man's being?

Ans. The adjustment of the self and the not-self. This is the result of the development of the mind which becomes a neutral field—a universal solvent—in which the opposites of consciousness are capable of meeting in mutual understanding.

How may we know one who has succeeded in this adjustment?

Ans. We can know him as one who sees the divine lesson in the little things overlooked by the world in its endless rush. The one who sees the clearest is the one who sees God in the greatest number of things.

What is the reward of adjustment of life and its bodies?

Ans. Consciousness on all the planes of nature where the adjustments are made and communion with the central life within.

Who is the greatest failure at the present time?

Ans. Those who fail to recognize opportunity and conserve time by making every moment useful to all eternity—they are wasting God's most precious gifts.

What constitutes a successful speaker?

Ans. He is the one whose words, though few, still convey to the world with the greatest clearness the ideals which fill his consciousness. He is the one who speaks the truths that others dare not think.

Who has learned to listen most successfully?

Ans. The one who has learned to hear the voice that speaks from the silence of his own soul and who knows the meaning of its quiet words.

Who is the most successful thinker?

Ans. The one whose thoughts, like God's, are in harmony with the Divine plan. Man realizes the power of God when he learns to think God's thoughts; he knows the ways of the divine when he himself has walked them.

What is adjustment?

Ans. Adjustment is the arranging or balancing of things into harmony one with the other.

The Lord Of The Flaming Mountain

UP from the shadows of swaying palms and jungle underbrush a little group of pilgrims wound their way in and out among the broken lava rocks and stubble towards a mighty mountain that rose as a looming mystery to touch the deep blue of the tropic sky. From the top of this peak a thin trail of smoke poured eternally as though in truth this mystery of nature were the vent of Vulcan's forge. A strange group indeed it was that climbed up and up along the narrow path that led to the distant heights. They were a people we see no longer for already eternities have shrouded them in the mantle of forgetfulness.

First came a tall and aged man, his copper skin seamed and wrinkled but his face strong and resolute. He was robed in a cape woven of bird's feathers and tilted forward upon his head was a strange peaked cap from the point of which hung a pendant of gold and jewels which tossed and swayed as he walked. On his forehead was a cross, traced in white pigments, while the breeze blowing aside his cape disclosed the fact that his only other garment was a girdle of golden plates set with amethysts and rubies. In the center of the girdle was a strange face molded of solid gold, a face surrounded by a halo of flames in whose eyes sparkled rubies of a never-ending radiance. In one hand the aged man carried a carved staff painted in many colors and in the other a rattle hanging upon a tassel of human hair and composed of a gourd containing within its dried husk a tiny pebble. The long hair of the man was grey and hung in many plaits upon his shoulders while his beard, braided like an Assyrian's, hung half way to his waist. He was the priest of the Divine Lord, Master of the Great Fire, whose temple stood alone among the lava banks and ashes of the flaming mountain.

The second member of the party was a young girl some sixteen or eighteen years of age. She too wore a cape of bird feathers and upon her small feet were sandals inlaid with jewels. Her head was uncovered revealing braided hair which hung in two long coils nearly to her knees and was of the shiny blackness of the lava rocks that surrounded her. She was covered with golden ornaments and chains while her arms and ankles were encircled by bands of gold connected with links of silver and copper. But though adorned with the ransom of emperors, she seemed more a captive in bondage for her ornaments were like shackles and clanked dismally as she walked along.

Two other figures completed the group. Powerful men they were whose brown bodies glistened in the sunshine and whose forms and proportions were those of Greek athletes. They wore neither cape nor headdress but their bodies were adorned with golden bangles and strange animals were tatooed in many colors upon their skins. The heavy girdles they wore were weighted with plates of gold and each carried in his hand a feathered staff surmounted by a globe of fiery gold.

The four figures wound in and out among the rocks and as they neared the top of the lofty mountain thin streams of smoke rose up from the crevices at their feet; the air was filled with a moaning and rumbling, the earth shook and shivered like a thing alive; the heavy fumes of sulphurous smoke creeping up shrouded the little band in a semi-darkness while the sun shone as a ball of angry red behind clouds of swirling ashes.

Evening was falling before they neared the summit and as the sun sank to rest a strange lurid glow thrilled through the atmosphere, an eerie ever-changing radiance reflected in a million different ways from the clouds of mist and vapor. Still the little band climbed upward and upward ever nearer to the mighty crater that loomed like a gaping pit of hell before them.

Suddenly they reached a great rock and passing around its side were confronted by a tiny hut built of stones and lava, shielded by the projecting side of the cliffs but half concealed by the seething vapors of the volcano. Reaching the door of the hut, the old priest raised his staff while the other three fell to their knees.

"Behold! This is the Temple of Anguish built on the crest of Chetoka, the Mountain of Undying Fires. This is the Place of Wailing where we sinful mortals come to ask forgiveness of our Lord and Master! For, behold! our God speaks to us through the mountain of fire! Many days now has His voice been heard and the roaring and rumblings have whispered of His wrath. He has said to His priests: 'Bring from the people of earth a living sacrifice unto Me in the mountain of my fires!' And we have brought one even as He has said—for behold we have chosen from among our nation the lovliest and purest daughter of earth and brought her up this mountain to be the bride of the Fire King!"

He rose and entered the little hut and a fire, kindled with a broken stick, flared up, its ruddy glows revealing a massive altar above which a great flaming Face looked down—a face of gold and jewels from which poured forth streamers and rays of living light.

"Oh, Spirit of Fire! thy children obey thy call. For it was said of thee by our father's fathers that when thou criest out for vengeance for the forgetfulness of men—behold! there must be one of the people who shall climb to the heights of thy lofty shrine and die that thy children may be saved. For thine own voice has spoken saying there shall be one acceptable in the sight of our God who shall come to make offer of their life unto our God on Chetoka the sacred mountain—and only the pure in heart are acceptable as a sacrifice unto thee. Come—oh Lord of the Sacred Mountain!—and take unto thyself this one of our people who comes forth to sacrifice herself that thy wrath may not descend upon the world!"

The flaming Face gleamed and glowed in the flickering light, its eyes seeming to shine with a fire demonical. The old priest bowed and no sound broke the stillness except a broken sob from the prisoner in her golden chains.

Slowly the old priest left the little hut and, followed by the others, climbed up and over the side of the volcano, finally standing at the very peak of a great rock that jutted over the sea of molten lava. In the center rose a mighty cone and from it flames and sulphur came up in never-ending steam. A great rumbling and roaring rent the heavy stillness of the island night and the splashing of lava bubbles in the sea of molten rock beneath sounded like sobs on the air. All the figures were tinged red with the flames and standing alone on that pinnacle of rock in their robes of feathers and girdles of gold they seemed like fiery spirits of the dawn when creation was in the making instead living creatures in a world of flesh.

The old priest raised his hands and cried outward over the lake of flames:

"We have come, oh Master! as thy law has demanded. We have brought thee thy bride. Accept our sacrifice, oh Fiery One, and destroy not our people. Send not thy flaming rivers to burn our homes with consuming fire—send not the messengers of death—the ashes and the plagues—rock not the earth with thy vengeance—oh God of Fire! But accept this, the best we have to offer thee." He knelt upon the rock and the rumblings and roarings seemed to deepen while great clouds of flame and smoke rose from the volcano's depthless center and the rocks beneath their feet shook and quivered with a life divine.

Slowly the slender figure of the girl arose and with calm courage crossed the narrow shelf of stone. Dropping aside the robe of bird's feathers she stood poised upon the point of rock, beneath her the surging sea of molten lava. The flames sparkled on the jewels that she wore for these too were to be cast with her into the yawning mouth of the fire-god.

Suddenly as she stood there, there arose from the depths of the mountain a great streaming cloud of many-colored mists. It twinkled, swayed and twisted like a thing alive and instead of passing onward and outward into the heavens it hovered and floated over the center of the crater. Slowly the streaming lights took form, the many changing vapors gathered themselves together until a Mighty Being hovered over Chetoka.

The priest raised his hands in awe and trembling and shrank backward on the rock while the two that were with him moaned and groaned in fear and agony. But the thin figure still stood alone on the point of rock, her copper skin gleaming and glowing from the flickering flames of the volcano. The great mystery shadow shape became clearer as the moments passed and the Great One hovered closely over the volcano—a creature composed of the very flames themselves, his hair a mass of flowing sparks, his fingers tapering off into points of flame, his robes of crimson fire trailing off into the mist and vapor of the volcano. Great wings of flame and fire poured from him and his eyes shone like the molten lava of the crater.

A thundering voice spoke as the Great Creature swept over the surface of his volcano towards the pinnacle of rocks:

"Behold! I am angered at thee, thou puny children of men! It is well that ye have brought your sacrifice to the top of the mountain for ye have displeased the Spirit of the Fires. What boon ask you in exchange for the bride that ye have brought me?"

"Oh, Lord of the Flaming Mountain!" cried the priest, "for many days have the ashes poured upon our villages, for many nights has the dull glow of your anger brought terror to our hearts. We come to thee, oh Lord, asking peace and that ye shall not destroy us with the flames of thy wrath. Oh, King of the Salamanders! Son of the fiery Sparks of Fohat! accept this the purest gift of earth and freest from thy hate!"

The Lord of the volcano had reached the mighty cliff that edged his crater and reached out his arms of streaming flame to grasp in them the slender figure that stood upon the rock.

"Ye have brought your sacrifice, oh children of men, but know you not that you yourselves are the spirits of the fire? For many weeks and many years ye have wrangled and fought and hated in your villages and for that ye have brought upon yourselves the curse of the Lord of Flames. For, behold! to my mountain come the hates and griefs and wranglings of the people and from them are built the flames of my lofty peak, and were it not that ye battled in your villages my flames could not battle on this mountain peak. Ye sue for peace but that I cannot give you while to this crater come the flames of hate. The mumblings and the rumblings which ye hear are but shadows of your own hearts, the seething cauldrons of flames but whisper of the flames of passion within your own soul. I am the Lord of the Flames—I am the Regent of the Red World —I am the Voice of the Eternal Fire—I love the children of men and being strong in fire I would serve them. But they have taken my fire and desecrated it and as it seeths and boils within their own souls so the shadows rise upon my mountain. Go back to your village and say unto them that the Lord of the Flaming Mountain has spoken saying that only when the souls of men are at rest will my mountain slumber.

"Behold thy sacrifice is acceptable in my sight, the heart of one that is pure can sooth the flames of creation. It is said of the gods that through all the ages some must perish that many may be saved! Go ye now your way and I shall return to the heart of the flaming mountain taking with me the sacrifice that ye have made. Be not this sacrifice in vain, for it is not the first nor shall it be the last! Many a soul has perished to save the world from my wrath, many a courageous one has entered my flames that the world should have peace. But the Lord of the Flaming Mountain is not unkind—fear not for the one that ye have given nor fear ye for the sacrifice of your people. But come unto me with love and my flames shall warm their hearts."

Slowly the fiery figure gathered the form in its arms and floating out over the volcano passed slowly downward into its mighty center, clasping to itself the jeweled figure of the girl.

A great peace descended upon the mountain, the flames of smoke died out and the lava ceased to flow, the rumblings grew less and less until at last silence ruled supreme. The old priest rose and was turning away when a mighty voice spoke from the depths of the earth:

"I, the Lord of the Flaming Mountain, am at rest. A noble soul has sacrificed itself to bring me peace. In all the ages of the world I have gathered unto myself many but they are not mine. For behold the daughter of earth is not with me in my fiery mountain but with her God and my God! And, behold, she has passed through the flaming ring unscarred and in her great desire has redeemed not only you but herself also.

"Go ye unto your people and let not this sacrifice be in vain. Remember that only when ye learn to love one another shall my mountain be at rest, for when ye wrangle and discord among yourselves ye loose my flames and turn them on the worlds of men. Then my mountain cries out for vengeance and the sword of death is loosened as the thunder and lightening of the gods. Once more art ye forgiven—go and do better. Remember who was your answer and let not the martyr die in vain.

"The Lord of the Flaming Mountain is not dead but rests in peace under the spell of redemption. Wake him not with hate and lust for once awake he will never sleep until another be found to pacify him, send no more brides to the top of my mountain but live in your villages in peace as the most acceptable sacrifice unto my eyes. Fear me for I am great, obey me for I am kind, redeem me for I am salvation, and though my temple is on my mountain rather let it be in the soul of man. While there is one that is pure I will rest, lulled to peace by their love; but if ye live not one unto the other in friendship and in charity ye shall hear my voice again and the world shall know me and cry out in agony unto the Lord of the Flaming Mountain. But I can do nothing but use the flames which thou hast given me. Send me no flames of hate and I will not burn your homes. Live not in discord one to the other and my lava shall never flow again."

Faded Flowers

OFTENTIMES in wandering through an old home among the scenes of long ago one finds pressed away in a favorite volume—possibly the Bible or the family album—a faded rose crushed between the leaves. After many years of forgetfulness it will bring back memories of the past. Some loved one nearly forgotten in the battle of life—some dear soul we used to know—comes before the mirror of the mind. We hear a laughing voice, perhaps now hushed forever, and kind hands stretch out across the years to enfold us again in memory's embrace. How few of these faded flowers have a message to the world—yet each whisper something of the past to some responsive heart.

And how much like faded flowers are the hearts of suffering men and women wandering through life! Each faded rose was once the fairest blossom and in a distant day forgotten its dried and falling petals shone forth with all the glory of nature and its God. As we go along the road of life we see many wondrous blossoms filling the air with glorious fragrance and exquisite color but when we pass that way again we see them faded and returning again to the dust from whence they came. How like the faded flower is the life of man! The glowing ideals he came here to carry out he soon forgets—his dreams of glorifying the world vanish from his memory as he struggles through the sordidness of life. In truth, he cometh forth as a flower and is cut down.

But beneath the wilted petals and beneath that broken heart of a man there still glows in embers a light eternal. And some day the Great Magician is going to wander along that dusty road and with the touch of his magic wand bring back life to these faded flowers.

In the highways and byways of this world who shall be this Great Magician? Who shall play the fairy queen and raise to life again the dead? There is within each one of us the Great Magician—the good spirit—who can bring faded flowers to life and restore the broken blossoms from whose crushed petals have been formed a rosary that ends with a cross. There is this wondrous fairy-godmother who can bring to life the dead rose and make it bloom again in radiant beauty, and this mystic being—the good fairy—is the sweetness and compassion of love and hope that is hidden deep in the heart of every man. Each kind word, each sweet thought brings forth again the glow of life to the soul of some faded flower!

It is a glorious thing to have the power to make the world shine again with happiness. This is within the reach of every mystic, for into the hands of one who has earned this right—to bring back the blush of life to broken souls—a great privilege is given. No longer does he live for what the world can give him for he has more than it can ever know. He lives to wander through the gardens of humanity where flower and blooming shrub fade each year as the snows of winter come. Gathering up the dried and withered leaves he blesses them with the power of life and they brighten up again at his touch.

Where the mystic is there can be no faded flowers for he lives only to bring joy and life into the world. Hates and fears, sorrows and remorse—all these have withered the flowers of life. The roses of youth vanish from the cheek as the furrows of care appear and the eyes once bright with laughter soon grow dull with weeping. But the work of the master is to bring back the old time joy and although his own heart be sad he smiles serenely through his tears as he gathers the broken petals to mold them again into perfect flowers.

And man is walking in the footsteps of this Master. Every day, some where, he sees a withered rose whose petals would glow again if he would but nourish them with the waters of life. Just a kind word and the flower will become a thing of beauty in the garden of the Lord. We are to go forth in the name of the Father and gather close to our hearts these withered flowers—the broken children of men. In love and compassion we are to serve them, in humility and simplicity to protect them, in sympathy and brotherhood to assist them, that the spirit of joy may come again into their lives as the blossoming of a flower.

Somewhere in the soul of man—no matter how cold he may seem—there is something which cries out to smile, cries out to be happy—and being happy cries some more! This is a certain soul quality explainable and known only to those who have suffered and yet through it all are drawn by bonds undefinable back to the cause of their anguish. There is something very human about the world and while it may seem a cruel place the longer we are in it the less we desire to leave it. It is so much like each one of us that the bonds of understanding make us love the old earth more and more.

The glory of being alive is a wonderful thing but the still greater glory of giving life and expression to others fills the heart with a real purpose of being. And he who turns back again into the garden of the earth to nurture and care for those withered flowers, whose drooping petals bespeak the dying courage of an unawakened life, knows no other joy. It is a wondrous thing to feel that it is within our power—if we live as we should —to give these flowers new duty. From the soul of him who thus redeems the rose that was withered shall shine forth a star through the darkness—that star which is the mark of the Compassionate One.

The Sons of God labor eternally with man to build within him that sweet sadness—the sadness which is the great peace that surpasseth understanding. In simple symbol well known to our eyes the Sons of Compassion ever seek to teach us the way that we should go, seeking to build within us the realization of the path which they have walked. They never command us to go this way or that—they only show us the beauties of the path. They show us the faded flowers and then they ask if there can be anything more beautiful in all the world than a flower turned upward in adoration to the light of its God? They ask if anything is sadder than to see the blossom wither and fade away?

Then it is shown to us how we may go forth and bring to blossom the flower of spirit now budding alone in the endless deserts of materiality. So let us take their symbol of service and go out to labor in the world fields that the faded flower hidden within the heart of man—called the spirit of Christ—shall be raised from the dead to blossom forth unto perfect life.

Man is the little creator made in the image of the Great Creator containing in possibility all that God has in awakened energy.

A Discourse on the Eight Perfections
(Continued)

AND the Lord of Light spoke of the the Fifth Perfection which is Intelligent Living, saying:

"Know that the Fifth Perfection is that ye should live well to yourself and true in your dealings with others; that ye should be joyous among others but that your living be right in the eyes of the Lord. Know that of the many things which thou hast this sheath of stone which ye call a body is most useful to you at this time, for only through this body may ye learn that which is eternal. Realize that this body is not the Eternal I nor God but is rather of a demon of darkness; but you must treat it well that it may serve thee well unto the work for which God has designed it. By the Intelligence of Right Living know that he who liveth with nature in simplicity liveth with God in reality and he who would know how to live must search for life among the living and not among the dead. Man is dead, therefore search not for life there but look only unto God who is the One Life."

So saying, the Lord opened the fifth Petal:

"Of this Lotus the fifth Petal is the Perfection of Intelligent Living wherein ye shall learn that length of life is the prolonging of opportunities—when to this ye add Perception and Purpose. But the body liveth not of itself alone but of the life which is within it and which is the life of Brahma who is the Creator and Father who ever shall Be. Therefore in all your living, live moderately and wisely; live as a brother with all other things. Thereof it is spoken in the Sacred Bharatas: Live not of the body but of the spirit. But know that living means that the bodies be preserved for the spirit and that the spirit speaks through its own reflection in the mirror of eternity."

* * *

Wherein the Blessed Lord saith:

"This is all that I would speak of the Fifth Perfection. So listen unto the words of the Sixth Perfection which is Perfect Effort. Know that intelligent effort is the basis of all that expands and groweth great; effort is the measurement of reward and according to your effort so shall it be with you in that which is Eternal. Know, oh son! there is a reward for effort regardless of its works and know that right effort bringeth with it a sure promise of right reward. Nothing in this universe is without effort and those who do not labor shall some day be enfamine for that which they have not sown. Therefore know that in effort lies the secret of power and the Sixth Perfection is Intelligent Effort which ye gain through intelligent Perception, intelligent Speech, intelligent Purpose, intelligent Conduct and intelligent Living."

Thus spake the Lord of the Lotus as he pointed towards the heavens, saying of the Sixth Perfection:

"In the skies beyond the Blue Veil is the home of the saints in Sheta-loka, the home of those who have been tried and have labored for that which they are. For unto those who try is a sure reward, if ye strive with perfect effort. Ye gain not Nirvana through meditation alone; there must be works and perfect effort. Therefore, oh son, is effort greatly to be desired and when in doubt as to the labored to perform, strive with perfect effort and thy reward is sure."

* * *

Thus spake the Mighty One of the Sixth Perfection which is Intelligent Effort, and then He saith:

"I will now speak of the Seventh Perfection which is of the mind and is Intelligent Mindfulness. For in all thy seeking be not thoughtless lest in being such ye waste or injure. Be ye ever mindful of three things, oh son of earth! that thou mayest be perfect in Mindfulness. First, be mindful of thy conduct that it behooves thee well to watch as how thou shalt conduct thyself unto thyself. Second, be mindful of those responsibilities which are thine from the world; forget them not nor neglect them for they are Dharma and not to be overlooked. Third, be mindful that in your eagerness ye trample not your brothers under foot but are gentle and modest in the sight of men. It were good that ye should also be mindful of the will of God and the ways of His saints for although ye be mindful of men ye shall not succeed if ye forget the will of God."

Thus spake the Blessed Lord of the Seventh Petal as He sat in the Heart of the Flower:

"Be mindful also that every labor shall increase thee in the sight of God for by this is known the Seventh Perfection—that ye have no longer the power to hurt, the power to injure nor the desire to excel but that ye are eternally mindful and considerate of the needs of others. By this shall ye reach the feet of thy Lord and Master who is ever mindful of you, and thus shall it be known that you understand the Seventh Intelligence which is the Perfection of Mindfulness."

* * *

Whereupon the Lord of Light spoke once more saying:

"There is one more Perfection whereof I would speak, namely, the Intelligence of Contemplation wherein ye become as one with God through the Contemplation of Reality. For he who can contemplate within his own soul the wonders of creation and float over oblivion on the wings of intuition and and reason—he hath Perfect Contemplation which seeth life and death and yet is unmoved. Such a one shall himself live and die and yet be unmoved, whereupon may ye know that he is free from the Wheel of Birth and Death insomuch as he contemplates them as part of the Great Lesson but is not enmeshed in them as mortal man. He that is able to stand beside the universe and contemplate upon its wonders without himself being involved therein:—that one has Perfect Contemplation for he seeth all things, liveth all things, contemplateth all thing and is no part of them but is one with their source."

Thus spake the Great Lord of the Eighth Perfection which is Intelligent Contemplation, saying:

"Behold, oh son of man! the gods are perfect in contemplation and the universe is the fruit of their meditations. Therefore if ye would be one with the Eternal, contemplate also upon That which Is and you will be one with the Twelve Eternal Meditators in the Fields of the Infinite. For he who seeth in all things a lesson but in no thing the personality, he is perfect in contemplation; he who seeth in all things a personality, he is perfect in ignorance. All men stand between two things—perfection in ignorance and perfection in knowledge—while the god-man sits in contemplation upon the two. They are not wise for they are not the fruits of ignorance, they are not ignorant for the seeds of wisdom have not been planted there. Know that Perfection of Contemplation is that which sitteth between wisdom and ignorance and meditateth upon them but is neither."

* * *

"Whereupon I have finished my discourse upon the Eight Intelligences which are the eight paths of my wisdom and the Petals of my sacred Lotus. Know ye therefore, oh Chela! that the Blessed Lord hath spoken, whereof it is written in the Sacred Books of the Trees, of that which Is and ever shall Be because it has never been, for once being it must cease to be."

The Master Speaks
(Continued from page 11)

And this was my first great experience among worldly scoffers and it was there that I learned a lesson which I never forgot. In the words of my teacher I say:

"Fear not that your words will not express your hopes and ideals for he who is carrying the Master's message is never alone. When his own words are failing the Invisible Ones gather around and whisper in his ear. If you work and labor in truth and sincerity, never fear, for the Teacher is with you. He knows the words you need and whispers them when the moment comes.

(To be continued.)

ASTROLOGICAL KEYWORDS

Leo as the fifth sign of the Zodiac is of special interest to students of the occult sciences for several reasons. First, being the throne of the sun, the Lion is often used as a symbol of life and power and Christ who represents the sun-god is often referred to as the Lion of Judah. In Masonary Leo is very symbolical, for being the chief of the cat family the Lion is said to have the same peculiarity in his ability to see in the dark consequently is used by the ancients to symbolize the Eye of God which sees into the darkness of human affairs.

The Grip of the Lion's Paw is well known and it is symbolical of the returning of life when the sun, in his endless round, enters his throne in Leo bringing all things to life that have been dead through the long winter months.

Below we list the keywords of the sign of Leo in a simple, concise manner so that the student with slight practice will be capable of analyzing its most general characteristics. Leo is also of special interest at the present time insomuch as it forms the esoteric school of the Aquarian Age—its opposite in the Zodiac—and according to geocentric astrology the Aquarian Age which is so close at hand will bring with it a powerful spiritual ray from Leo the Lion of the Tribe Judah. Leo is always symbolical of life and fire and as in man it governs the heart, so in the cosmos it is the home of the sun, the heart of the solar system.

Leo the fifth sign of the Zodiac:
- Hot
- Dry
- Fiery
- Choloric
- Eastern
- Masculine
- Diurnal
- Northern
- Commanding
- Fixed
- Estival
- Brutish
- Barren
- Four-footed
- Broken
- Changeable
- Fortunate
- Strong
- Hoarse
- Bitter
- Violent
- Long Ascension

The day and night home of the Sun
The detriment of Saturn
Feral
Furious

General Characteristics:
- High resolve
- Royal
- Unbending
- Ambitious
- Quick-tempered
- Changeable
- Generous
- Free
- Courteous

The Leo person takes his general characteristics from the animal in question, namely, the lion. Like that animal he chafes under confinement, rebels against over-lords and is monarch of all he surveys. If crossed or attempt is made to curb him he is quick-tempered and noted for his roaring, ranting and cantankering. But it does not last long and he soon quietens down. This sign is usually in important positions of trust, fond of the occult sciences, and under normal conditions makes its mark in the world of affairs.

Physical Appearances:
- Usually a large body
- Broad shoulders
- Austere countenance
- Large eyes
- Dark yellow, reddish or brown hair given to curling
- Strong voice, sometimes hoarse
- Full-blooded
- Oval countenance, sometimes rather choppy
- Later part of the sign produces weaker body with lighter hair
- Large round head
- Staring and goggle eyes
- Middle stature but heavy
- Narrow sides
- Fierce countenance
- High sanguine complexion

Health:

While Leo is considered a healthy sign we do find considerable sickness especially that due to circulation and blood conditions. It governs the heart and back and its most common diseases are:

- Pains in the back and ribs
- Convulsions
- Fainting
- Fevers
- Pestilences
- Smallpox
- Measles
- Jaundice
- And all hot and inflamatory diseases
- Entirely barren sign
- Sore eyes
- The plagues
- Heart trouble
- Denotes accidents by fire, explosion and combustible materials
- Subject to sprains, falls, shocks, etc.

Domestic Problems:

Leo can only be said to be happy in the home when it rules the home. Monotony and drudgery does not rest well upon the Leo types and their fiery dispositions often break their homes. If they find someone, however, who is willing to allow them to do just what they want to they are usually faithful but not overly domestic, being turned more to public things.

Countries under Influence of Leo:

Italy	West of England
Bohemia	The Alps
France	Turkey
Sicily	Silesia

Cities Ruled by Leo:

Rome	Prague
Bristol	Syracuse
Bath	Ravenna
Taunton	Philadelphia
Cremona	Damascus

Colors:

Yellow	Red
Brown	Green

According to Ptolemy the stars in the head of Leo are in effect like Saturn with a ray from Mars; the three in the neck are like Saturn with some of Mercury; the bright one in the heart called Regulus agrees with Mars and Jupiter; those in the loins and the bright one in the tail are like Saturn and Venus; those in the thighs resemble Venus and in some degree Mercury.

According to Henry Cornelius Agrippa, of the Twelve Orders of Blessed Spirits Leo rules the powers; of the Twelve Angels over the Twelve Signs, Verchiel rules Leo; of the months Leo rules the 20th of July to the 20th of August; of the Twelve Tribes, Asher; of the Twelve Prophets, Hosea; of the Twelve Apostles, Peter; of the twelve plants, ladies' seal; of the twelve stones, jasper; of the twelve principle members, the heart; of the Twelve Degrees of the Damned, the jugglers of darkness.

The Night Of Brahma

AT THE end of every cosmic cycle of action there follows a period of rest and this is the ebb and flow of energy which marks one of the fundamental expressions of the eternal plan. The periods of activity are called the Days of Brahma when the world outpouring itself from the Unknown expresses its energized and rejuvenated qualities, and with greater courage, power and speed carries on the work of universal unfoldment because of the periods of rest. At the end of each day of manifestation the Universe, the Sun of Necessity, is dissolved or swallowed up in cosmic night which was called by the ancients "Pralaya."

For every action in this world, which implies the expending of energy, there must ensue a period of inaction during which time nature rebuilds the tissues and revivifies the bodies torn down and scattered by the activities of mental, physical or spiritual expression. There is no one who can entirely set aside the periods of rest and while for many years, lives perhaps, a powerfully constituted organism may sustain itself upon comparatively little relaxation, still at some time or other even the gods must pass into cosmic or universal sleep.

Death is merely an expression of the return of bodies to sleep. Paul says we die daily and this is a spiritual truth for each day we tear down the body cells and life forces which we are forced to expend in our manifestation and growth here. During the periods of cosmic sleep the universe rebuilds its shattered vehicles and when they return to life they start with a great impetus similar to the buoyancy we feel when we awaken from peaceful slumber. When we do not feel refreshed from sleep it is a certainty that the vehicles have not been relaxed and that through unwise eating or physical derangement the spiritual consciousness has not completely separated itself from its vehicle of expression. The withdrawal of the life from the form constitutes death, the temporary withdrawal without rupturing the connecting links between bodies is called sleep, and this is the period of physical regeneration for night is illuminated by the moon, the generator of bodies and the ruling principle of those vitalizing forces which rebuild the depleted tissue of vehicles under the direction of the elemental intelligences.

Brahma, the incarnated intelligence of the universe, is called the Grand Man and He is supposed to be endowed with the qualities of man in a grander and more perfect degree. The sleeping and waking, the birth and death, of Brahma, is correlated to the shorter periods of manifestation of man and the analogy is quite perfect. One of the greatest works that confronts the student is to accurately learn to understand the use and application of the powers of relaxation. The continued over-exertion of a body, a brain center, or an organ of consciousness will shorten the length of its life. It is true that all parts of man grow stronger with exercise but exercise must be balanced by rest for exercise tears down the walls of resistance and saps the stores of energy used to give expression to a body or organ. Therefore, a cretain part of the time we must allow certain centers to rest and recuperate from our unbalanced use of them.

The child in school tires of arithmetic in an hour or so and then you transfer his attention to spelling or geography bringing into play an entirely different series of sense centers. This results in the relaxation of the tired organ during which time the mind recuperates from the strain placed upon it and preparaes for further active expression. The forty-three faculties of the human brain must all be given alternately exercise and rest, the result being a well balanced consciousness and an adaptable mind. The mental breakdown is the result of the abuse of a single faculty or trying to make an organ run both night and day, year in and year out, without rest.

There are two grand phases of force. One is that expression which pours into the reservoir to supply the needs of expression; the other is that which pours out of the reservoir in active manifestation. Nothing can come out of man that has not already gone in for he has not yet acquired the miraculous pitcher of the gods. He can go no further than the energy stored in the reservoir; he can be no stronger than the involuted energies which he radiates. Therefore, the involution of power is absolutely necessary to the evolution of form. These two laws are intra-dependent one upon the other, for man cannot pour into his organism safely energy unless he expends a certtain amount in his daily life. If he does not do this he runs over. On the other hand the amount within measures his capacity to draw forth. Man involutes the expressions of this force in his material and spiritual thoughts, actions and desires.

All life is an ebb and flow of energies. These energies pour into man from the planes of consciousness to which he has attuned himself through his own works and thoughts. They can produce no higher results than the plane of consciousness from whence they came and the quality of inflowing energy is limited by the vehicles of attraction which gather it from the cosmos.

The problem of the days and nights of Brahma is to man a divine allegory expressing as it does the requirements of his own life. Two forces govern man, solar and lunar; the solar govern the higher man, the lunar, the bodies. Each of these must alternately be given opportunity for self-expression in order that they may carry on their respective duties. So at night while the body is undisturbed by conscious mental or physical reaction, the reparatory powers of nature take charge of the organism and prepare it to support and express the life within it during the following period of action. In the daytime the spiritual consciousness is ushered into its vehicle where its own growth is carried on at the expense of the lower bodies. The result is a divine balance of the periods of recuperation and destruction.

Wise and careful seekers after things spiritual have learned to recognize the vital importance of giving their bodies and centers of consciousness the proper amount of exercise and relaxation. All of man's bodies have a great similarity. Our minds and emotions are subject to the same general ailments before which the physical body must bow and all through nature the law of action and repose is a governing factor. Man in his haste fails to properly consider and study the law of periodicity, consequently he must pay the price in broken health and inefficiency. Those who would be like God in dynamic powers must develop their organism in accordance with His laws which are the individualized needs of His composite progression.

So through the ages the days and nights of Brahma go on. Worlds come in and worlds go out and in shorter periods of time man passes through similar conditions which to him seem very terrible but which in reality are his greatest blessings, for God does not die when his vehicles are asleep, He is functioning in other worlds in finer and more sensitive bodies, and it is only the exhausted appendage of consciousness that is dropped and its centers allowed to rest, while in higher and finer words the consciousness is making further plans for its unfoldment and final union with the form which now it is forced to vampirize in order to exist during the days of Brahma.

Note

It may be of interest to some of our readers to know that we are preparing mimeograph notes of some of our lectures which may be secured by those desiring them on the same free-will offering basis that is used in all of our publications. The edition is limited but we will be glad to supply them while they last.

We have the following prepared for distribution at the present time:

Total Eclipse of the Sun and Effect Upon World Affairs.

This is an astrological analysis of the effect of the September eclipse upon the geographic, political, economical and weather conditions of the world.

The Sex Problem.

These are the notes of a lecture given in Los Angeles about the effects of the modern sex teachings upon the race.

The Einstein Theory of Reletivity.

A simple analysis of this intricate problem, applying it to the practical problem of human relationship.

Talks for Teachers, Parts I, II and III.

These three separate lectures deal with three phases of the work of preparing pupils for the world ministry and the labors of the coming age.

The Masters, Parts I and II.

Two lectures dealing with the Masters of Wisdom and the work of preparing oneself to be become their conscious assistants.

Books for Occult Students.

A list of nearly two hundred books and authors valuable to the student of occult teachings, which should be read and studied by all aspiring candidates on the path of self unfoldment.

Occult Masonry

THE TRIANGLE ON THE MASON'S RING

(Continued from May Issue)

In the first issue of our magazine we started an article on the symbolism of the triangle, especially the flaming triangle as it is understood in the inner Masonic lodges and mystic centers of spiritual knowledge.

The three sides of the triangle represent of course the three outpourings of life and energy which are molding the threefold body of man. The triangle is composed of two substances and is shown in two ways. The upright triangle is white symbolizing the up-pointing spiritual tendencies of man, the turning God-ward of the three human expressions of thought, emotion and form; while the triangle with the point downward is symbolical of the three spiritual flames descending downward from the heavens to impregnate and vitalize man. These two with their points together form an hour-glass which is the ancient symbol of time well known to Masons.

There are two flames in the universe—the golden flame and the black flame. The golden fire belongs to heaven and the realms of truth and light, while the black flame belongs to oblivion the home of eternal darkness. The degenerate individual is symbolized by the black flame while the regenerated individual is typified by the golden up-pointing fire.

The Yod or Dot in the triangle represents God who is only known or cognized through the expression of the Triangle. He is the life within or behind the glass of manifestation and the unformed, unexpressed energy manifests through the three witnesses of air, fire and water-earth. God manifests only through His creations. When He wishes to send us a great truth needed for our development He expresses it through the triangle of spirit, mind and body. Spirituality is a child born of three parents: a clean body, a pure heart and a balanced mind. This child must be nurtured and cared for as any physical baby. From this guarding and care is born the soul which shines forth as a great aura of light and is symbolized by the glow which surrounds the Masonic triangle.

Of all the ancient and honored religious doctrines there are none as old as the worship of the Flame. From the most ancient of times down to our modern days the Great Unknown, the spiritual power of the universe, has been loved, protected and revered by mankind and called the Eternal Flame. The ancients used as a symbol of this Flame the upright triangle—which preceeds the G. as the sacred symbol of Masonry. In Greek, God is Deus and the first letter, D., is made in the form of an upright triangle. This upright triangle signifies the awakening of God within man as a wonderful threefold flame which divides itself through the nourishing of the three bodies. It is the thirty-third degree symbol of the Masonic Order which, surrounded with its glowing flame, stands for the God-consciousness in man.

The flaming triangle is made of three absolutely equal angles and symbolizes the divine balance in the threefold constitution. The balancing of his three bodies and their uniting to express a single central power is the basis of the thirty-third degree of Freemasonry and is the end to which all Masons aspire.

The salt, sulphur and mercury of the ancients is a divine allegory used to conceal the secret of the philosopher's stone which is nothing more or less than the union of spirit, mind and body—the endless symbol of the human ultimate. The realization of this great truth is the beginning of true wisdom.

Thirty-third degree Masons are evolved not ordained and their ordination in the spiritual things is the result of having lived the mystic truths of the Masonic life. Without this no true spirituality is possible. When the God in man, the flaming center of the triangle, is capable of expressing itself through three perfect instruments, built by man and dedicated by the lower upon the altar of the divine, then can God find the perfect expression and the Mason himself becomes the flaming triangle surrounded by the glowing garments of his living soul.

The triangle is truly a wonderful symbol and as the Mason carries it upon the ring he wears let him realize that its eternal plea is for the balancing of the threefold constitution united in the expression of a single divinity.

(The End)

Pearly Gates Gazette

MEMBER OF ASSASSINATED PRESS · EXTRA · UNLIMITED CIRCULATION

VOL. 30000001 — OCTOBER, 1923 — No. 1000000000005

SCANDAL UNVEILED IN HEAVEN'S "400"

War On Children Waged

PROHIBITION ENFORCEMENT NOTICE

The Pearly Gates Drys had a convention here last week at the Skydome Auditorium. Mr. Ryan spoke announcing the fact that a large percent of the crime wave in heaven is due to the demoralizing effect of saloons where nectar and ambrosia is served, often to minor angels. A petition has been sent to the Pearly Gates City Council to enforce a prohibition measure, making it illegal to serve ambrosia which is over two per cent. The Drys believe this will be of great assistance in combatting the ever increasing evil of drunkenness among the people.

NEW PICTURE GREAT SUCCESS

The Pearly Gates Motion Picture Syndicate has just finished work on a new five-reel earthquake picture. The original scenario is by Algernon Wheeze a man of many words and some of the scenes were supposed to be laid in Hell. But as Purgatory was closed for three days while the Devil was at the Sulphur Spring the photographers and cameramen with a small staff of specially picked actors went to the planet Earth where they found all the realism and location they were prevented from securing in Hell. His Satanic Majesty was invited to the pre-view at the studios last week. He threw up his hands in despair and threatened to abdicate feeling that he had failed to live up to his reputation as chief devil. Announcements have been made that Hell will probably be moved to Earth where conditions seem more appropriate. The picture is entitled "Ten Days in Pandemonium or Life on Earth" and is of an educational nature, starring Ananias in the role of a Wall Street broker. Further announcements later.

SCANDAL IN UPPER SET

Nehemiah is involved in a bigamy charge which has rocked heaven's Five Hundred to the very core. Mrs. Nehemiah No. One and his five children are receiving the consolation of a large number of friends since it was found that the prophet was keeping two households. Mrs. Nehemiah No. Two claims to be ignorant of the fact that the prophet was previously married. The case will be taken before the grand jury when it convenes next spring early in Pisces. Nehemiah is very miserable according to last reports.

RIOT AT CURB MARKET

Feathers flew at the Pearly Gates Stock Exchange yesterday morning when Negative Magnetic took a slump. Several well known Wall Street magnates got out just before the slump. A riot followed in which several angels were badly injured. Several small constellations were completely wiped out by the slump. War bonds were the only things that remained up to par. Sulphur also stayed fair.

KING SOLOMON OPENS PENNY DANCE

Dancing has become quite a rage in heaven this spring among the younger angels and King Solomon has opened a municipal dance hall with a syncopated Jazz Band. Several new dances are very popular here but the Wingywabble and the Feather-flutter are undoubtedly the most popular. Barney-Google and Chicago are the song hits this season in heaven and may be heard by anyone passing the dance hall in the evenings. Prof. Snick gives dancing lessons every afternoon while Saturday afternoon is turned over to the children.

So many complaints have come to the Pearly Gates Childs Welfare Association that it has become necessary for a law to be passed prohibiting children from coming to heaven. Three small boys woke the Seven Sleepers last night, have tied tin cans to the tail of Canus Major, broken three windows in the sedan of Mr. Neptune, woke the Lord in the middle of the night siccing two cats together and landlords announce that every apartment house in heaven is closing its doors to children owing to the fact that not one moment's peace can be had by tenants while there are children in the place. This condition is becoming very serious, a board meeting yesterday afternoon which met to discuss municipal typhoon arrangements was forced to disband because of three children, one with an old automobile horn, another with a washboiler and a third with a tin whistle who chased around the building about four hundred times. One angel went into distractions and pulled all of the feathers out of his wings whereupon two others had to assist him home. The cause of the condition seems to be that these wild children, most of whom come from earth, have not been properly raised but are neglected and allowed to run loose consequently they become a nuisance to heaven, earth and hell. The patriarch Jeremiah called on a mother yesterday to ask damages for his tall silk hat which a young hopeful had knocked off of his head and stepped on. The mother became very indignant against the patriarch, claiming that she had a perfect child. Jeremiah is suing her for a hat.

SUBWAY LINE OPENED

A subway between Pearly Gates and Hell has just been opened making direct transportation between these two points possible. In the past it was necessary to use the shortline via Earth but this new improvement simplifies matters decidedly.

SPECIAL ANNOUNCEMENT!
SECOND EDITION
(First Edition exhausted in one week)

"The Ways of the Lonely Ones"
When the Sons of Compassion Speak
By MANLY P. HALL

This is the latest work of this author and approaches the problem of spiritual enfoldment and growth in a manner both new and unusual.

The book contains six allegorical stories dealing with the spiritual development and initiation of mystical characters EACH ONE OF WHICH CAN BE PLACED IN THE LIFE OF THE STUDENTS OF THE WISDOM TEACHINGS. THE READER IS THE HERO OF EACH OF THE MYTHS, and concealed under the fables are many of the very deepest principles of occultism.

The book contains the following chapters:

The Maker of Gods.
This deals with the regeneration of matter and the transmutation of bodies.

The Master of the Blue Cape.
In this chapter the mystic meaning of the elixer of life and the philosophers' stone is given to the reader. Also the inner meaning of Alchemy.

The Face of The Christ.
The mystery of the last supper and the great problem of the second coming of the Christ is taken up from the occult standpoint, and presented in an understandable way.

The Guardian of the Light.
The duties and labors of one who seeks to be given charge of the Divine Wisdom are set forth in this chapter. Also the price of the Mystic Truth.

The One Who Turned Back.
This is the allegory of one who reached the gate of Liberation and renounced freedom to return again into the world. A study in Mystic Initiation.

The Glory of the Lord.
What happens to those who seek to enter the presence of the Lord without purifying themselves according to His laws? Read what happened to one, in the Tabernacle of the Jews.

The book is well printed on good paper and bound in boards stamped in blue. It contains sixty-four pages closely written.

This work like all of these publications is presented to the public without fixed price, leaving it to your own higher sentiments to show you your part in the work we are carrying.

The edition of this book is limited, so if you are interested send at once enclosing the contribution that you wish to make, not to pay just for the book but to help the work along, and you will receive your copy in the return mail.

Address all orders to Manly P. Hall, P. O. Box 695, Los Angeles, Cal.

These booklets by the same author may be secured by sending to Postoffice Box 695, Los Angeles, California, care of Manly P. Hall.

Price. These publications are not for sale but may be secured through voluntary contribution to help meet the cost of publication.

The Breastplate of the High Priest

A discussion of Old Testament symbolism showing how the spiritual powers of nature reflect themselves through the spiritual centers in the human body which we know as the jewels in the breastplate of Aaron. This booklet is out of print but an attempt will be made to secure a few copies for any desiring them. Illustrated.

Buddha, the Divine Wanderer

A new application of the life of the Prince of India as it is worked out in the individual growth of every student who is in truth seeking for the Yellow Robe.

Krishna and the Battle of Kurushetra

The Song Celestial with its wonderful story of the Battle of Life interpreted for students of practical religion. The mystery of the Blue Krishna and his work with men.

The Father of the Gods

A mystic allegory based upon the mythology of the peoples of Norway and Sweden and the legend of Odin the All-Father of the Northlands.

Questions and Answers, Part One
Questions and Answers, Part Two
Questions and Answers, Part Three

In these three booklets have been gathered about fifty of the thousands of questions answered in the past work gathered together for the benefit of students.

Occult Masonry

This booklet consists of the condensed notes on a class in mystic Masonry given in Los Angeles. It covers a number of important Masonic symbols and the supply is rapidly being exhausted.

Wands and Serpents

The explanation of the serpent of Genesis and serpent-worship as it is found among the mystery religions of the world and in the Christian Bible. Illustrated.

The Analysis of the Book of Revelation

A short study in this little understood book in the Bible, five lessons in one folder as given in class work during the past year.

The Unfoldment of Man

A study of the evolution of the body and mind and the causes which bring about mental and physical growth, a practical work for practical people.

Occult Psychology

Notes of an advanced class on this subject dealing in a comprehensive way with ten of its fundamental principles as given to students of classes in Los Angeles on this very important subject.

Parsifal and the Sacred Spear

An entirely new view of Wagner's wonderful opera with its three wonderful acts as they are applied to the three grand divisions of human life, the Legend of the Holy Grail, which will interest in its interpretation both mystics and music lovers.

Faust, the Eternal Drama

This booklet is a companion to the above and forms the second of a series of opera interpretations of which more will follow. The mystic drama by Goethe is analyzed from the standpoint of its application to the problem of individual advancement and its wonderful warning explained to the reader.

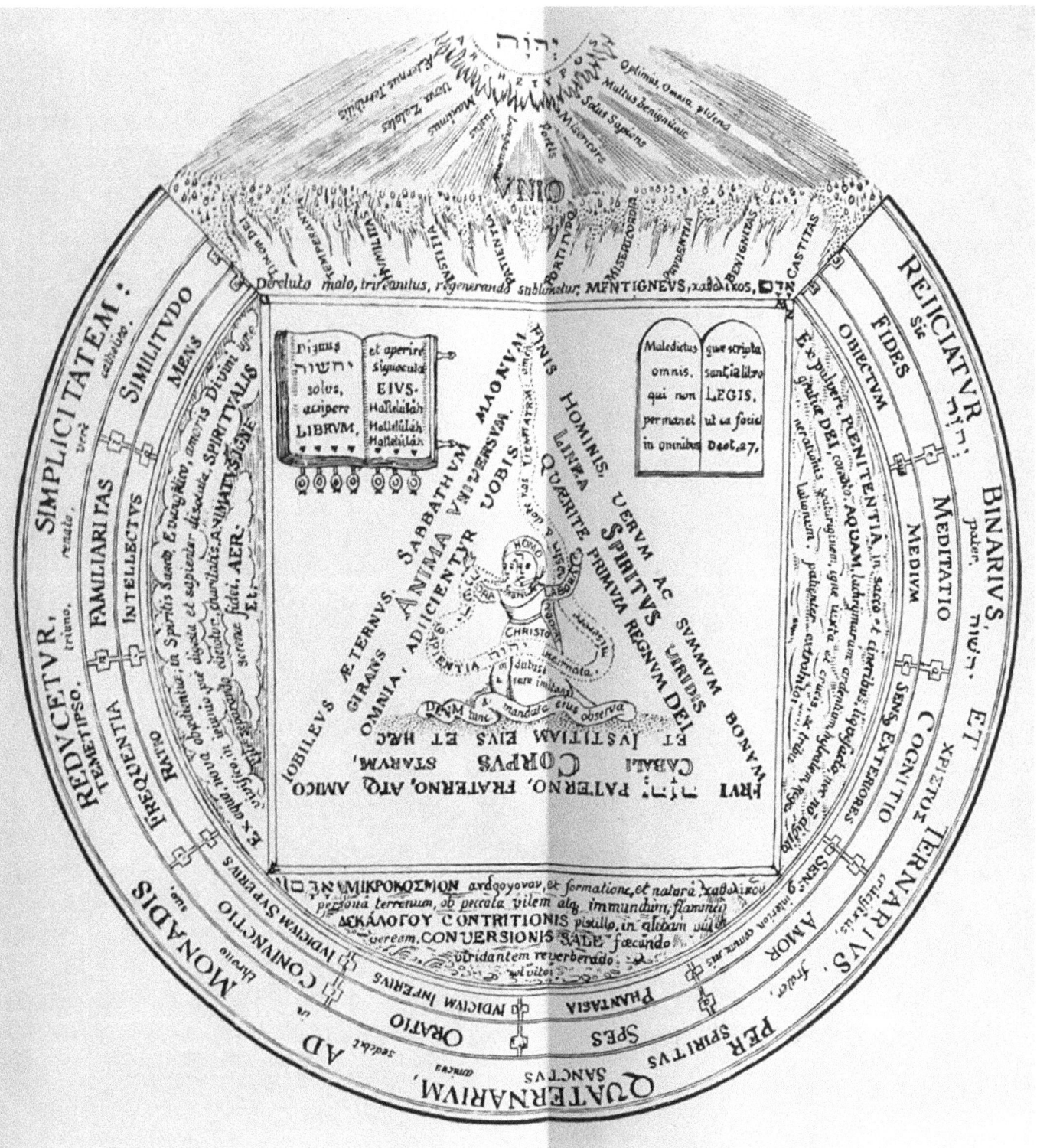